The Diffusion of Social Movement

Actors, Mechanisms, and Political

D1534245

It is widely recognized that social mov~~e~~ from one site to another. Such diffusion, however, is a complex and multi-dimensional process that involves different actors, networks, and mechanisms. This complexity has spawned a large body of literature on different aspects of the diffusion process, yet a comprehensive framework remains an elusive target. This book is a response to that need, and its framework focuses on three basic analytical questions. First, what is being diffused? This question directs attention to both the protest repertoires and interpretive frames that actors construct to define issues and mobilize political claims. Second, how does diffusion occur? This book focuses attention on the activist networks and communication channels that facilitate diffusion, including dialogue, rumors, the mass media, the Internet, nongovernmental organizations, and organizational brokers. Finally, what is the impact of diffusion on organizational development and shifts in the scale of contentious politics? This volume suggests that diffusion is not a simple matter of political contagion or imitation; rather, it is a creative and strategic process marked by political learning, adaptation, and innovation.

Rebecca Kolins Givan is Assistant Professor at Cornell University's School of Industrial and Labor Relations. She received her PhD from Northwestern University and has previously held positions at Cardiff Business School and the London School of Economics. She has published in the areas of health care work, trade unions, and comparative industrial relations.

Kenneth M. Roberts is Professor of Government and the Robert S. Harrison Director of the Institute for the Social Sciences at Cornell University. He received his PhD from Stanford University and has previously taught at the University of New Mexico. He is the author of *Deepening Democracy? The Modern Left and Social Movements in Chile and Peru*, along with other writings on populism, party systems, and political change in Latin America.

Sarah A. Soule is the Morgridge Professor of Organizational Behavior at the Stanford Graduate School of Business. She received her PhD from Cornell University and previously taught at the University of Arizona and Cornell University. She is the author of *Contention and Corporate Social Responsibility* and a coauthor (with David Snow) of *A Primer on Social Movements*. She has published papers on social movements, organizations, and political change in the United States.

The Diffusion of Social Movements

Actors, Mechanisms, and Political Effects

Edited by

REBECCA KOLINS GIVAN
Cornell University

KENNETH M. ROBERTS
Cornell University

SARAH A. SOULE
Stanford University

CAMBRIDGE
UNIVERSITY PRESS

CAMBRIDGE UNIVERSITY PRESS
Cambridge, New York, Melbourne, Madrid, Cape Town, Singapore,
São Paulo, Delhi, Dubai, Tokyo, Mexico City

Cambridge University Press
32 Avenue of the Americas, New York, NY 10013-2473, USA

www.cambridge.org
Information on this title: www.cambridge.org/9780521130950

© Cambridge University Press 2010

First published 2010

Printed in the United States of America

A catalog record for this publication is available from the British Library.

Library of Congress Cataloging in Publication data

The diffusion of social movements : actors, mechanisms, and political effects / edited by Rebecca
Kolins Givan, Kenneth M. Roberts, Sarah A. Soule.
    p.   cm.
Includes bibliographical references and index.
ISBN 978-0-521-19373-3 (hardback) – ISBN 978-0-521-13095-0 (pbk.)
1. Social movements.   I. Givan, Rebecca Kolins, 1975–   II. Roberts, Kenneth M., 1958–
III. Soule, Sarah Anne, 1967–   IV. Title.
HM881.D54   2010
303.48'4 – dc22   2010003656

ISBN 978-0-521-19373-3 Hardback
ISBN 978-0-521-13095-0 Paperback

Contents

List of Tables

List of Figures

Contributors

Kenneth T. Andrews, University of North Carolina, Chapel Hill

Michael Biggs, Oxford University

Valerie Bunce, Cornell University

Sean Chabot, Eastern Washington University

Lance Compa, Cornell University

Jennifer Earl, University of California, Santa Barbara

Rebecca Kolins Givan, Cornell University

Jayson Harsin, American University of Paris

Ronald J. Herring, Cornell University

Katrina Kimport, University of California, San Francisco

Kenneth M. Roberts, Cornell University

Conny Roggeband, Free University of Amsterdam

David A. Snow, University of California, Irvine

Sarah A. Soule, Stanford University

James E. Stobaugh, University of California, Irvine

Sidney Tarrow, Cornell University

Sharon Wolchik, George Washington University

Preface and Acknowledgments

Students of social movements have long been fascinated by the ways in which they influence or spread from one site to another – in short, how they diffuse. Recent scholarship has shed light on different dimensions of the diffusion process, including the actors, networks, and mechanisms that make diffusion happen. This volume is an attempt to pull together different strands of this research into an integrated and comprehensive understanding of the diffusion process.

Most of the contributors to this volume participated in a conference at Cornell University in November 2007 that explored how social movements create linkages and frame issues under contention. The conference was an initiative of an interdisciplinary theme project, "Contentious Knowledge: Science, Social Science, and Social Protest," sponsored by Cornell's Institute for the Social Sciences. This project brought together scholars who study contentious politics with others who explore the social construction (and contestation) of authoritative knowledge. The dialogue among these scholars sparked considerable interest in the diffusion of mobilizing tactics and frames across activist networks. It also revealed the need for a single volume to integrate what we know about the diffusion of social movements and identify some of the new research frontiers on the topic. We hope this volume contributes to these goals.

Our collaboration has greatly benefited from the generous support of the Institute for the Social Sciences (ISS) at Cornell University, which funded a series of seminars and workshops related to this topic and provided an enriching intellectual environment where theme project members could work. ISS Director Elizabeth Mannix and Associate Provost David Harris offered unwavering support for our interdisciplinary research, and Anneliese Truame and Judi Eastburn devoted their considerable organizational and administrative skills (not to mention their patience) to our project. We are indebted to project members Steve Hilgartner, Maria Cook, Durba Ghosh, Janice Thies, Jason Frank, Tom Medvetz, Kyoko Sato, and Susan Spronk for intellectual inspiration, and especially to project leader Ron Herring for his tireless search for common ground. Sidney Tarrow recognized early on the potential for producing a single volume on movement diffusion, and we thank him for prodding us in that direction. We also thank Lewis Bateman at Cambridge University Press for his support for our volume, and Emily Spangler for ushering it through the production process. Finally, we are grateful to Noelle Brigden, Stacy Diaz, Timothy Perry, and Diane Yates for very competent assistance with copyediting tasks.

Introduction

The Dimensions of Diffusion

Rebecca Kolins Givan, Kenneth M. Roberts, and Sarah A. Soule

The concept of *diffusion* is widely used by social scientists to refer to the spread of some innovation through direct or indirect channels across members of a social system (Rogers 1995). Diffusion effects are often recognized, for example, in the spread of new technologies, the adoption of policy reforms (see, e.g., Soule and Zylan 1997; Weyland 2006; Simmons et al. 2006), and changes in political regimes (Hagopian and Mainwaring 2005; Brinks and Coppedge 2006). One of the most prominent areas of research on diffusion, however, is in the field of social movements (Strang and Soule 1998; Soule 2004). Observers, participants, and scholars of "contentious politics" have long been intrigued by how social movements (or some element thereof, such as a tactic, frame, symbol, issue, or outcome) spread or diffuse from one site to another. It is commonplace in both media and scholarly accounts of social movements to remark about how some issue or form of protest has spread across a country – or, in some cases, from one country to another.

Indeed, diffusion undoubtedly helps to account for the wavelike character of protest cycles and other types of social mobilization (Tarrow 1998a). Simply put, social movements in one site (or time period) are often inspired or influenced by movements elsewhere. One cannot understand social movements – how they evolve, how they expand, how they engage the political arena – without understanding the dynamics of diffusion. It is little wonder, then, that prior research has explored many different facets of the diffusion process, including the spread of protest repertoires (Soule 1997; Bohstedt and Williams 1988), the construction of overarching issue frames (McAdam and Rucht 1993; Snow and Benford 1992), the role of mass media and other forms of communication in the diffusion process (Singer 1970; Myers 2000; Olesen 2005), and the social networks (Gould 1991) and institutional conditions (Strang and Meyer 1993; Hedström et al. 2000) that foster coordination and collective action.

One of the central insights of this body of research is the multidimensionality of diffusion processes – a multidimensionality that reflects the plethora of actors, networks, and mechanisms involved in the spread of social movements.

This multidimensionality poses a challenge to scholars who study social movements, however, as it complicates the development of a comprehensive framework for the analysis of diffusion effects. Even the most sophisticated research may capture only a narrow slice of more complex realities. The primary purpose of this volume – to our knowledge, the first of its kind to provide a comprehensive overview of diffusion dynamics in social movements – is to promote a more integrated understanding of the diffusion process. Such an understanding must start by "unpacking" the concept of diffusion to identify its core elements and explain how they relate to one another in a larger process of movement transformation. The book is thus designed to pull together different strands of the literature on diffusion into a more coherent theoretical understanding of a dynamic and multidimensional process. It provides an overarching analytical framework to help organize the field and assess existing research, and it presents new research on a number of empirical cases to illuminate the key dimensions outlined in the theoretical framework.

To develop this overarching framework, the contributions start with a straightforward question that too often elicits muddled responses: "What is being diffused?" Protest tactics or collective action "repertoires" often spread from one movement site to another, or sometimes from one social movement to another. But so also do the interpretive frames that actors construct to define the issues, codify problems and solutions, target responsible parties, and mobilize political claims. Protest tactics and interpretive frames interact in complex ways, and they are often adapted or modified by new actors as they diffuse across movements or sites. Indeed, appealing to new constituencies – an integral part of the diffusion process – often requires some reframing of the issues and/or a retooling of the collective action repertoire. Diffusion, then, does not simply mean that tactics or frames are transplanted in whole cloth from one site to another; creative borrowing, adaptation, and political learning are often vital to its success.

Second, our contributors ask, "How does diffusion occur?" This question focuses attention on the mechanisms by which protest repertoires and interpretive frames spread. Diffusion is often a highly social or, as Tarrow (2005) calls it, a "relational" process, whereby repertoires or frames are transmitted through interpersonal contacts, organizational linkages, or associational networks. The study of relational diffusion typically entails tracing the diverse ways in which individuals and groups come into contact with each other and learn, borrow, or adapt the collective action repertoires or frames that have been adopted in one of the sites. Diffusion can also occur in the absence of social contacts, however, as when instantaneous global communications transmit images that elicit demonstration effects among social actors that are otherwise unconnected. Diffusion can also occur through indirect network contacts, such as when two activist groups are not directly connected to each other, but are each connected to a third, mediating, group or actor that brokers the spread of tactics or frames. Arguably, globalization and technological modernization have increased the prevalence and importance of such indirect and nonrelational forms of diffusion, as movements can learn, borrow, and coordinate across distant sites through the Internet, satellite television, and the rise of transnational nongovernmental organizations (NGOs) and activist networks. Consequently, the mechanisms of diffusion are best understood by examining the activist networks, organizational brokers, and communication channels that facilitate the spread of norms, frames, tactics, and images.

Third, our contributors ask, "What is the impact of diffusion?" by exploring its relationship to shifts in the scale of contentious politics (McAdam et al. 2001; Tarrow and McAdam 2005). When a particular type of movement or protest diffuses horizontally from one site to another, it enlarges the scope of contentious politics. When actors at these different sites begin to coordinate with one another, or create new representative or coordinating bodies to articulate their claims in larger political arenas, a "scale shift" has occurred. In the process, a local-level protest or social actor may become linked to contentious struggles being waged at the national or even transnational level. Diffusion, then, is not synonymous with scale shift, but it is often integral to it; by spawning new actors or sites of contention, diffusion creates incentives to build intermediary institutions and "scale up" the level of coordination for waging political struggle. The distinctions between diffusion and scale shift, and the complex linkages between the two processes, are not well understood in the field today, and they cry out for a more systematic delineation.

As the contributions in this volume make clear, diffusion may be driven by identifiable mechanisms, but it is far from being a mechanical process. It is heavily conditioned by political agency, and it almost always involves the interaction between formal and informal institutions. The character and content of diffusion are shaped by the efforts of political actors to proselytize, to engage in dialogue, to borrow and adapt, or to frame and reframe the issues under contention. Some actors are receptive to outside influences, whereas others are more closed or resistant. Diffusion, then, is a creative and strategic process, one that is marked by political learning, adaptation, and innovation; it is not a simple matter of political contagion or imitation.

Consequently, political agency – both individual and collective – will play a central role in the patterns of diffusion analyzed in this volume. Because the role of political agency has been undertheorized and underresearched in previous scholarship, one of our primary goals is to shed new light on the diverse ways in which actors shape the mechanisms of diffusion. The empirical cases in this volume are thus drawn from a variety of national and transnational contexts, and they profile several different types of political actors. These actors vary widely in the material, organizational, and human resources they are able to mobilize, so the mechanisms of diffusion and the prospects for scale shift are inevitably conditioned by resource availability and constraints.

WHAT IS BEING DIFFUSED? THE ALIGNMENT OF REPERTOIRES, FRAMES, AND CONTEXTS

The study of diffusion is often plagued by ambiguity about the nature of the innovation being spread from one site to another. This problem is hardly unique to the study of diffusion in social movements. In his analysis of policy diffusion, for example, Weyland (2006: 17–18) distinguishes between the spread of specific policy "models" and the more abstract "principles" or guidelines that may be compatible with a range of distinct policy choices. The fact that policy diffusion is often associated with certain types of institutional innovations merely adds to the complexity of identifying what is being diffused. Such complexity is also apparent in the study of social movements, which are inherently multidimensional social phenomena. What does it mean, then, to say that a movement has diffused to another site? Along which dimensions(s) should diffusion be tracked? In short, what is being diffused?

The content of diffusion (that is, the innovation that is diffused) can occur along two primary dimensions of social movements: behavioral and ideational. The behavioral dimension involves the diffusion of movement tactics or collective action repertoires. Strikes, riots, protests, sit-ins, boycotts, petition drives, and other forms of contentious action may occur in waves, spreading from their original site of contention to others through a variety of mechanisms that are explored in the next section (Soule 1997; Myers 2000). Tactical diffusion signifies that part of the repertoire employed in one site finds resonance in others, and is deemed to be a legitimate or effective instrument for pressing claims on a given target.

Diffusing innovations, however, can also occur on an ideational plane through the spread of collective action frames that define issues, goals, and targets. As Snow and Benford (1992: 135–136) emphasize, and as a long tradition of scholarship on collective action problems (Olson 1965; Lichbach 1998) and resource mobilization (McAdam 1982; McCarthy and Zald 1977) demonstrates, social movements do not arise inevitably or even naturally from shared interests or grievances. To mobilize participants, social movements engage in a dynamic and interactive struggle "over the production of ideas and meanings" (Snow and Benford 1992: 136). Such meanings are shaped by structural conditions or positions, but they are not directly determined by them. They are ultimately social productions that construct reality, or at least interpret it, for movement participants, antagonists, and bystanders.

Frames, then, are "interpretive schemata" (Snow and Benford 1992: 137) that give meaning to collective struggles. They determine which claims or grievances are chosen as focal points of contention; how these are interpreted in relationship to specific collective interests, values, or identities; and how they are bundled or separated in the mobilization of different constituencies. Frames help define the objectives of collective action and the political or institutional targets against which specific claims are directed.

As several chapters in this volume demonstrate, framing is an inherently political process that combines the creative construction of social meaning with strategic considerations of political efficacy. Collective action frames are formed and shaped by concrete social struggles, but they are also refined by actors who continually assess how different meanings and tactics will resonate with movement adherents, targeted opponents, and noncommitted observers.

Frames, therefore, are not fixed; they are subject to strategic revision or innovation as conditions change, issues evolve, or new social actors enter a contentious arena. Such innovations may facilitate the diffusion of frames to new actors or sites of contention, and they allow movements to adapt over time in response to changing strategic environments. Adaptation across sites of contention can be seen in Conny Roggeband's chapter on the politicization of sexual harassment, as feminist movements in Europe strategically borrowed and refined collective action frames that originated in the United States to press claims in different national and transnational institutional settings. Likewise, strategic adaptation of frames can take place within a given site over time; as James Stobaugh and David Snow discuss in their chapter, a series of court rulings induced faith-based movements opposed to the teaching of evolution in public schools to shift their focus from a creationist frame to one emphasizing intelligent design.

Such strategic adaptations demonstrate that contentious issues and claims can be framed in different ways, highlighting the centrality of political agency in the spread of social movements. This does not mean that movement activists have free rein to adopt or alter frames to their choosing; collective action frames that are too detached from social realities and prevailing cultural meanings or identities are unlikely to resonate with targeted audiences. Nevertheless, social realities and cultural meanings can be constructed around alternative interpretive schemes, and these have major implications for the ways in which issues and interests are defined, identities are invoked, and claims are made. In Lance Compa's chapter on the U.S. labor movement, for example, workers' struggles that were traditionally conceived in terms of class interests were reinterpreted through a human rights frame that recast the claims around which contention occurred, potentially broadening the scope of their appeal. Similarly, the initial focus of the U.S. civil rights movement on issues of desegregation in the 1950s shifted to a more ambitious and encompassing set of claims around economic justice and democratic citizenship rights, including effective rights to suffrage, during the 1960s. In so doing, elements of the civil rights frame eventually diffused to other aggrieved groups – such as women, Native Americans, immigrant farm workers, and gay and lesbian citizens – that mobilized claims for expanded rights and equal protection under the law.

The political implications of alternative framing strategies are readily apparent in Ronald Herring's chapter on the anti–genetically modified organism (GMO) movement. As Herring demonstrates, the framing of threats and benefits associated with transgenic technologies in pharmaceuticals is quite different from their framing in agriculture, and the framing of the latter in Europe diverges sharply from that in the United States. Indeed, the European threat-based anti-GMO frame diffused through transnational activist networks to developing countries and heavily influenced the construction of an international regulatory regime – one that is routinely skirted by farmers with material stakes in the adoption of new technologies.

Such patterns of diffusion raise important questions about the alignment of actors, tactics, issue frames, and the socioeconomic or political contexts in which contention occurs. Often diffusion takes place among actors who are located in different sites but share similar structural positions that create a common set of interests, claims, or grievances around which to mobilize. Students subjected to a draft for an unpopular war may conduct protests or sit-ins that spread rapidly from one university campus to another. A successful land invasion by a peasant community or a group of urban squatters may encourage similar groups to attempt the same tactic. Food shortages or price hikes may trigger riots by the urban poor in one city that quickly diffuse to neighboring cities, whereas a labor strike that wrings concessions from business owners or the state for one union may induce other workers to wield the strike weapon as well.

So-called IMF riots in low-income countries during the 1980s provide a clear example of how similar actors, tactics, issue frames, and socioeconomic contexts can be aligned in contentious struggles across multiple sites (Walton and Seddon 1994). These riots were common responses of the urban poor to economic austerity measures imposed by debt-strapped national governments under pressure from foreign creditors and the International Monetary Fund (IMF), which often made new lending conditional on the adoption of specific economic adjustment policies. The outbreak of protests in multiple sites around a common set of issues or claims, however, does not suffice to demonstrate that diffusion has occurred, as such protests may be independent responses to structurally similar economic or political grievances. Diffusion requires that movements across these multiple sites be linked together through activist networks, or at least informed and inspired by media-transmitted images or shared cultural understandings of popular struggles in other settings, as discussed later. The chapter by Valerie Bunce and Sharon Wolchik on the diffusion of citizen protests against electoral fraud in postcommunist societies provides a textbook example of how such networks can develop and operate transnationally. In their account, "electoral revolutions" diffused through a range of personal contacts, organizational linkages, and communication strategies that defined a common set of democratic citizenship claims and a collective action repertoire for contesting autocratic political authority in the electoral arena.

Such forms of diffusion rely on an "attribution of similarity" (Tilly and Tarrow 2006: 95), whereby similar groups with closely related claims or grievances adopt a common set of tactics in different locations. Other patterns of diffusion, however, rest on a less thorough alignment of these different dimensions of struggle. As Tarrow (1998a: chapter 3) points out, some tactics are highly portable or "modular" in their application; rather than "belonging" to a specific cause or group, they can be adopted by diverse collective actors mobilizing around quite different types of interests, grievances, or causes. Sean Chabot's chapter provides a striking example of such modularity – namely, the diffusion of the Gandhian repertoire of nonviolent direct action from India, where it was integral to the nationalist struggle for independence from colonial rule, to the United States, where leaders and participants in the civil rights movement consciously borrowed tactics from the Gandhian repertoire in their struggle against segregation and disenfranchisement. Similar tactics were thus employed by very different types of actors in pursuit of widely varying claims and grievances.

Even where movement actors, tactics, and issue frames are broadly similar, the contexts of collective action may vary widely. The chapters by Roggeband and Herring, for example, show how similar issue frames operate differently in distinct national or regional settings; hence, feminist mobilization against sexual harassment in Europe is conditioned by national and transnational legal institutions that are different from those in the United States, and the material interests of farmers in low-income countries alter the response on the ground to an anti-GMO frame originating in Europe.

Clearly, tactics vary in their degree of modularity. Workers, students, pensioners, homemakers, and the unemployed may all find cause to protest against government austerity programs, and all are capable of doing so, but only workers can effectively wield the strike weapon. Similarly, collective action frames vary in their degree of specificity or generality – that is, in their ability to incorporate or articulate a range of interests, issue areas, and grievances within a common interpretive scheme. Diffusion is facilitated when "master frames" are developed "to articulate and align a vast array of events and experiences so that they hang together in a relatively unified and meaningful fashion" (Snow and Benford 1992: 137–138). Democratization, for example, may provide a master frame for diverse struggles over human rights, economic justice, and citizenship claims when regime change is conceived as an overarching precondition for the attainment of more specific goals. Likewise, antiglobalization frames may amplify and connect otherwise separate claims related to environmental protection, workers' rights, and local or national autonomy. Diffusion, then, is not limited to structurally similar groups articulating the same claims or grievances; the construction of master frames plays an integral role in the magnification and diversification of collective action, transforming particular struggles into more general ones, and facilitating the transition from local to national or even transnational forms of contention.

The recognition that diffusion may involve the spread of both collective action repertoires and interpretative frames begs the question of how it actually occurs. This question directs attention to the causal mechanisms and dynamic properties of diffusion processes, to which we now turn.

HOW DOES DIFFUSION OCCUR? RELATIONAL AND NONRELATIONAL MECHANISMS OF DIFFUSION

After we have identified what is diffusing, the next step is to try to understand the mechanisms that give a diffusion process its dynamic properties. That is, we should ask the question: How has the diffusion occurred? Furthermore, what types of actors, organizations, and institutions set the process of diffusion in motion?

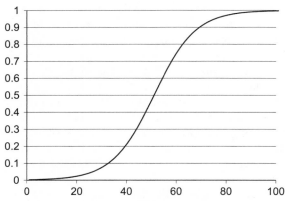

FIGURE 1.1. S-Shaped Curve of Diffusion

Classic diffusion scholarship identifies four kinds of actors that are central to the diffusion process. First, there are *innovators*, who are the adventurous first actors to adopt an innovation. Typically innovators have connections to others outside a given social system; these connections are what allow innovations to be introduced to the social system. Second, there are the *early adopters* who help to legitimate the innovation in the eyes of other actors who have yet to adopt. In the language of *protest cycles* (Tarrow 1998a), innovators and early adopters may be thought of as central to "early riser" movements, which help to set a protest cycle in motion. Third, there are the *later adopters* who come slowly to the process of adoption, but who nonetheless choose to adopt the innovation, often after careful deliberation. And, finally, there are the *nonadopters*, or those who have not yet (and may not ever) adopt the innovation. The actions of these four kinds of actors lead to the classic "S-shaped curve of diffusion," as depicted in Figure 1.1.

The S-shaped curve depicts the rate of adoption of a given innovation as a function of the number of actors in the population who have adopted the innovation. The figure shows that initially there are no adopters, but after a few innovators begin to use an innovation, adoption catches on as early adopters begin to embrace the innovation. At some point along the curve, the innovation is deemed legitimate, which leads to the steep increase in the number of adoptions. Finally, the rate of adoption slows as the population of nonadopters approaches zero.

This S-shaped curve characterizes diffusion dynamics in many different social and institutional settings, but the mechanisms that account for upward shifts along the curve may vary for different types of diffusion. In other words, the mechanisms that drive the diffusion of social movements are not necessarily the same as those fostering other types of diffusion, such as technological, institutional, or policy innovation. For example, competition is often a driving force behind the diffusion of innovations in technology and organizational design. Business firms operating in a competitive marketplace, or military institutions locked in a security rivalry, are pressured to adopt technological or organizational innovations that have proven successful elsewhere or provided a competitive advantage for their rivals. In other contexts – for example, the global diffusion of economic liberalism and political democracy in the waning decades of the twentieth century (Simmons et al. 2006; Levitsky and Way 2005) – processes of norm compliance and institutional leverage may play a central role in the spread of innovations. States may embrace internationally sanctioned policy models or institutional forms because of their normative appeal or perceived efficacy, but they may also feel compelled to conform as a condition for gaining access to global financial circuits or membership in international organizations. Diffusion, therefore, may rest in part on the capacity of global power centers to exert leverage for norm compliance on potentially recalcitrant actors.

Such forms of competitive pressure and institutional leverage are less central to diffusion among social movements, which tend to rely more heavily on processes of political learning and what McAdam (1982) called "cognitive liberation." Learning occurs when actors in different sites find tactics or frames employed elsewhere to be useful tools for articulating their own grievances, mobilizing support, or pressing claims on their targets. As such, it is a highly instrumental process. Although such learning can occur among existing social groups or activist networks, it can also activate new ones, thus expanding the scope of political contention and social mobilization. Indeed, the notion of cognitive liberation suggests that movement diffusion occurs not only through instrumental learning, but also through the construction of new meanings, identities, and issue frames that mobilize new actors by altering their conception of what is politically feasible or desirable. Diffusion, in short, often entails a transformation of political consciousness.

Diffusion conceived as a process of instrumental learning, cognitive liberation, or both is dramatically different from early scholarly treatments of the phenomenon. These treatments were framed by an interest in psychology and micro-level cognitive processes, and they tended to interpret diffusion as a form of contagion between individuals in groups or crowds. Maladaptive and aggressive impulses were to be feared, because they were thought to spread from person to person and drive collective action. Observers of race riots, lynching, Nazism, fascism, McCarthyism, and Stalinism viewed individuals as nonrational and thus susceptible to contagion effects in contexts of failed social integration (Kornhauser 1959).

With the development of the resource mobilization tradition in the 1970s, and its focus on social movement organizations and the rationality of movement actors, it became possible to consider diffusion as something other than a simple process of contagion. Scholars thus began to study diffusion as a function of connections between different organizations and other mechanisms of strategic innovation. We might usefully classify these mechanisms into three very broad categories: *relational, nonrelational,* and *mediated mechanisms* of diffusion.

Relational mechanisms include a variety of different direct, interpersonal networks that exist between individuals and organizations. Network ties are a generally efficient channel along which information may flow, as they tend to be based on interpersonal trust. However, because networks tend to be segregated, diffusing items often remain within networks. Thus, whereas networks are an efficient mechanism of diffusion, how far the innovation will travel depends on at least some members' connections beyond a given network.

In some instances, researchers are able to track the presence of ties and communication between people or between organizations, such as in classic network studies. For instance, Singer (1970) interviewed 500 African American men about their sources of information on the Detroit riot of 1967 and found that the chief source of information, according to his informants, was personal communication. The chapter in this volume by Sean Chabot points to precisely this mechanism of diffusion; that is, Chabot discusses the importance of direct, interpersonal communication processes to the diffusion of the Gandhian tactical repertoire.

When scholars are not able to obtain precise data on who spoke to whom (or who is connected to whom directly), it may be possible to infer that direct contact has happened and has facilitated diffusion. For example, some research focuses on the way in which the emergence of transportation and trade routes brought people from disparate locales together (e.g., Rude 1964). The connections forged via these routes were necessary for the dissemination of information of various kinds, including that about politics and social movements. For example, Bohstedt and Williams (1988) show that dense community networks formed through market transactions facilitated the imitation of food riots across communities in Devonshire in the late eighteenth century. Following a similar line of reasoning, Hedström, Sandell, and Stern (2000) find that the diffusion of the Swedish Social Democratic Party (in 1894–1911) followed the travel routes of political agitators at that time.

Another way that direct, interpersonal communication is inferred is via shared organizational memberships. That is, scholars often infer that people are sharing ideas, communicating, and facilitating the diffusion of social movements because they belong to the same movement organizations. Because individuals often have multiple organizational affiliations, they serve as conduits of information across organizational boundaries. This idea is implicit in much of the research on the sit-ins of the 1960s, such as Morris' (1981), which shows that the sit-ins were not spontaneous and uncoordinated activities, but rather preexisting organizational ties facilitated communication necessary for the emergence and development of this protest tactic. Likewise, research on social movements in Latin America suggests that labor union members were important actors in the development of militant grassroots neighborhood organizations in low-income urban communities in Peru (Stokes 1995), whereas Catholic Church activists inspired by liberation theology contributed to the spread of peasant associations in rural El Salvador that eventually provided a social base for insurgent collective action (Wood 2003).

Scholars also infer that interpersonal communication occurs via geographic proximity, adjacency, or both. For example, Petras and Zeitlin (1967) show how the Chilean mining industry spawned high levels of Marxist ideology and activism, which spread to agricultural municipalities via proximity. Likewise, Gould (1991) demonstrates that the district-level insurrection against the impeding Versailles army in Paris in 1871 depended on the level of resistance in other districts to which the district was directly linked.

Whether the presence of direct ties is established or inferred, most scholars recognize that direct network ties and relational diffusion are only part of the story. In addition to direct connections among individuals, organizations, or both, indirect ties can also facilitate the diffusion of protest – what we refer to as nonrelational mechanisms. We noted earlier that relational networks of diffusion are efficient, but can be limiting given the tendency for networks to be segregated. Nonrelational mechanisms may be even more efficient, but because individuals are not in direct contact with one another, interpersonal trust and influence do not facilitate the diffusion of an innovation.

One type of indirect tie is the shared cultural understanding of similar activists or organizations in different locales, what we referred to earlier as "attribution of similarity." Although they are not directly connected, activists who define themselves as similar to other activists may imitate the actions of others. An example of this process is the imitation by activists in Seabrook, New Hampshire in 1976 of a mass demonstration at a nuclear site in Germany in 1974 (McAdam and Rucht 1993). In related work, Soule (1997) shows that innovative student protest tactics diffused among educational institutions that were similar along certain dimensions. The construction of categories of similarity served as indirect channels between colleges and universities in the mid-1980s, leading to the diffusion of the shantytown protest tactic during the student antiapartheid movement.

Part of the story of nonrelational diffusion is that theorization, or "a strategy for making sense of the world" (Strang and Meyer 1993: 493), facilitates the process by which an item diffuses to unconnected actors. Theorization, in many ways, relates to our earlier discussion about framing in that both processes require that a complex set of ideas and policies or tactics are distilled into easily understandable (and modular) units that are more easily imported into a variety of different settings, even if actors are not directly connected. As Strang and Meyer (1993: 490–491) suggest, "linkages may be cultural as well as relational," and the "cultural understanding that social entities belong to a common social category constructs a tie between them" that facilitates diffusion through a process of "rational mimicking." Because "cultural linkages generally outstrip direct relations," Strang and Meyer emphasize the role of theorization in allowing "globally available models" to be "imported into local situations." As such, they view "culturally legitimated theorists" as "central conduits of diffusion" processes (1993: 492–494, 498).

Clearly, for diffusion to occur in the absence of direct personal or organizational relations, mechanisms must be found to inform actors in different sites of the tactical repertoires or collective action frames employed elsewhere. The mass media often perform this function, and thus play an important role as indirect channels of diffusion. Noting that the urban riots of the late 1960s appeared to cluster in time, Spilerman (1976) hypothesized that riots diffused throughout urban, black areas, and were facilitated by television coverage of civil rights activism, which helped to create solidarity that went beyond direct ties of community. To Spilerman, then, the media served as an indirect channel of diffusion by creating a cultural linkage among African Americans in different metropolitan areas. Television, he argues, familiarized individuals all over the country with both the details of riots and the reasons that individuals participated in riots. Singer's (1970) aforementioned work on the Detroit riot of 1967 points to the media (as well as interpersonal or direct communication) as a leading source of information on the riot in that city. In more recent treatments, Myers (2000) finds evidence for the claim that riots that received national media attention increased the subsequent national level of riots, whereas smaller riots that received only local media attention increased riot propensities only in the local area. Andrews and Biggs (2006) also point to the importance of the news media to the diffusion of sit-ins in the civil rights movement. In this book, the chapters by Jayson Harsin and by Jennifer Earl and Katrina Kimport both explore the ways in which technology, and in particular the Internet, is affecting the diffusion of social movements and political tactics in important ways. The Internet can facilitate the sharing of information and interpretive frames, and it can help coordinate protests, petition drives, and other forms of contention among groups that otherwise may have little contact with each other. According to Harsin, it may also spread rumors and images that heavily condition the interpretation of political events.

Finally, brokerage or mediation is a third mechanism of diffusion, which is akin to nonrelational forms of diffusion in that individuals and organizations are not directly connected to one another. However, in mediated diffusion, actors are similarly connected to a third actor, who is able to facilitate the diffusion of information and actions. In such cases, the broker or mediator is an important facilitator of diffusion, yet the diffusion process can be influenced by mediators' preferences, beliefs, and interests. Thus, it is possible to imagine cases in which mediators' self-interests can affect the diffusion of an item to the detriment of the actors who are connected via this broker. In this volume, Bunce and Wolchik imply brokerage when they discuss the role of NGOs in connecting social actors in the various postcommunist regimes that they study. Likewise, NGOs play an important brokerage role in Ronald Herring's account of the diffusion of the anti-GMO movement from Western Europe to developing countries.

The importance of brokerage and mediated forms of diffusion is undoubtedly magnified in an era of globalization, when social struggles in one national setting may influence or coordinate with those in another without establishing direct personal or organizational relations (Tarrow 2005). As Keck and Sikkink (1998) demonstrate, transnational activist networks may form to mediate otherwise separate national struggles over human rights, women's and indigenous rights, environmental protection, and social and economic justice. Such networks create mediated linkages between local or national organizations, NGOs operating at a transnational level, and parallel groups or solidaristic organizations in other national settings. These transnational networks often mobilize external support for local or national struggles in an attempt to enhance their political leverage when pressing claims on domestic governments. They may also spawn new, transnational institutional forms that are explicitly designed to link and coordinate disparate national actors – a point that is taken up later.

WHAT IS THE IMPACT OF DIFFUSION?

Finally, the contributors in this volume offer some insight into questions about what impacts the diffusion of social movements have on other social processes. For example, Michael Biggs and Kenneth Andrews ask an important follow-up question about the diffusion of sit-ins associated with the civil rights movement in the 1960s. They ask how the diffusion of sit-ins affected the subsequent growth and founding of civil rights organizations in 334 cities in the southern United States. Diffusion, then, may leave an important imprint on the organizational forms and associational networks of civil society. And as Roggeband and Herring each suggest, diffusion can foster institutional change in the form of new legal and regulatory frameworks to process societal claims and manage contentious issues.

Indeed, diffusion often plays a central role in shifting the scope and scale of contentious politics. It can transform a local protest into a national movement, or a national movement into a transnational one. In so doing, it may foster the development of new and larger organizational forms to articulate and coordinate societal claims, and induce higher-level political institutions to respond to such claims. These dynamics, and the broader patterns of interaction between diffusion and political institutions, are explored in Sidney Tarrow's chapter on the relationship between diffusion and scale shift. Political institutions are generally at the heart of contentious politics; as Tarrow points out, they can focus, channel, and constrain social mobilization, but they are also frequently transformed by such mobilization. Autocratic regimes, for example, that manipulate elections to hold onto power provide a focal point for social mobilization against electoral fraud, sometimes culminating in regime change. At the transnational level, the prominence of institutions such as the World Trade Organization, the World Bank, and the International Monetary Fund in defining the rules and policies for economic integration made them targets of antiglobalization protesters who mobilized around a diverse set of issue claims. Indeed, they provided a stimulus for the counterorganization of new transnational resistance institutions, such as the World Social Forum and its summit meetings of activist groups – an archetypal example of crossborder movement diffusion facilitated by brokerage networks and culminating in the scaling up of new political institutions (Bandy and Smith 2005). Such forms of transnational organizing may induce institutional or policy change at various points of contention; examples include the World Bank's formal recognition of environmental concerns in its lending policies, the adoption of labor-rights provisions in the North American Free Trade Agreement and other international trade accords, and the development of the Cartagena Protocol governing the use of genetically modified seeds in agricultural development.

Although scale shift can engage social actors in larger coordinating bodies that pressure higher-level political institutions for policy change, at times it may generate new institutions that become contenders for political power in their own right. Contemporary Bolivia provides a compelling example. Social actors that articulated a diverse but largely disconnected set of particularistic claims – including peasant and indigenous groups that resisted coca eradication policies, community organizations opposed to the privatization of municipal water services, and labor unions that fought against economic austerity measures – eventually converged in a series of mass protests against the government and its free market policies. The rapid diffusion and coordination of antigovernment protests after 2000 was facilitated by a master frame of nationalist opposition to neoliberal globalization. The protest movement not only forced an elected president to resign, but also spawned a new political party (see Van Cott 2005) that entered the electoral arena and captured the presidency in 2005. The transformation of popular struggles from the Cochabamba "water wars" of 2000 to the capture of national executive office five years later thus entailed both a diffusion of protest repertoires across the social spectrum and a scaling up of organizational forms as social actors entered formal institutional arenas to contest state power.

LAYOUT OF THIS BOOK

The sections of this volume are organized around these three primary questions, with the first section focused on frame adaptation and tactical diffusion, the second on mechanisms of diffusion, and the third on the impacts of diffusion on scale shift and organizational development. The first section includes four chapters that explore how frames adapt and evolve across space and time as movements respond to different contexts and appeal to new audiences. Conny Roggeband analyzes how women's movements in Europe strategically adapted the sexual harassment frames developed by their American counterparts, and Lance Compa examines the labor movement's adoption of a human rights frame to assess workers' right in the United States. Frame adaptation over time in response to changing social, political, and legal contexts is explored in James Stobaugh and David Snow's chapter on the creationist movement from the Scopes Monkey Trial in 1925 to the intelligent design case in Dover, Pennsylvania in 2005. Alternative framings of transgenic crops and their implications for the political contestation of scientific knowledge are analyzed in Ronald

Herring's chapter on the anti-GMO movement as it spread from Europe to developing regions.

The second section includes four chapters that analyze different mechanisms of diffusion. Sean Chabot explains how personal contact and intergroup dialogue facilitated the diffusion of the Gandhian repertoire from India to the American civil rights movement. Jennifer Earl and Katrina Kimport dissect the role of the Internet in the diffusion of protest tactics within "movement societies." Valerie Bunce and Sharon Wolchik analyze how direct contact and movement brokers facilitated the diffusion of electoral revolutions in post-communist Eurasia. Finally, Jayson Harsin examines John Kerry's presidential campaign to understand how political rumors shape public images and "brand" political figures, in the process reframing media coverage of more substantive or policy-related issues.

The third section includes two chapters that explore the relationships among diffusion, scale shift, and organizational change. Michael Biggs and Kenneth Andrews study the organizational effects of student sit-ins during the U.S. civil rights movement, asking whether the diffusion of sit-ins affected the subsequent growth of preexisting organizations and the formation of new ones. Sidney Tarrow concludes with an assessment of scale shift in contentious politics and its relationship to movement diffusion and political institutions. These diverse case studies and analytical approaches shed new light on the different dimensions of diffusion processes and how they interact in the spread of social movements.

PART I

DIFFUSION AND THE FRAMING
OF CONTENTIOUS POLITICS

2

Transnational Networks and Institutions

How Diffusion Shaped the Politicization of Sexual Harassment in Europe

Conny Roggeband

Diffusion is often conceptualized as a random, voluntary, almost "natural" process, which is reflected in synonyms such as "contagion," "spread," or "flow." In this chapter, instead, I want to draw attention to diffusion as a strategic process and highlight the crucial role of "framing" in this. In line with Schneiberg and Soule (2004), I see diffusion as a political process in which actors at different levels (strategically) adopt and adapt foreign examples to make national and transnational claims and to change institutional and legal settings, build alliances, and exert pressure. Institutional encounters affect the framing of social movements (see Tarrow, Chapter 11). To get their message across, social movements must adapt their frames and align them to the dominant frames of other relevant actors. Strategic framing efforts are thus central in shaping this political process and, as I will demonstrate in this chapter, are crucial in allocating power and positions in this process.

In recent decades, social scientists have been paying increasing attention to the central role of diffusion in shaping social movements, policies, and institutions (see also Chapter 1 of this volume). Examples of these are studies of democratization, the globalization of the human rights discourse, and transnational mobilizations that demonstrate convergence not only of strategies, ideas, and slogans, but also of policies and legislation. These studies, however, provide us with little insight into how these processes occur and into the intracountry dynamics. As stated in Chapter 1 of this volume, diffusion is a multidimensional process that reflects the plethora of actors, networks, and mechanisms involved in the spread of social movements. What happens in transnational processes of reception and translation of foreign ideas and models? And to what extent are similar concepts understood differently in specific cultural and institutional contexts? Processes of diffusion in national settings often imply framing processes at different levels, not just at the (meso) level of adopting social movements, but also at the macro level of the public debate, the political arena, the legal norms, and so on. We therefore need a multilevel approach that pays attention not just to processes between movements, but also to processes between movements and institutions, and to diffusion at the institutional level.

This chapter focuses on the issue of sexual harassment, which first emerged as a social movement issue within the United States and then diffused from the grassroots level to European national and transnational legal settings and policies and to other social movements (Roggeband 2002; Saguy 2002; Zippel 2006).

HORIZONTAL AND VERTICAL DIFFUSION

Two different (sometimes simultaneous) processes of diffusion can be distinguished. A first process, *horizontal* diffusion, is between social movement organizations, national or international. Tarrow (2005) lists three different types of horizontal diffusion: relational diffusion (in case of existing links or direct ties between organizations), nonrelational diffusion (diffusion among people with no or few ties, mostly through mass media and electronic communication), and mediated diffusion (in which brokers link unconnected sites).

A second form of diffusion, vertical diffusion, labeled *scale shift* by McAdam, Tarrow, and Tilly (2001), is diffusion from local social movements to other transnational movements. Scale shift implies "a change in the number and level of coordinated contentious actions to a different focal point, involving a new range of actors, different objects, and broadened claims" (McAdam et al. 2001: 331). The process of scale shift may operate in two directions: upward (when local action spreads to a higher level) and downward (when a generalized practice or idea is adopted at a lower level). Tarrow (2005) identifies a number of similar as well as different mechanisms that are at work in both processes. Scaling up local action requires *coordination* – that is, creating "instances of cross-spatial collaboration" (Tarrow 2005: 122). This process is helped by *brokerage* to build bridges and *theorization*, a concept borrowed from Strang and Meyer (1993), which "permits the generalization or abstraction of a core causal idea from a particular reality into a general frame that can be applied to other realities" (Tarrow 2005: 122). Scaling down, according to Tarrow, also requires brokerage and diffusion. More important, he claims that *certification* – that is, "the validation of actors, their performances, and their claims by authorities" – is a crucial precondition for downscaling (2005: 194).

The parallel processes of cross-national diffusion and scale shift create a multilevel dynamic among grassroots levels, national governments and state institutions, and supranational institutions. In the case of sexual harassment, this means a complex dynamic among grassroots organizations operating in different contexts, national states and nonstate actors, and the European Union, with its structure of multilevel governance. Interactions and negotiations among these different actors and levels imply processes of translation and transformation. In addition, actors are operating under very different conditions, with diverging opportunities and resources. To enable communication, to translate different local experiences, and to overcome differences between them that may hinder exchange, the actors involved are actively engaged in framing processes (Snow and Benford 1999; Chabot and Duyvendak 2002; Roggeband 2004; 2007). Framing is a crucial facilitating process in complex multilevel diffusion.

THE ROLE OF FRAMING IN MULTILEVEL DYNAMICS

Framing activities take place on at least three different levels: first, in horizontal diffusion processes between social movement organizations active in different contexts; second (vertically), in processes of scale shift from local level to transnational coalitions and networks; and third, in making claims at the level of the national state or the supranational level.

In horizontal diffusion processes this framing process consists of two essential elements: *reception* and *recontextualization* (Roggeband 2007). Reception refers to the way social movement actors perceive and interpret a new idea or a practice developed within a different context. Actors must appreciate the innovative qualities of the diffusion item and think it is applicable to their own context before considering the use of a foreign example. Recontextualization emphasizes how actors deal with differences between the source of a new idea and themselves, and the different constraints and opportunities of the context in which they operate. This involves much creative reinvention and pragmatist agency on the part of receiving actor.

In processes of scale shift, framing is necessary to help built a common frame of reference that applies to different contexts and contains shared claims. Tarrow (2005) argues that upward scaling requires *theorization*, whereas for downscaling *certification* is a crucial framing activity. Theorization may result in shifting claims and targets, and in some case a shift in identity, as boundaries between actors may alter (Tarrow 2005: 122). Certification serves to legitimize claims and actors, but is also a selective mechanism because only a limited set of actors, performances, and claims is recognized (ibid.: 194).

In the diffusion of movement ideas to national and supranational institutions, framing helps to build legitimacy, claim recognition, attribute positions and responsibilities, and create strategic coalitions. Social movement actors engage in purposeful action to shape the frames of others and try to link their goals to the goals of organizations or actors they wish to involve (Verloo 2005). Stone (1989) distinguishes among four strategic functions of frames that may be used deliberately and strategically by the different actors involved: (1) challenging or protecting social order, (2) identifying causal factors or agents responsible for the problem, (3) legitimizing and empowering problem "fixers," and (4) creating new political alliances (Stone 1989: 295).

These framing efforts at different levels are both enabled and hindered by national institutional and cultural settings or supranational settings that create specific opportunities or constraints for entering these new frames into the public and political domain (Ferree et al. 2002). The different actors involved in the bureaucratic framing process (social movements and advocacy groups, state actors such as policy makers and member of the justice system, supranational entities, and independent experts) compete over different definitions of a problem. At stake in policy contests is what is represented as the problem, and by whom, and the different assumptions that underpin these representations. Some definitions of issues are organized into politics, whereas other definitions are organized out; some aspects of social reality are included and others are left undiscussed. A careful analysis of this process aims to understand how frames are negotiated and how the object of diffusion transforms in this process through the shaping impact of social and political contexts and dominant systems of meaning. Whether the frames advocated by nonstate actors will resonate with their targets is contingent on the dynamic interaction of both the political opportunity structure in which they are embedded and the mobilizing structures they have at their disposal.

The example of the way sexual harassment became a central issue across Europe serves to demonstrate how diffusion is a political process in which actors at different levels adopt and adapt foreign examples to make national and transnational claims and change institutional and legal settings, build alliances, and exert pressure. I examine how the issue of sexual harassment diffused from the United States to Europe and how the issue was framed within a European context. Also, I analyze the process of up- and downscaling the issue in the European Union (EU). In particular, I focus on the agents of brokerage crucial in this process and the framing activities in which they were engaged to make their framing resonant with opportunities at different levels.

CASES AND DATA

In this chapter I reconstruct how European feminists adopted the issue of sexual harassment, which first emerged within the American context, and translated this issue to their own social and political contexts. Sexual harassment provides an interesting case to study cross-national diffusion processes, because it is a relatively new concept, originating only in the 1970s in the United States and consequently becoming an important feminist issue in many other countries (Roggeband 2002; Saguy 2002; Zippel 2006). The American example has influenced developments in Europe and provides an instructive case to understand how it has affected the framing and politicization process in Europe, where cultural and (political and legal) institutional settings differ significantly. This makes it possible to examine how foreign examples shaped national debates and how feminists dealt with national particularities they were facing.

The data I use for this reconstruction are mainly drawn from my own studies of the Dutch and Spanish feminist struggle to politicize sexual violence (Roggeband 2002, 2004, 2007; Roggeband and Verloo 1999). For my reconstruction of sources, channels, and mechanisms of diffusion in the Netherlands and Spain and to study the considerations and decisions of the actors involved, I analyzed written materials from women's organizations against sexual violence in both countries. These ranged from leaflets and papers to minutes of meetings and correspondence. I also analyzed policy documents and minutes of meetings in national and EU parliaments and documents of the European Commission (EC) and Council of Ministers. My frame of analysis was based on Axelrod (1976) and van de Graaf and Hoppe (1992), who designed a method to reconstruct the structures and lines of argumentation in discourse. Also, I used Snow and Benford's concept of collective action frames (1992) to compare problem definitions and proposed solutions of the different groups. To complement this material I conducted twenty oral history interviews with feminist activists, trade union leaders, policy makers, and politicians who were involved in getting the issue of sexual harassment on the agenda of women's organizations as well as trade unions and state and supranational institutions. During the interviews, I asked the respondents not only about their international contacts and their perception, use, and adaptation of foreign examples, but also how they tried to negotiate their ideas and strategies in different arenas.

For this chapter my own empirical material is complemented with studies of diffusion processes and politicization of sexual harassment in France (Saguy 2002) and Germany and the EU (Zippel 2006), which enables me to reconstruct the wider context of feminist international cooperation on this topic.

SOCIAL MOVEMENT DYNAMICS: DIFFUSION AT THE GRASSROOTS LEVEL

In the 1970s, sexual violence became a central and "new" issue within the second-wave women's movement worldwide. Feminists argued that male violence served as the main agent of the perpetuation of male domination over women by force (Brownmiller 1975: 209). The concept of "sexual harassment" originated in the United States. In a consciousness-raising group in 1974, American feminist Lin Farley discovered that each member of the group had "already quit or been fired from a job at least once because we had been made too uncomfortable by the behavior of men" (Farley 1978: xi). The term "harassment" was invented because this came "as close to symbolizing the problem as language would permit" (ibid.). Within a relatively short period of time this "new" problem became a central issue and subject to a body of law.

Within the American context activists benefited from antidiscrimination laws such as the Equal Pay Act of 1963 and the Civil Rights Act of 1964 that helped to frame sexual harassment as a form of sex discrimination on the job. Particularly influential became the work of Catherine MacKinnon, a feminist legal scholar on sexual harassment. Her 1979 book *Sexual Harassment of Working Women* argued that sexual harassment is discrimination because it constitutes unequal treatment of men and women at work and because it affects the economic rights of women as a group. Women risk job loss if they refuse sexual favors to superiors or may quit jobs because of harassment by colleagues. She thus framed sexual harassment as a workplace/discrimination issue and an issue of violence/sexuality, linking economic to sexual rights (Zippel 2006: 15). MacKinnon distinguished between two different forms of sexual harassment: "quid pro quo" harassment or sexual blackmail by superiors, and

"hostile environment" harassment, sexual or sexist behavior by peers that dete-
riorates the working conditions of the employee. Feminists also made a broader
argument about the harm to all women caused by sexual harassment as a form
of sexism.

The feminist framing of the problem, but also strategies and legal frameworks developed within the American context, served as an important source
of inspiration for European feminists.

TRANSNATIONAL DIFFUSION FROM THE UNITED STATES TO EUROPE

In the early 1980s, the issue of sexual harassment "traveled" to Europe. In
some cases, as I found out in interviews, European feminists traveled to the
United States to learn more about ideas and practices that had been developed
in that context.

In 1980, two Dutch feminists, one of whom had been living in the United
States for several years, decided to investigate the incidence of sexual harassment in the Netherlands. For this purpose, they copied an American survey that
had been issued by the popular women's magazine *Redbook*. Their initiative
attracted much attention and reactions in the media. The initiators invited the
women's department of the largest Dutch trade union to form a working group
on sexual harassment, the *werkgroep ongewenste intimiteiten op de werkvloer*
(Working Group on Unwanted Sexual Intimacies on the Workfloor). Likewise, French feminists formed an association to combat sexual violence against
women at work in 1985 called the *Association européene contre les violences
faites aux femmes aux travail* (AVFT, the European Association against Violence toward Women at Work). This initiative was also informed by American and French Canadian examples (Saguy 2002: 250). In Spain, trade union
women asked the Union General de Trabajadores to commission a study of the
incidence of sexual harassment in Spain in 1986. Their initiative was supported
by the International Confederation of Free Trade Unions, which in that same
year published a special guide to advise trade unions about how to deal with
this issue. In Germany, the first awareness programs against sexual harassment
in the workplace, organized by feminist advocates, took place in the late 1980s
and were inspired not only by American feminism, but also by other European
examples (Zippel 2006: 164).

These European initiatives against sexual harassment emerged about five
to ten years later than in the United States and were clearly informed by
the American example through direct links such as international feminist networks, personal contacts, and visits, but in some cases also through the media,
or available (feminist) literature. Although the issue of sexual harassment was
rapidly adopted across Europe, European feminists were also rather critical of
the American approach to sexual harassment. I will examine how European
feminists received and translated foreign feminist concepts and ideas. Differences in national political, legal, and cultural traditions importantly shaped
this process, but, as I will demonstrate, feminists across Europe have also tried

to overcome these differences and develop international strategies and coalitions to frame sexual harassment as a problem that requires a transnational, European answer.

RECEPTION

Reception is a first central step in the diffusion process – the way an actor perceives and interprets a new idea or practice is decisive for her willingness to consider using a foreign example. The issue of sexual harassment caused ambivalent reactions across Europe. On one hand, feminists recognized the problem of gender and power at work in which sexuality and harassment were used as tools both by superiors and colleagues to keep women in subordinate positions. As a Dutch feminist active within the largest Dutch trade union observed:

[W]e knew it was happening, it was by no means a new problem. Unwanted sexual behavior had occurred ever since men and women were working together. But it was a taboo subject, part and parcel of being a woman active on the labor market, but something you did not speak of.

> (interview with Els Hoogerhuis, women's section of trade union FNV in Roggeband 2002: 213)

On the other hand, some doubts were present. Another Dutch activist explained that she viewed sexual harassment as a specific cultural problem:

In my view sexual harassment at first appeared a largely American phenomenon. I considered the sexual culture of the US to be different, with very specific ideas about how women ought to be dressed at work, very feminine.... I somehow thought the problem would be less extensive here. Thinking of it now, it is a bit strange that I had these doubts, because I myself had experienced harassment, but never labeled it that way and simply perceived it as an incident.

> (interview with Mieke Verloo, initiator of first Dutch survey on sexual harassment, in Roggeband 2002: 212)

Similar doubts were present in Spain and France. Even though most feminists agreed that harassment was a common phenomenon in their country, they were suspicious about the high incidence reported within the American context. Therefore, the first step for many feminists across Europe was to investigate the extent of the problem in their own countries. Explorative studies in the Netherlands and Spain indicated that equally high numbers of women had experienced some form of sexual harassment.

The study we ourselves conducted and other European studies, like in the UK, helped to convince us that sexual harassment was a common problem across Europe, not just in the US.

> (Elvira Llopes, women's section of trade union CC.OO, in Roggeband 2002: 216)

Research thus served to raise consciousness on the issue and "transport" the issue to the European context. It also served as an important legitimating tool to request social and political attention for the problem.

RECONTEXTUALIZING THE AMERICAN FRAME

European feminists drew heavily on ideas and strategies developed in the United States. The French feminist Marie-Victoire Louis, an important French pioneer, stated that the American and Canadian feminist work on sexual harassment "saved years of reflection" (Saguy 2002: 253). Similarly, a Spanish feminist of the major trade union UGT remarked that the feminist analysis that linked harassment to gender and power was particularly useful to understand the problem (Roggeband 2002: 213).

Feminists across Europe coincided in framing sexual harassment both as a workplace issue and as an issue of violence against women. There was, however, much discussion about how to translate the concept of sexual harassment. Initially, Dutch feminists decided to translate the issue as "unwanted intimacies" (*ongewenste intimiteiten*), putting emphasis on the right of women to define what behavior they perceived as unwanted. The concept was often ridiculed in the press and on the workfloor ("what intimacies do you want?"), however, and was therefore later replaced by the concept of "sexual intimidation." The French feminists of AVFT defined sexual harassment as a specific form of sexual violence in the workplace and labeled it as *"violences faites aux femmes aux travail,"* although later the French Canadian translation *"harcelement sexuelle"* was adopted. In Germany feminists chose the translation of *"sexuelle belästigung"* or mobbing, which refers to bullying, but can also be used for physical attacks and intimidation by superiors. The Spanish translation, *"acoso sexual,"* remained closest to the American concept.

Although in all four countries feminists agreed on a broad definition of sexual harassment that included both forms of sexual harassment distinguished by Catherine MacKinnon, quid pro quo and hostile environment sexual harassment, both French and Spanish feminists decided to put a stronger emphasis on the struggle against sexual blackmail than on hostile environment sexual harassment. They considered that by framing the issue this way they would be more successful in getting sexual harassment on the political agenda. Also, they feared that hostile environment harassment would not be taken seriously in a cultural context in which kissing, friendly touching, and hugging are seen a common greeting practice for women and men. It was argued that southern European culture in this sense differed too much from the American culture. American discussions and regulations were perceived as exaggerated and puritan, and therefore counterproductive.

In France, there was a pervasive criticism of the American situation. The press regularly reported about "American excesses": "the simple act of holding the door open for a women can elicit a severe reprimand and that most men admit to being more cautious in their dealings with women in the workplace"

(Saguy 2002: 260). Also, public intellectuals and lawmakers argued that sexual harassment bills *à l'americaine* would disrupt existing gender relations and sexual culture and threaten everyday seduction. Françoise Giroud, former Secretary of Women's Rights, contrasted the French "harmonious relations between the sexes" with American "gender warfare" and argued that French women would be able to negotiate most situations well on their own (Saguy 2002: 261). This resistance against legislating sexual harassment forced French feminists in favor of legislation to be careful in addressing the issue and actively counteract caricatures of the American situation. French feminists therefore tried to disarm potential adversaries by limiting their focus to only sexual harassment of an employee by his or her boss (ibid.).

Likewise, Spanish feminists feared that the issue of sexual and sexist behavior of peers would not be taken seriously in a cultural context in which touching and making positive remarks about one's looks (*piropear*) is generally seen as a positive cultural value.

> Some of the American regulations were seen as very rigid and exaggerated, not appropriate for this context. Our culture is much more direct, more physical contact and so on. I therefore think that the radical position of some American feminists forced us to come up with our own strategy.
>
> (Maria Jesus Pinto, trade union CC.OO, cited in Roggeband 2002: 221)

Like their French counterparts, Spanish feminists opted to start their lobby for legislation with an emphasis on sexual blackmail, which they considered as "easier to sell" (Roggeband 2002: 222). French and Spanish feminists thus strategically reframed the issue to create legitimacy and look for potential alliances.

Feminist activists also borrowed other strategies, such as consciousness raising, documenting sexual harassment through surveys, and mobilizing protests around specific incidents, from the American movements. As a result, in the early 1980s, media attention on sexual harassment in some EU member states began to raise public awareness of the issue. Publicizing the results of national surveys in the Netherlands, Belgium, and Spain helped to convince the wider public of the nature and extent of the problem.

POLITICIZING SEXUAL HARASSMENT: CHALLENGING THE INSTITUTIONAL LEVEL

In most countries with active trade unions, feminists chose a double strategy of targeting both the state and trade unions. Although it appeared easier to raise the issue within the trade unions because of the existing feminist alliances within these organizations, female union members encountered strong resistance. Sexual harassment was trivialized and considered a "women's issue" of less political relevance. Furthermore, it constituted a potential conflict of interest within the organization when sexual harassment occurred among union members. Dutch feminists who raised the issue within the country's largest trade union, for instance, were accused of "placing under suspicion all men" and thus threatening the solidarity principle within the union (Roggeband 2002: 65). For this reason, it was easier to find support for the issue of sexual blackmail within the trade unions. In their framing efforts, trade union feminists decided to focus exclusively on sexual harassment by employers. By doing this the conflict between workers and employers was emphasized, which fostered rather than threatened union solidarity (Roth 2003: 148).

The issue of sexual harassment also lacked legitimacy within the national political arenas. In the Netherlands, opportunities to get the issue on the political agenda at first appeared favorable. Hedy d'Ancona, a well-known feminist activist, became state secretary for women's affairs in 1981 and supported the claim of the *werkgroep ongewenste intimiteiten*. The framing of sexual harassment as a particular form of violence against women helped her to incorporate the "new" issue into her plans for an integral policy to combat sexual violence against women. The recommendation of the *werkgroep ongewenste intimiteiten* to start a national complaints office was adopted in the policy document. In 1984, the group received state funding to create this office. The complaints office, which was given the activist name *Handen Thuis* ("Hands Off"), started as a service for victims but after a few years developed into a consultancy office for labor organizations. The complaints office was a highly innovative project within the European context, which gave the Netherlands the status of pioneering the issue within the EU. The Dutch government, however, did not take any further steps to legislate against sexual harassment and instead maintained that the EC should legislate (Roggeband and Verloo 1999). The Dutch feminist organization Handen Thuis therefore pressured the government to use the Dutch presidency of the Council of Ministers to position the Netherlands as a European forerunner and innovator. This lobby was successful and the Dutch presidency organized a conference on the issue in 1986.

In France, the AVFT also employed a strategy that pressured the French government to reform its penal code and labor laws (Saguy 2002). There was, however, no political support for this plan. Yvette Roudy, a member of the Socialist party, proposed a law against sexual harassment but this plan was not backed within her party:

When I proposed it to the socialist group, the first reaction was "You aren't going to prohibit flirting. We are not in the United States."
(*Liberation*, 30 April 1992, cited in Saguy 2002: 261)

Hence, instead, the AVFT successfully applied for initial financial support from the EC and, in subsequent years, they also received government support.

The issue of sexual harassment was not given priority at the national level and no national government in the EC passed laws addressing it. Because they faced limited opportunities or even resistance at the national level, feminist groups across Europe instead started lobbying to place sexual harassment on the agenda of supranational organizations, mainly the EC.

SCALING UP TO THE TRANSNATIONAL LEVEL: CREATING TRANSNATIONAL ADVOCACY NETWORKS

By turning their attention to the EC, feminists decided to use an additional layer of opportunities that was more flexible and open for influencing policy than most national institutional contexts. By turning their attention and pressure to the EU level, activists were able to create a new venue for EU action (Roggeband and Verloo 1999). The EC, in particular, was busy promoting and building an agenda of gender equality within the European Union and therefore actively supported the development of transnational advocacy networks (TANs) in general and the TAN on gender equality in particular (Zippel 2006: 91). The French AVFT, UK WaSH (Women against Sexual Harassment), and Dutch Hands Off served as brokers to initiate an informal TAN by establishing contacts with feminist and gender-sensitive actors from within and outside the EU institutions. Their aim was not only to lobby at different levels, but also to create a shared European frame and joint strategy to promote EU and national legislation against sexual harassment. The network drew extensively on experiences and ideas developed within the United States and Europe. In particular, the U.S. policy model was exemplary in formulating measures against sexual harassment (ibid.: 99). Sexual harassment was framed both as a workplace issue, and thus under the purview of the EC, and as an issue of violence against women.

The network successfully targeted members of the EU Parliament and Commission to promote legislation. In 1983, socialist members of the European Parliament, Fuillet (France) and Cinciari-Rodano (Italy), presented a draft to the European Parliament demanding action against the sexual exploitation and blackmail of women in the workplace (Zippel 2006: 94). In 1984, the Dutch former state secretary d'Ancona, now a member of the European Parliament, was appointed as special *rapporteur* for the EC on sexual harassment. In 1986, the European Parliament passed a resolution on violence against women, recommending action on the part of the Commission (OJC 175, July 14, 1986). That same year, the Council of Ministers, under Dutch presidency, organized a conference and the Council of Ministers commissioned an EU-wide study (Roggeband 2002: 70).

THEORIZATION: CREATING A EUROPEAN SEXUAL HARASSMENT FRAME

The result, Michael Rubenstein's report *The Dignity of Women at Work*, was published in 1987 and incorporated feminist ideas and proposals from the United States and the UK, but used these elements to strategically develop a distinctive European model (Zippel 2006: 93). Sexual harassment was framed as conduct affecting the dignity of women and men at work: "Sexual harassment means unwanted conduct of a sexual nature, or other conduct based on sex affecting the dignity of women and men at work. This includes unwelcome physical, verbal or nonverbal conduct" (OJ No C 157, 27. 6. 1990, p. 3).

Defining harassment as the "violation of dignity" drew on the continent's tradition of workers' rights and the international UN discourse on human rights (Friedman and Whitman 2003). In this way the more contentious frame of sexual harassment as sex discrimination was avoided. Sexual harassment was linked to the existing legitimate field of intervention on equal treatment of women and men at the workplace as defined by the Equal Treatment Directive of 1976. The Rubenstein report revealed that only a few member states had adequate legislation and made several suggestions for EU-level directives and a code of practice (Roggeband 2002).

Certification by the European Commission

Member state governments, however, resisted the creation of the new directive or expanding the existing Equal Treatment Directive. Within the EC no consensus could be reached regarding the conduct that would constitute sexual harassment (Zippel 2006: 94), but agreement could be reached for nonbinding soft law measures. In 1990, the Council of Ministers passed a resolution on the Protection of the Dignity of Women and Men in the Workplace (OJ No C 157, June 27, 1990). With this resolution, the EC encouraged policy transfer between member states. This strategy promoted crossnational exchange of policy models. In 1991, the EC issued a recommendation and Code of Practice on sexual harassment in the workplace to stimulate member states to develop national legislation. The Code of Practice defined sexual harassment as unwanted sexual behavior with negative implications for the working conditions of an employee. Just as in the United States, the EU defined sexual harassment from the point of view of the victims. When an employee feels harassed, the code said, his or her complaint should be taken very seriously and not be denied or played down.

According to Evelyn Collins (1996), who worked for the Equal Opportunity Unit of the EC, these soft law measures were the result of the lobbying efforts of the transnational advocacy network, in particular groups such as AVFT, Hands Off and WaSH. The demands of these groups are visible in the feminist framing of the issue visible in the Code of Practice (92/131/EEC):

As sexual harassment is often a function of women's status in the employment hierarchy, policies to deal with sexual harassment are likely to be most effective where they are linked to a broader policy to promote equal opportunities and improve the position of women.

Feminists across Europe used the transnational advocacy network on sexual harassment to exchange information and knowledge, which enhanced learning processes about failed and successful frames and strategies. The TAN on sexual harassment thus helped to create a specific transnational expertise that proved to be an important resource to bridge national cultural, political, and legal differences among countries. As Zippel argues, "professional, scientific language" became "the currency" in transnational communication among feminists, policy makers, and politicians (2006: 91).

Despite the success of creating a common frame and getting the issue on the EC agenda as a workplace issue, feminists active in the TAN on sexual harassment were disappointed that no binding legislation was developed. The heated debates in EU member states made it unlikely that an agreement at the EU level would be reached. Therefore, more lobbying work was necessary at the national level.

SCALING DOWN TO THE NATIONAL LEVEL

Feminists from different EU member states tried to capitalize on the transnational soft law measures to shape national policies and institutional arrangements. One of the strategies used by feminist groups across Europe was to compare their countries to other, more "advanced," countries. Feminists framed their country's position and role in combating sexual harassment either as potential "forerunner" or "laggard." The EU soft law measures served to justify a "moderate" European way of defining sexual harassment and designing policies. Advocates in Spain and France were now able to avoid mentioning U.S. laws or studies as examples and instead used the Rubenstein report and Code of Practice to legitimize their claims. Ironically, the EU definition was almost identical to that of the United States, but could now be "sold" as typically European.

According to Marie-Victoire Louis from the French AVFT, the EU measures were an "extraordinary tool":

The [European] Council's decisions and recommendations allowed us to push the [French] legislation. It was an extraordinary tool. [Our use of it] was strategic. The association got its first concrete financial support from the EC. So Europe allowed us to live financially and we could draw on those different declarations to argue our case.

(Louis in Saguy 2002: 253)

Furthermore, France became one of the first countries to pass a law on sexual harassment following the EC recommendations.

Spanish feminists seized the opportunity that their country had just become a new EU member and used the argument that Spanish gender relations needed to be "Europeanized" (Valiente 1998). Rubenstein's study revealed that Spain had no adequate regulations to combat sexual harassment. Feminists within the ruling Socialist party (PSOE) proposed to amend the "Workers' statute" and add a paragraph to ensure respect for a person's intimacy and dignity, including protection against verbal or physical insults of a sexual nature. This legal measure was defended by indicating that other economically and politically "more developed" countries were ahead in combating sexual harassment (Valiente 1998: 217). In 1995, the Penal Code was reformed to include sexual harassment by superiors and, since 2000, the Social Offences and Sanctions Act also covers coworker harassment.

The Dutch feminist lobby for national regulation initially met resistance from the social partners. Both unions and employers were not in favor of state regulation and instead argued that the problem should be addressed through collective agreements. Hands Off found an important ally in a former union employee, Elske ter Veld, who was appointed as Secretary of Social Affairs and Employment. In 1994, she was able to add a paragraph to the law on labor conditions in which employers became obliged to protect their employees against sexual harassment. The law, however, requires no specific mechanisms and leaves room for employers and employee representatives to work out means to handle harassment (Roggeband and Verloo 1999; Roggeband 2002).

Compliance with EC measures thus became an explicit and powerful argument for promoting legislation at the national level. Feminists across Europe successfully used the European recommendation and Code of Practice to overcome resistance at the national level and legitimize national policy measures. The response of nation states, however, differed enormously, and therefore the TAN on sexual harassment continued its lobby for more binding legislation at the EU level.

AND UP AGAIN

In 1999, a new window of opportunity opened at the EU level when Anna Diamantopoulou of Greece was appointed as Commissioner for Social and Employment Affairs. She announced that she would promote a new directive on gender equality and make sexual harassment one of her priorities. The resistance of the Greek government to adopt soft law measures convinced her that more binding regulation should be developed at the EU level. Her intentions were backed within the EC, but met resistance from Austria, Ireland, Sweden, and the United Kingdom (Zippel 2006: 118). In addition, the European employers union UNICE actively lobbied against a new directive. The TAN on sexual harassment published a new study indicating that across Europe 40 to 60 percent of working women suffered from harassment that deteriorated their working conditions and forced women to leave their jobs. These results helped to establish a link between sexual harassment and sex discrimination. Also, the network successfully lobbied to get support from the European Trade Union Confederation (Zippel 2006: 119).

In 2002, almost twenty years after sexual harassment was first mentioned in EC documents, a new equal treatment directive was proposed, including a binding definition of sexual harassment as sex discrimination, in line with original U.S. regulations and the original feminist framing. The directive required member states to revise or adopt laws by 2005 encouraging employers to prevent sexual harassment.

CONCLUSIONS

Concerning the issue of sexual harassment, national movements tried to bypass their often reluctant governments by directly searching out European allies and mobilizing additional resources for their domestic struggle. In that way, they attempted to bring pressure to bear on their hesitant government from outside. Thus, feminist efforts created a multilevel dynamic in which activism, in particular framing efforts, and policy impact occurred both at the level of member states and the supranational level. Strategic framing served as a central instrument. Feminists active in transnational advocacy networks developed a joint collective action frame by adapting American ideas and strategies to the European context. The TAN was actively engaged in sharing knowledge and experiences in the different EU member states through international conferences and sponsored empirical studies to examine the scope of the problem across Europe.

The findings of this chapter led to several conclusions in relation to processes of diffusion and scale shift. Diffusion is by no means a linear process, but a dynamic cooperative process of up- and downscaling, in which actors jointly recreate frames and strategically adapt them to make them resonate with opportunity structures at different levels. My empirical data draw attention to a dual diffusion dynamics of "localization," in which activists strategically frame their issues and actions as local and adapted to the specific national context (culture, legal settings, figures, political opportunities, necessities), and "transnationalization," seeking broader responses and coalitions by stressing commonalities in the nature of the problem, international political opportunities, and the like. Transnational diffusion of ideas and practices often results in scale shift and creates transnational advocacy networks or other forms of coordinated action. In relation to the diffusion and scale shift of the issue of sexual harassment, these TANs were central for strategically reframing the issue of sexual harassment. By defining harassment as the "violation of dignity," they managed to create a shared "European" frame of sexual harassment (theorization). This strategic adaptation of the frame had several important functions (Stone 1989; Tarrow 2005). First, it was crucial for further diffusion. Second, it helped to build a broad strategic alliance. Third, it was crucial to gain legitimacy for action (certification by the EU). Creating a transnational expert frame and using policy learning experiences and comparative research results not only made the feminist framing of sexual harassment gain acceptance and legitimacy for the ideas, but also helped feminist organizations alter the political opportunity structure and create new venues for action.

My findings show the advantage of a multilevel dynamic for mobilization and politicization: "Scaling up" to the European level helped the European advocacy groups working against sexual harassment to gain legitimacy and to pressure the member states to take action. What started as a "simple" diffusion process between social movements resulted in complex multilevel brokerage, framing, and negotiating with different actors, all of which implied major gains both at the national and transnational levels.

3

Temporality and Frame Diffusion

The Case of the Creationist/Intelligent Design and Evolutionist Movements from 1925 to 2005

James E. Stobaugh and David A. Snow

In this chapter, we seek to expand our understanding of how frames travel over time and especially of some of the factors that affect the temporal diffusion of frames. We do so by examining the extent to which the various frames associated with the creationist/intelligent design movement and the evolutionist movement have evolved and mutated from the famous Scopes Monkey Trial in 1925 to the intelligent design (ID) trial in Dover, Pennsylvania in 2005, and by exploring some of the factors contributing to this process of frame change and evolution. We explore these changes within the context of the legal institution, focusing on legal framing in the major court cases involving the teaching of evolution and creation science in public schools in America since the famed Scopes trial. We are not the first to explore legal framing, as Pedriana (2006), among others, has examined competing legal frames within the women's movement. We extend this research by focusing on framing between oppositional movements mobilized around the issues of creationism and evolution.

We begin to answer our questions by providing an overview of the relevant diffusion and framing literature and the issues not sufficiently examined by this literature. We then consider the ongoing debate over teaching evolution and creationism in the schools as it has played out over the years in the American judicial system. Next, we discuss our data sources and procedures. We then elaborate our findings and consider their implications for understanding the interplay of framing and diffusion over time. In addition to accenting the importance of time in understanding the ebb and flow of social movement frames and framing strategies across time, our analysis highlights the dynamic, interactive character of framing in relation to diffusion.

THEORETICAL ISSUES AND FOCAL QUESTIONS

Students of collective behavior and social movements have long been interested in diffusion-related topics and processes, dating back at least to 1897 and

LeBon's *The Crowd*. Until recently, however, "contagion" was the operative, umbrella concept for the spread of some behavioral, emotional, or ideational phenomenon among a collectivity. Indeed, in the 1987 (third) edition of their now classic text on collective behavior, Turner and Killian still classified the "contagion perspective" as one of the three dominant perspectives on the coordination that makes collective behavior truly collective rather than the aggregation of parallel individual behaviors. But, as Turner and Killian's analysis suggested and as subsequent work has made clear (e.g., McAdam and Rucht 1993; McPhail 1991; Snow and Benford 1999; Soule 1997, 1999, 2004), the idea of contagion as represented in the work of LeBon ([1897] 1960), Tarde (1903), Park and Burges (1921), and Blumer ([1939] 1972) was – and is – essentially a flawed explanatory concept. The core problem with the idea of contagion as the mechanism through which behaviors, sentiments, or beliefs and ideas are spread is that it suggests a nonrational and nonagentic process. This problem is aptly illustrated in Blumer's famed contention that contagion is predicated on "circular reaction" rather than on "interpretive interaction" ([1939] 1972), which is said to characterize nonhabituated human interaction.

The upshot of Turner and Killian's (1987) and McPhail's (1991) critiques, Soule's various empirical studies (1997, 1999), and McAdam and Rucht's (1993) and Snow and Benford's (1999) theoretical elaborations is that the long-standing contagion perspective has been pushed aside, as the contagion concept is now seldom used by students of collective behavior and social movements. Instead, we now speak of diffusion, as it has become the operative, umbrella concept for considering the spread or flow of social behaviors, moods or sentiments, and various cognitions or cognitive clusters or perspectives among individuals, organizations, and even nations and nationalities.

As with any evolving area of inquiry, theoretical inquiries and empirical research tend to focus on some relevancies or areas of concern to the exclusion of others. Such has been the case with the recent body of work on diffusion within the context of collective action and social movements. To date, the bulk of this research and theorizing has focused primarily on the diffusion of certain protest tactics, as with "sit-ins" in the southern civil rights student movement (Morris 1981) and the "shantytown" in relation to the anti-apartheid movement (Soule 1997) and the effect of such bridging or facilitative mechanisms as network linkages, the media, mutual identification (e.g., shared identity), and spatial proximity in the spread or diffusion of tactical practices and symbols (see Soule 2004 for a summary).

Much less attention has been devoted to the matter of time and whether, and to what extent, the passage of time affects the item diffused or the character of the process. Most diffusion studies of collective action cover a relatively brief period of time, as with the spread of riots across American cities in the late 1960s (Myers 2000; Spilerman 1976). But we do not know much about the diffusion of items over an extensive period of time, as in the case of four or five decades. There has also been less research on the diffusion of clusters of ideational and symbolic elements as encapsulated in what has been called collective action frames.[1]

Additionally, there has still been little attention given to the role of the various sets of actors implicated in the diffusion process. We know that some number of actors will be involved in the transmission of the object of diffusion, with others functioning as adopters, but we do not know much about how these, and possibly other actors as well, modify the cultural practice or item being diffused, even though Snow and Benford (1999) directed attention to this agentic aspect of diffusion nearly ten years ago. Finally, some research suggests that collective action frames change with changes in relevant events (Ellingson 1995; Noonan 1995; Rothman and Oliver 1999), but the relationship between the character of the frame change and the kinds of events or challenges encountered still calls for further investigation and elaboration.

In this chapter we attempt to shed some empirical light on these insufficiently researched and theorized areas by examining the following questions in relation to the evolution and mutation of the creationist and evolutionary science frames within the educational and legal institutions: (1) What are the objects of diffusion for both the proponents of creationism and evolutionary science, and how have they been framed over time within the court system? And, most interestingly: (2) How and why did the way in which the objects of diffusion were framed change course through the eighty-year period from 1925 to 2005? More concretely, what factors account for the changes or mutations observed?

THE CREATION SCIENCE AND EVOLUTIONARY SCIENCE DEBATE

To provide a context for the research, we begin with a brief history of the creationist/intelligent design movement in America. The earliest and historically most celebrated clash between the creationists and evolutionists occurred in

---

[1] Collective action frames are the resultant products of framing activity within the social movement arena. They are relatively coherent sets of action-oriented beliefs and meanings that legitimate and inspire social movement campaigns and activities. Like everyday interpretive frames, collective action frames focus attention by specifying what is "in" and "out" of frame; articulate and elaborate the punctuated elements within the frame so that a particular meaning or set of meanings is conveyed; and, as a result, often transform the meanings associated with the objects of attention, such that some situation, activity, or category of individuals is seen in a strikingly different way than before, as when everyday misfortunes are reframed as injustices or status groups such as the homeless and cigarette smokers are framed as legitimate targets for social movement protest. But collective action frames differ from everyday interactional frames in terms of their primary mobilization functions: to mobilize or activate movement adherents so that they move, metaphorically, from the balcony to the barricades (action mobilization); to convert bystanders into adherents, thus broadening the movement's base (consensus mobilization); and to neutralize or demobilize adversaries (counter-mobilization). For discussion of collective action frames and their elements, see Gamson (1992) and Snow and Benford (1988, 1992); for review and discussion of research on framing and social movements, see Benford and Snow (2000) and Snow (2004).

1925 in Dayton, Tennessee, and became immortalized as the Scopes Monkey Trial. It was here that high school teacher John T. Scopes went on trial for teaching evolution, which was prohibited by state law. The two sides in the debate sent their best to the tiny Tennessee courthouse, with the creationists represented by William Jennings Bryan and the evolutionists by Clarence Darrow. In what has become one of America's best-known legal stories, Bryan took the stand and was submitted to a grueling cross-examination by Darrow. This moment was commemorated in the American consciousness through the play and film *Inherit the Wind*.

People often think back to the Scopes trial as the end of the stranglehold on teaching of evolution in the schools because of Darrow's brilliant and ardent cross-examination of Bryan, as it received so much positive press in the national media that it has become the accepted "narrative" for the event, when in reality the outcome was quite different. Not only was John Scopes found guilty of violating state law and fined, but he eventually lost an appeal as well, although the court did drop the fine on a technicality. These decisions not only constituted a legal victory for the creationist movement, but also provided the symbolic and legal impetus to press for laws in other states to forbid the teaching of evolution.

Faced with several states passing laws prohibiting the teaching of evolution, science textbook publishers bypassed the mention of evolution in their textbooks so they could be marketed in all states. This clearly was a victory for the creationists, as they had effectively closed the door on evolution in the classroom. In time, this led to a rupture between advances in evolution science that were taking place in the academy and the teaching of evolution science in American public schools. This fissure continued through the 1960s when the Biological Sciences Curriculum Study (BSCS) was commissioned by the National Science Foundation with the mandate to produce a textbook that would feature evolution as a salient aspect of the science curriculum (Toumey 1994: 28).

The 1960s were marked by a reversal of dominance of the creationist movement. This was most prominently illustrated in the 1968 U.S. Supreme Court case, *Epperson v. Arkansas*, which challenged an Arkansas law prohibiting teaching evolution because it conflicted with teaching Protestant Christianity. The court ruled that this prohibition violated the First Amendment, saying that a law cannot be used to protect religion from science. With this setback the creationists had to find another means of countering the teaching of evolution (Binder 2002). Their strategy was two-pronged: First, it entailed creating a new theory, dubbed "creation science," which could be taught alongside evolution and thus challenge it. The second prong of their strategy was to target local and state school boards of education, pressing them to authorize teaching creation science in the classroom and to get this perspective included alongside evolutionary theory in the textbooks that the school districts purchased.

This double-edged tactic was employed by the creationist movement from the late 1960s through the mid-1980s. In so doing the creationists hoped that students either would be convinced that creation science was the correct explanation for the creation of the earth and life on it or would be so confused by the competing claims that they would, at the very least, reject evolution. The creationists realized that they could not keep evolution out of school but they hoped they had found a way to keep it from being taught as fact.

This tactic continued with some success. In July 1981, for example, Louisiana passed the Balanced Treatment legislation, which held that when the origins of the earth were discussed, both perspectives – evolution and creationism – would have to be discussed and neither could be treated as scientific fact (Binder 2002: 140). The argument for this law was that it protected academic freedom and was neutral toward any specific religion. Upon its passage, the American Civil Liberties Union (ACLU) sued the state of Louisiana, arguing that balanced treatment was in fact tantamount to teaching religion. The case made its way up to the U.S. Supreme Court and in 1987 the court ruled, in *Edwards v. Aguillard*, that teaching creation science was in fact promoting religion and was therefore unconstitutional. This decision was a setback for the movement that had, for nearly two decades, pursued a course of getting creationism taught side by side with evolution in the public schools. It became clear, based on the *Epperson* and *Edwards* decisions, that the Supreme Court was unconvinced by the efforts of the creationist movement to frame itself as a science and that if the movement was going to gain a footing within the educational system, it would have to find a way to overcome the hurdles set by the Supreme Court in keeping religion out of public education.

The vacuum created by the *Edwards* decision left the movement searching for an alternative to evolution, one that could stand up to the scrutiny of the judicial system. What the movement needed was a rival theory that would embrace the ideals of creation science but would not be seen as promoting one religion over another. The movement found such a program in "intelligent design," which came onto the stage in the early 1990s not just as an alternative to creation science but also as a reframing of it. The theory of intelligent design was proposed by UC-Berkeley law professor Phillip Johnson as an alternative to evolution. Many have argued that the fact that it was crafted and promulgated by a lawyer was a sign that it was shaped to pass constitutional muster with the legal system (Forrest and Gross 2003). Advocated mainly by the Discovery Institute, a partisan think tank based in Seattle, the intelligent design frame claimed that scientific evidence does not support the theory of evolution, largely because the world is too complex to have been created by chance mutations. It is thus argued that the complexity inherent in the world and universe can be explained only by the presence of some intelligent entity.

The institute and other proponents of the intelligent design frame have been very careful to state not who or what this creator is, but only that there simply must have been one. Care is also taken to present intelligent design as nonsectarian and nonreligious. Furthermore, it is argued that because there are cracks in evolutionary theory, intelligent design should be taught as an alternative rival explanation; hence, the evolution of the "Teach the Controversy" frame.

The "Teach the Controversy" frame has been taken up as the battle cry of proponents of intelligent design throughout the country, with the school boards of Dover, Pennsylvania and the state of Kansas actually approving its insertion into the curriculum in their respective educational jurisdictions. These successful efforts spurred counter-movements leading to elections in each jurisdiction that brought in new slates of board members who overturned the pro-intelligent design initiatives. Kindling was added to the debate when George W. Bush weighed in on the issue, stating that he favored multiple perspectives being taught in the science classroom. The Dover case wound its way into the court system and was adjudicated in federal court in 2005, with the proponents of intelligent design claiming that their proposed theory was scientific rather than religious and therefore should be taught alongside evolution in high school science classes. Ultimately, the federal court ruled that intelligent design is religious and cannot be taught in the classroom.

Although not a thoroughgoing history of the battle between the creationist and the evolutionist movements, the preceding provides a sketch of the ways in which the movements have transformed over time and, in doing so, hints at the role of framing in the process. What we want to do now is consider more analytically how the objective of teaching creationism in the schools traveled and mutated from the Scopes trial to the present by examining the different ways in which that objective was framed in relation to the proponents of evolutionary science. Additionally, we seek to identify and elaborate some of the key factors that account for the frame mutations across time.

DATA SOURCES AND PROCEDURES

The data we use to track these questions come from the legal documents associated with the five key cases in which the contest between creation science/intelligent design and evolutionary science played out in the courtroom over the eighty-year period from 1925 to 2005. The five cases examined are *Scopes v. State of Tennessee* (1925), *Epperson v. State of Arkansas* (1968), *McLean v. State of Arkansas* (1981), *Edwards v. Aguillard* (1987), and *Kitzmiller v. Dover Area School District* (2005). Table 3.1 shows these cases along with the main issues addressed and the major holding of each case. These cases were chosen because they are cited in the relevant literature as the important cases in the movement opposing evolution teaching (Binder 2002; Forrest and Gross 2003). In addition, these cases provide variance in the level which they were adjudicated, with one settled at a lower state court (*Scopes*), two settled by federal courts at the district level (*McLean* and *Kitzmiller*), and two settled by the U.S. Supreme Court (*Epperson* and *Edwards*). This variation allows us to assess whether differences in the legal setting affect the character of the frames that are invoked.

We examine several types of legal documents, but the primary documents are the legal briefs filed in the courts by the proponents and opponents of teaching evolution. These documents are important because they include examples of

TABLE 3.1. *Cases, Issues, and Holdings*

Case	Year	Issue	Decision
Scopes v. State of Tennessee	1925	Teaching evolution	Upheld ban on teaching evolution
Epperson v. State of Arkansas	1968	Teaching evolution	Curricula should not be required to align with a particular religion
McLean v. State of Arkansas	1981	Creation science	Creation science violates the establishment clause
Edwards v. Aguillard	1987	Creation science	Teaching creationism in public schools is unconstitutional
Kitzmiller v. Dover Area School District	2005	Intelligent design	Teaching ID is unconstitutional because ID is not science

the frames projected to the court and the logic behind the frames. In addition to looking at the briefs, we also examined transcripts of available testimony and depositions given by witnesses and experts in these cases. Their testimony presents another way that movement frames are projected in the courts.

The majority of the documents were obtained from the Westlaw and Lexis-Nexis legal services. Older documents pertaining to the Scopes trial were obtained from a website at the University of Missouri-Kansas City, which hosts a collection of legal documents relating to the trial (Linder 2005).

For one case, *McLean v. State of Arkansas*, we were unable to obtain actual trial transcripts or legal briefs because the official records have been lost. Instead, we relied on detailed notes by ACLU attorneys on the witnesses' testimony. Although these notes might appear biased because the ACLU consistently has aligned itself with the evolution camp, this is not the case. These notes needed to be as detailed, factual, and accurate as possible because they would be used in preparing the closing arguments and might be necessary in preparing future cases. Because of this, these notes provided an acceptable source of data for a case in which this information is no longer available in other forms.

In the *Kitzmiller* case, briefs and motions were obtained through the aforementioned legal services, but trial transcripts were obtained from the Wikipedia site that had them linked in PDF format (Wikipedia 2006). Although Wikipedia has its limitations based on its nature as an open encyclopedia that any user can edit, the documents we analyzed were the actual scanned pages of the trial testimony in a format that does not allow for them to be altered by the public.

All told, we analyzed more than seventy-eight individual documents containing more than 1,000 pages of text. The documents were loaded into Atlas.ti and analyzed for specific issues, topics, or themes. One of the co-authors read through the documents in chronological order, line by line. When he identified a specific issue, topic, or theme, he would see if there was a code for it; if not, a new code would be created. Upon completion of coding we had a total of 101 codes. After the codes were identified we then went back through the documents, again in chronological order, and recoded them.

After the systematic coding was completed, the codes were aggregated into what Snow and Benford (1988; also see Benford and Snow 2000) identify as the diagnostic and prognostic components of collection action (collective problem solving) frames. These two components, along with motivational framing, constitute the three core framing tasks of collective action frames. For the purposes of this chapter we analyze the frame mutations in terms of changes in diagnostic and prognostic framing.

Diagnostic framing entails the diagnosis of some event or aspect of life as troublesome and in need of repair or change (problematization), and the assignment of blame or responsibility for the problem (attribution). For this project, diagnostic framing was indicated whenever a party addressing the court presented the problem that the party was confronting. Because of the logical and structured nature of the legal briefs we analyzed, the problem was usually expressly stated and easy to identify. After reviewing all the documents, we identified five key diagnostic framings, three that were used by the anti-evolutionist movement and two that were used by the evolutionist movement.

Prognostic framing, in relation to collective action, addresses the Leninesque question, "What is to be done?" More specifically, it articulates a solution to or remedy for the diagnostically framed problem. Within the context of the legal system, and particularly the courtroom, it is important to bear in mind that each of the contestants is appealing to the court for a remedial decision, and therefore the proposed remedy is framed in a fashion that the court can accept as a legal reason for siding with one contestant rather than the other. Unlike the diagnostic framings presented earlier that were specific to one contestant or the other, the prognostic framings of both movements – the anti-evolutionists and the evolutionists – were found to be similar, although the framings were employed in very disparate ways, which will be discussed subsequently. All told, five major prognostic framings were identified and used over the period in question.

FINDINGS

Having elaborated our data sources and the coding scheme and logic behind it, we now present our findings based on the analysis of the data. We present separately the findings for both the diagnostic and prognostic frames.

Diagnostic Frames

As noted earlier, diagnostic frames identify the problem(s) with which the movement or collectivity is confronted and attribute blame for that problem. As also noted, we identified five core diagnostic frames, three of which were constructed and employed by the creationist/intelligent design movement and two by the evolutionist movement.

Creationist/Intelligent Design Diagnostic Frames. The first and earliest diagnostic frame, employed by the creationists in the 1925 Scopes Monkey Trial, was the "Protect Religion" frame. The problem that this frame was diagnosing was the perceived threat of evolutionary theory to religious teachings, specifically Christian teachings. "Religious Belief," "Science and Religion Conflict," and "Science and Religion Different Realms" were some of the different codes that clustered under this frame.

This frame was articulated clearly by the famous creationist and presidential nominee, William Jennings Bryan, who argued that evolution must be banned from the schools because it posed a threat to the religious morals of the schoolchildren. He couched the problem in strong dichotomous terms, with religion and all that was good on one side versus evolution and all that was corrupt on the other. This is illustrated in his closing argument:

The case has assumed the proportions of a battle-royal between unbelief that attempts to speak through so-called science and the defenders of the Christian faith. . . . It is again a choice between God and Baal.   (William Jennings Bryan, 1925 [in Linder 2005])

It is clear that Bryan viewed the realms of religion and evolution as being at odds with one another. The problem for Bryan, and the other creationists of the day, was that not only was evolution viewed as heretical, but it was also seen as a real threat to the religious views that they espoused. Their central argument was that teaching that a theory exists that is antithetical to the creation story might lead children to question their faith and be led away from religion. Thus evolution was problematized as a threat to religion, which now was thought to require protection.

The "Protect Religion" frame was once again used in the *Epperson* case in 1968. In this case the state of Arkansas argued, much as the state of Tennessee did in the *Scopes* case, that evolutionary theory is "contrary to Christianity" (Jurisdictional Statement 1967). However, in this case the state was defending a law that made it illegal to teach a "theory or doctrine that mankind ascended or descended from a lower order of animals" (Initiated Act No. 1, 1929). When challenged in this case by the evolutionists, the creationists claimed, as before, that religion needed to be protected from teaching evolution. Eventually the Supreme Court ruled that governments could not bar the teaching of evolution simply to protect religious interests.

The next two cases, *McLean* (1981) and *Edwards* (1987), jettisoned the "Protect Religion" frame in favor of a newly constructed frame captured by the plea to "Teach Both Sides." Here the problem was framed diagnostically as the closed-door policy in the public schools to alternatives to evolutionary theory. Codes indicating this frame – such as "God-Fearing Country," "Teach Both," and "Still Teach Evolution" – emphasized that alternative viewpoints should be introduced because the United States is a religious nation, and therefore the biblical perspective should be taught as well as the scientific perspective.

This second creationist frame evolved in response to the constraints of the previous court ruling that forbade the exclusion of evolution from the public school classroom. Because evolution was now a standardized feature of the science curriculum in public schools, the problem was reframed from one of protecting religion to one of including the creationist point of view within the curriculum so students could be exposed to an alternative argument. For the creationist, it was inconceivable that evolutionary theory would be taught without something to "balance" it. This emphasis on inclusion and balance became the intersecting problem around which the creationist movement coalesced. This two-sided issue was captured during the *McLean* case in the testimony of a witness for the state, Dr. Larry R. Parker, who said, "Teaching only one view is tantamount to indoctrination" (Geisler 1982).

This fight continued in the *Edwards* case, which made its way up to the U.S. Supreme Court in 1987. Because of tactical considerations, *McLean* was never appealed higher; instead the creation scientists waited for a case that they thought would provide a better chance for success. They thought that *Edwards v. Aguillard* was the special case, framing the argument even more clearly. As noted in a 1986 brief of the Christian Legal Society and the National Association of Evangelicals:

Furthermore, the Act is neutrally "inclusive," allowing the teaching of both evolution-science and creation-science as scientific models, and not "exclusive," preferring one over the other.

> (Brief of the Christian Legal Society and National Association
> of Evangelicals as Amici Curiae Supporting Appellants 1986)

Thus the problem of keeping the creationist point of view in the schoolhouse shifted from protecting it from evolution to including it as an alternative, competing theory. But once again the creation scientists lost in court.

This defeat was followed by a third creationist/intelligent design diagnostic frame: the "Shut Out of Science Discourse" frame. This frame problematized the fact that alternatives to evolution, even those that claimed not to be religious, were summarily dismissed from the scientific debate and classroom presentation of human origins. Codes illustrating the presence of this frame were "Limit Scientific Inquiry," "Science Must Have Debate," and "Teach the Controversy."

This frame, promulgated during the 2005 *Kitzmiller v. Dover* case, was largely the child of the intersection of the *Edwards* defeat and the "intelligent design" frame developed principally by Phillip Johnson and the Seattle Discovery Institute. It constituted not a shift from but a transformation of the creation science frame (Forrest and Gross 2003). As noted earlier, the biblical creation idea was dropped and the reality of evolution was acknowledged, but it was now argued that complexity of life presumes a grand watchmaker-like entity, albeit not a blind one akin to Richard Dawkins's watchmaker (1986). With this new master frame in hand, and spurred by both the previous defeats and a still-unflinching commitment to the idea that students ought to be exposed to alternatives to the evolutionary theory, the creationists/anti-evolutionists, now in the guise of scientists, articulated a new frame with which to continue the battle. The problem now was that the intelligent design perspective was being excluded from academic and scientific discourse despite being framed as scientific, with the implication that creationism and creation science before them were religious and unscientific. This charge was clearly articulated in the brief filed by the several pro-ID biologists and Ph.D.s testifying in court in Dover:

Efforts to ban the scientific theory of intelligent design from the classroom, whether by a narrow definition of science or by a discriminatory attack on the personal motives of the scientists conducting scientific research into intelligent design, should be rejected by the Court.

(Brief of Amici Curiae Biologists and Other Scientists in
Support of Defendants 2005)

With this new frame constructed to shift attention away from religion to science, and the movement thus claiming that ID should have standing within the science curriculum, the long-standing contention between creationists and evolutionists had now come full circle, with science now the gatekeeper and proponents of creationism and ID now seeking entry into the schoolhouse.

Evolutionist Diagnostic Frames. In addition to the three aforementioned diagnostic frames associated with the creationist/intelligent design movements, we also identified two diagnostic frames proffered by evolutionists. The first pro-evolution frame was simply the "Teach Evolution" frame, which was used in the early part of the period of analysis during the *Scopes* case in 1925. The central problem from the vantage point of this frame was the fact that evolutionary theory was prohibited from being taught in the science classroom. In this case it was the evolutionists standing outside the schoolhouse door clamoring for entry. They were not rejecting the teaching of alternatives to science; they just wanted to be included. Some of the codes indicative of this frame were "Evolution Not Harmful" and "Scientific Standard." These codes illustrate the problem by making the case why evolution should be taught: first, it meets the scientific standard and therefore is appropriate for the science classroom; and second, it is not harmful, particularly to the religious sensibilities of the students.

This "teach evolution" framing did not carry much weight with the court, however, and languished on the vine, in what might be described as a long period of frame dormancy, until the 1968 *Epperson v. State of Arkansas* case.

It is important to note that in this intervening forty-year period the United States developed increasing interest in scientific knowledge, which accelerated during World War II and picked up greater speed with the space race, which began in 1957 with the launching of *Sputnik 1* by the Soviet Union. This race was another front in the escalating Cold War and thus seen as being fundamental to the country's political survival. If America was to catch up with and pass the Soviets it would need the top scientific minds, which required refocusing and ramping up scientific education in the classroom. It is against this changing cultural backdrop, in conjunction with various pertinent scientific advances, that the evolutionists mobilized in 1968 to counter efforts to have alternative perspectives included in the classroom.

So, for *Epperson v. State of Arkansas*, the evolutionists articulated a diagnostic frame that categorized "Challenges to Evolution as Religion." For the evolutionist proponents of this diagnostic frame, the problem they were advancing was that the different theoretical alternatives were religious and therefore should not be taught in the science classroom. Creation science, in particular, was seen as religious at its core and therefore inappropriate for the science curriculum and classroom. As stated quite clearly in one of the evolutionists' briefs:

[O]ne of the great arguments of the proponents of the "anti-evolution" statute is this Biblical inconsistency, which, perforce, casts the argument to that extent into a religious role.
                                                                (Jurisdictional Statement 1967)

Codes such as "Creation Science Is Religious" "ID Is Religious," and "Religious Motives" were markers of this frame,which was not only resonant with the cultural and political ascendance of science, but was also exclusionary, just as were the anti-evolutionists forty years earlier.

Discussion. Thus far we have elaborated the different diagnostic frames used in the courts that were associated with both the creationist/intelligent design movement and evolutionists, but the questions of why these frames mutated and when they did still beg answers. One part of the answer can be inferred from the pattern observed. The pattern, sketched in Figure 3.1, suggests that each mutation or change followed on the heels of a legal defeat. This makes sense, as the legal system is built in part on the theory of *stare decisis*, or let the decision stand, in which what was decided in the previous case should hold in the current case. The consequence of this for the contestants in the cases examined herein is that previously successful movements or challengers were highly likely to continue doing what they did before because this strategy had already been successful. The expectation is that it would succeed again and, therefore, there would be no reason to change the current framing strategy.

In contrast to the optimism that the system of precedents breeds for the winners, it produces a more difficult situation for the losers. Now not only are they arguing a current case, but they also must deal with the specter of past defeats. This creates a severe handicap. One of the key ways that a movement can overcome the problem of precedent is to construct a different diagnostic frame, which helps to reshape the issue involved and can hopefully move the issue out from under the purview of the previous precedent.

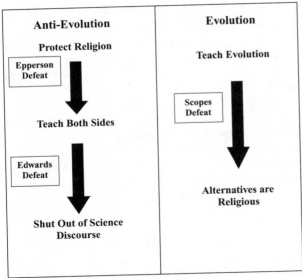

FIGURE 3.1. Diagnostic Frames

Our findings help bear this out. Each time the challengers, on both sides, experienced a defeat they regrouped and created a different diagnostic frame.[2] This adjustment did not happen so clearly in the *McLean* case but it did in the *Edwards* case. However, as we previously argued, *Edwards* was really just an extension of the earlier issues raised in *McLean*. The *McLean* decision was never appealed and it was not until the *Edwards* case six years later that the issues were fully adjudicated in the American legal system because of the belief by the creation science supporters that *Edwards* had a higher likelihood of success. In the face of an opposition movement with precedent on its side, it thus appears that the only option in the legal setting is to change the diagnostic frame and recast the problem so that the precedent no longer matters.

Prognostic Frames

As indicated earlier, prognostic frames prescribe some action as a remedy to the problem identified. We identified five major prognostic frames used over the eighty-year period by the two sets of contestants. They include Academic Freedom, Constitutional, Curriculum, Religion, and Science frames. Unlike the diagnostic frames presented previously, which were specific to one contestant or the other, we find that the contestants employed all five of these prognostic frames, but they did so in quite disparate ways at different times. It is thus useful

---

[2] This finding is consistent with Andersen's research, which revealed that the battles around LGBT issues in the legal system were essentially conflicts about "how a given gay rights claim should be understood" (2005: 210).

to keep in mind that although two different actors may be using the same frame to justify or call forth an action, that surface similarity may gloss over the way in which different elements of the frame are articulated and elaborated (see Snow and Clark-Miller 2005) or the way in which it is employed. This can be seen in the following sketch of each of the five prognostic frames.

The Academic Freedom frame was constituted by alternative constructions of what "academic freedom" meant and thus entailed appeals to the courts to protect the proffered version of academic freedom. For creation scientists, the appeal was framed as securing students' right to learn all theories that exist concerning the origins of man; for evolutionists, the appeal was framed in terms of teachers' freedom to teach science in their classrooms. Codes that indicated the presence of this frame included "Academic Freedom" and "Hurt Student."

The second prognostic frame was the Constitutional frame. This frame was used to provide a constitutional argument in support of the respective sides. The most common examples include appeals made in terms of the First Amendment in relation to right to freedom of religion and the Fourteenth Amendment in relation to the due process clause, which empowered the courts to place limits on government's ability to restrict freedom of religion and speech. Not surprisingly, both contestants drew on the very same amendments but interpreted them in differing ways that favored their respective positions. Examples of codes for this frame include "First Amendment Not Absolute," "Fourteenth Amendment," and "Church-State Separation."

The third prognostic frame was the Curriculum frame, which addressed the issue of who should dictate the curriculum. The anti-evolutionists argued that the state and community had the right to establish the scientific curriculum, as well as the broader curriculum, for the public schools; the evolutionists argued that, where the teaching of science was concerned, the experts in the area and the broader scientific community should dictate the curriculum. Codes indicative of this frame included "State Freedom," "Set Curriculum," and "Improves Science Education."

The fourth prognostic frame was the Religion frame, which concerned mainly issues regarding biblical literalism, the religious nature of the country, and the religious motives of those involved in the cases. Codes marking the presence of this frame included "Compulsory Religious Education," "Biblical Literalism," and "History Is Religious."

The final prognostic frame was the Science frame, which typically addressed differing views on what constitutes science. Both sides in this debate cast themselves as remaining true to the scientific standard and accused the other side of engaging in pseudoscience. Both movements appealed to the court to accept that they were in fact the true standard-bearers for science and to reject the competing arguments on both sides. Codes reflective of this frame were the "ID Not Scientific," "Evolution Central to Biology," and "What Is Science?"

In addition to noting variation in the way in which the contestants interpreted and employed what appears on the surface to be the same frame, it is also important to keep in mind that a number of the frames may be used in the same hearing, with one or two usually dominant. For the ease of presentation, we focus on and present the dominant frames employed. Table 3.2 highlights this presentational consideration by showing which frames were dominant for each of the contestants during each of the trials. We present and discuss the use of these frames by trial chronologically.

The *Scopes* case was heard in a low-level state court in Dayton, Tennessee. It was appealed to a higher state court, where the decision affirming the banning of teaching evolution was upheld. The dominant prognostic frame during the trial for the creationists was religion, followed by the curriculum frame, whereas on the evolutionists' side it was also religion, but followed by science. For the creationist, the issue was clear: Evolution had to be kept from the public schools to preserve Christianity. Bryan made this point clear when he wrote:

A bloody, brutal doctrine – Evolution – demands, as the rabble did nineteen hundred years ago, that He be crucified. That cannot be the answer of this jury representing a Christian state and sworn to uphold the laws of Tennessee. . . . If the law is nullified, there will be rejoice wherever God is repudiated, the savior scoffed at and the Bible ridiculed. Every unbeliever of every kind and degree will be happy. If, on the other hand, the law is upheld and the religion of the school children protected, millions of Christians will call you blessed.   (Bryan, 1925 [in Linder 2005])

We can clearly see from this framing that the only solution is to defend Christianity from the evolutionary theory. The issue of religion is paramount in this case; recall that the diagnostic frame from this period is that of Protecting Religion. It makes sense that the prognostic frame would be crafted such that the only solution is to reject evolution and embrace the Christian teachings.

The evolutionists sought to use the religion frame as well, although their use highlights the differences and versatility that are possible with these frames. For them religion should not be an issue. As Mr. Malone, a lesser-known member of the legal team defending Mr. Scopes, stated:

We are here as lawyers with the same right to our views. I have the same right to mine as a Christian as Mr. Bryan has to his, and we do not intend to have this case charged by Mr. Darrow's agnosticism or Mr. Bryan's brand of Christianity.
                                                        (1925 [in Linder 2005])

Here Malone attempted to show that he had just as much right to the Christian identity as Bryan but that religion, or the lack thereof in Darrow's sense, should not be the issue around which this case revolved. Thus, evolutionists were attempting to use the religion frame to make religion a nonissue.

In the *Epperson* case, which made its way to the Supreme Court, the religion frame ceased to be the dominant frame. Instead, the Curriculum and Constitutional frames were dominant for the creationists and the Constitutional and Academic Freedom frames were dominant for the evolutionists. An excerpt

TABLE 3.2. *Anti-Evolutionist and Evolutionist Prognostic Frames by Case, 1925–2005*

Frames Case	Constitutional		Science		Religion		Academic Freedom		Curriculum	
	Anti-Evolution	Evolution	Anti-Evolution	Evolution	Anti-Evolution	Evolution	Anti-Evolution	Evolution	Anti-Evolution	Evolution
Scopes v. State of Tennessee	S	S	S	D	D	D	S	S	D	S
Epperson v. State of Arkansas	D	D	S	S	S	S	S	D	D	S
McLean v. State of Arkansas	S	S	D	D	D	D	D	D	S	S
Edwards v. Aguillard	D	D	S	D	D	D	D	S	S	S
Kitzmiller v. Dover Area School District	S	D	D	D	S	D	D	S	D	S

D = Dominant Frame
S = Secondary Frame

49

from a brief by the attorney generals representing Arkansas helps to illustrate the Curriculum and the Constitutional frames of the creationists:

The statutes are a valid exercise of the state's power to specify the curriculum in its public schools and is not an unreasonable encroachment upon Mrs. Epperson's freedom of speech.   (Appeal from the Supreme Court of Arkansas Brief for Appellee 1968)

The solution the creationists were proposing is that the state should have the ability to decide what is taught in its schools. Without this they feared that anything could be taught.

Turning to the other side, the ACLU and the American Jewish Congress partnered on a brief opposing Arkansas's ban on teaching evolution. They used the Academic frame, joined with the Constitutional frame, to make their case. As noted in their brief:

This is particularly true in a First Amendment case, for the restraint on the teacher's freedom to teach is simultaneously one upon the student's freedom to learn. The student has a personal stake in the teacher's freedom, a stake that cannot be bargained away in a private agreement between state and teacher.

(Brief of American Civil Liberties Union and American Jewish Congress, as Amici Curiae 1968)

We can see that the evolutionists are framing academic freedom as warranting protection for both the teacher and the students. But in this instance they tied Academic Freedom to the Constitutional frame by appealing to the First Amendment, highlighting the fact that these two issues can be articulated in such a way that the frames overlap in a supportive fashion.

In *McLean*, the Academic Freedom, Religion, and Science frames were dominant for the creation scientists, whereas the Science, Religion, and Academic Freedom frames were paramount for the evolutionists. It is interesting to note the return of religion as a dominant frame and that both sides invoked the same set of dominant frames, although in a slightly different order. The following statement issued before the court illustrates how the creation scientists used academic freedom in a different way than their opponents did in the previous case:

The main point of academic freedom is allowing the student to be exposed to a wide range of materials and ideas.   (Dr. Larry R. Parker, 1981 [in Geisler 1982])

Creation scientists thus argued that the best way to ensure academic freedom is to expose children to several different theories so that they can have a better understanding of what the options are, which differs widely from the previous case, in which it was about supporting the teacher's right to teach what he or she deemed appropriate.

The Science frame was the most prominent frame invoked by the evolutionists in the *McClean* case. This frame specifies what is and is not science and, by implication, what should be rejected. This is illustrated in the testimony of Michael Ruse, philosopher of science and expert witness for the evolutionist side. When asked whether creation science was science, he stated that "creation-science is not science, it's religion," and that it "invokes miracles." He added, "Nobody's saying religion is false, they are saying it's not science," and then noted, for emphasis, that creation science is not grounded in "natural law" and is not "explanatory" (ACLU notes on Dr. Michael Ruse's testimony, 1981 [Geisler 1982]). This framing, which bounds and seals off "real" science from creation science, was invoked repeatedly in this case and in the following ones, making it one of the most frequently used frames by the evolutionists.

In *Edwards*, which made it to the Supreme Court, the creation scientists relied primarily on the Academic Freedom, Constitutional, and Religious frames, whereas the Constitutional, Religious, and Science frames were dominant for the evolutionists. Not surprisingly, given the locus of the trial, the Constitutional frame became a dominant frame again for both sides. Also, Academic Freedom was again center stage for the creation scientists. Arguing on their behalf, the Catholic League, invoking Louisiana's Balanced Treatment Act as a constitutionally valid precedent, pleaded for a balanced treatment of ideas in the classroom:

Louisiana's Balanced Treatment Act does not violate the Establishment Clause. An examination of the Act's language clearly reveals that the Act has a secular purpose of promoting academic freedom through increasing public school students' exposure to varied theories of origins.

> (Brief for the Catholic League for Religious and Civil Rights,
> Amicus Curiae, in Support of Appellants 1986)

The opponents of creation science countered with their constitutional frame, as voiced in a brief by the American Federation of Teachers:

Louisiana's "Balanced Treatment For Creation-Science and Evolution-Science Act" violates the First Amendment because the Act's purposes and effect are to promote a religious doctrine and restrict secular instruction perceived as inconsistent with that religious doctrine and because the Act would excessively entangle public education – and public school teachers – with religion.

> (Brief of Amicus Curiae American Federation of Teachers,
> AFL-CIO in Support of Appellees 1986)

These two examples illustrate how the two movements made different tactical framing decisions regarding when and how to invoke one frame rather than another depending on the court level and what they thought would resonate with the court.

Finally, in the *Kitzmiller v. Dover* case, Science was the dominant frame for both sides, with Curriculum and Academic Freedom following closely behind for the proponents of intelligent design, and Religion and Constitutional being used by the evolutionists. This is an interesting case because both movements used a Science frame. It became a war of words, with each side accusing the other of being wrong and misguided. Eventually all that was left in this battle was to throw credentialed experts at one another, as the next two excerpts show. First, the Discovery Institute, the torchbearer for the intelligent design movement, made the case that intelligent design is science by invoking a Dr. Meyer to laminate the claim with a veneer of scientific legitimacy:

Based on the false claim that design theory postulates an omnipotent deity, plaintiffs and plaintiffs' witnesses have argued that the theory of intelligent design is not testable, and therefore not scientific. This claim is incorrect. As Dr. Meyer has demonstrated in his expert report, the theory of intelligent design is not only testable, but is testable in precisely the same way as is neo-Darwinism and other scientific theories about the past history of the natural world.   (Brief of Amicus Curiae, the Discovery Institute 2005)

Not to be outdone, the evolutionists trotted out their cadre of scientists to counter any scientific frames proffered by the intelligent design proponents. This move was clearly evident in the opening statement of the evolutionists' side:

But intelligent design is not science in its infancy, it's not science at all. You will hear from Kenneth Miller, a biologist; Kevin Padian, a paleontologist; Robert Pennock, a scientific philosopher; and Brian Alters, an expert on teaching science. They will testify about how science is practiced and taught, why evolution is overwhelmingly accepted as a scientific theory, and why intelligent design has no validity as a scientific concept.
(Rothchild 2005)

Not only does the lawyer make the claim that intelligent design is not science, but he also has a laundry list of scientists willing to agree with that assertion.

Ultimately, the judge in this 2005 case ruled in favor of the evolutionists and rejected the claim that intelligent design is science.

Discussion. It is clear from our findings on prognostic frames that such frames are not always presented the same way in each and every case but instead are strategically constructed in relation to several factors. These factors include the legal arena in which the case is being heard, which frames were successful, and which frames the opponents are expected to use. Each of these considerations appears to have been taken into account when the movement contestants were deciding which prognostic frame to deploy.

The court level at which each case was heard appeared to function as a significant constraint on frame construction and deployment for both sets of contestants. We found that prognostic frames presented in lower-level state courts differed from those presented at the federal level, and that both of those differed from the prognostic framing done before the Supreme Court. We argue that this change occurred because of two main reasons. The first is that different courts are charged with different legal tasks. State courts are charged with adjudicating cases based on state and federal law, but they are also likely to be somewhat responsive to community sentiment and pressure because often the judges are elected officials who must face the community on a semiregular basis. In contrast, federal judges, who are appointed for life, can afford to be less responsive to public sentiment. The Supreme Court is charged only with looking at the constitutionality of the case at hand; therefore any case brought before it must relate to a constitutional issue. These considerations suggest that the layered character of the legal arena may constitute a constraint on movement framing in general and on prognostic framing in particular.

The second factor that appears to affect prognostic framing is each side's expectations about what frames the other side is likely to deploy. Because the legal setting provides an opportunity for each side to engage in a framing contest, the contestants are likely to be aware of how the other side will frame its case, especially if its opponents were previously successful. And, in turn, the contestants are likely to adopt a similar frame to counter or neutralize the opposition. This can be seen most clearly with the prognostic framing during the recent *Kitzmiller* case, in which the proponents of intelligent design projected a scientific frame. They tried to claim that intelligent design was just as scientific as evolution, if not even more so. This was done because they recognized that the science frame, which had been employed for decades by the evolutionists, was now more resonant legally and culturally. Thus, if the creation scientists/intelligent designers hoped to succeed in getting their argument into the classroom, they needed to adopt a similar framing strategy. And so they did in the 1970s and 1980s, when they attempted to reframe their claims as scientific. But apparently the courts saw through the creation scientists' efforts, as they read their claims as still religious at the core and sided with their opponents.

The foregoing observations indicate that prognostic framing within the legal institution is affected by the level or venue in which the hearing occurs, prior legal outcomes of relevant cases, and contestants' expectations about their opponents' likely framing strategies. Considered together, these factors help illuminate further the process by which frames are transmitted and diffused within legal contexts across time.

CONCLUSIONS AND IMPLICATIONS

We have sought to expand our understanding of diffusion processes by focusing on the intersecting questions of how frames travel over time and what factors affect their temporal evolution. We have pursued these questions by examining the extent to which the various frames associated with the creationist/intelligent design movement have mutated from the famous Scopes Monkey Trial in 1925 to the intelligent design trial in Dover, Pennsylvania in 2005, and by exploring some of the factors contributing to this process of frame change and evolution.

Overall, we think our findings and analysis extend and refine current understanding of diffusion processes. Specifically, they extend our understanding of diffusion within the legal arena, and suggest by implication that different institutional contexts may impose different sets of constraints on framing processes that in turn affect the character of what is diffused. For example, we found that whether the case was heard at the state, federal, or Supreme Court level affected the character of the frame and the probability of its resonance. The interactions with different legal institutions and their inherent constraints help draw attention to the importance of institutional effects on the diffusion process that Tarrow identifies (Chapter 11, this volume) and should be considered by scholars attempting to model diffusion processes. Our findings and analysis also refine our understanding of diffusion processes by directing attention to mitigating factors other than the now usual suspects, such as network linkages, identification processes, and spatial and social proximity. In particular, our analysis highlights (1) the effects of winning or losing on subsequent framing strategies, with winning leading to a continuation of the successful strategy and losing prompting a change in framing strategy; (2) what might be called contestant or combatant mimicry, in which the winning, and thus resonant, frame provides a model for imitation during the next encounter or skirmish; (3) the extent to which frame diffusion is beholden in part to the requisite of context or situational adaptation; and (4) the extent to which the salience or carrying power of frames tends to vary across time, in large part because the grounds for frame resonance often shift over time. If we cannot step into the same river twice, as the Greek philosopher Heraclitus is said to have exclaimed, then what was put in motion upstream is not likely to be quite the same when it emerges downstream. This, we would argue, is also the case with most objects of diffusion.

A goal of this volume is to elucidate how diffusion occurs and the factors that affect it. Our findings and observations suggest, consistent with Snow and Benford's earlier observations (1999), that various ideational, interpretive schemata, such as frames, are probably rarely diffused whole cloth but are more often reconstituted in a fashion in which core ideas or values are laminated with ideas and constraints that are consistent with the temper of the times and the institutional structures in which the collectivity or movement is embedded. In short, this suggests that frame diffusion – and, we suspect, diffusion in general – is more often than not a very dynamic, contingent process that is affected by a number of interacting factors. We have elaborated a number of these factors – such as the institutional contexts in which diffusion occurs, the ways in which the actors involved can influence each other, and how these and other factors can vary over time – that we think should be incorporated into subsequent models of diffusion processes.

Although we have accented several key factors in diffusion processes, there clearly are other important variables to be addressed. Chief among these is the issue of culture, which we touched on only briefly. Future research will want to explore the impact of changing culture, both societal and political, on the process of frame diffusion and adoption over time. The impact of the space race and growing deference to scientific knowledge in the post–World War II era clearly had an impact on the construction and deployment of frames by the evolutionist movement, whereas the creation science and intelligent design movements were clearly bolstered by statements of support by Ronald Reagan and George W. Bush, respectively. Such observations are suggestive of the impact of culture on frame construction and diffusion, but that relationship needs to be explored more fully than we have done within the scope of this chapter.

4

Framing Labor's New Human Rights Movement

Lance Compa

INTRODUCTION

Framing strategies have always been central to advancing working class interests in an often unfavorable economic and political climate. The threshold
reaction to collective struggles by workers is skeptical at best, and often hostile, in a society that celebrates individualism, control of private property,
and entrepreneurial success. The fact that workers' methods of mobilization
involve disruptive tactics such as protests, strikes, picketing, and boycotts only
amplifies knee-jerk antipathy toward organized labor in the United States, even
though these are time-honored methods of contestation in a democracy.

How workers and their unions define terms, present arguments, tell stories, amplify resonance, and evoke responses is critical to the outcomes of
their struggles in the workplace and in society. The trade union movement has
always needed middle-class reformist, professional, and intellectual allies to
make organizing and collective bargaining gains and to win legislation favorable to workers. This chapter examines how workers have framed their appeals
to potential allies in the past decade using new human rights arguments alongside more traditional economic justice arguments, and how changing discourse
affects prospects for success or failure in such alliances. In particular, it looks
at framing strategies in labor's efforts to win labor law reform after Barack
Obama became president of the United States in 2009.

Workers and unions win syndical struggles when they promote a discourse
that resonates in layers of society besides their own. The toughness and solidarity of auto workers in their forty-four day occupation of General Motors'
factories in Flint, Michigan in 1936 was essential to the sit-in strike's success, but so was their support from "clergymen, writers, professors and public
figures" – and even some GM stockholders (Kraus 1947). So was "lawyer-to-
lawyer" colloquy between United Auto Workers attorney Maurice Sugar and
Michigan Governor Frank Murphy, who ultimately refrained from sending in
the National Guard to clear the plants (Kraus 1947; Fine 1969).

The United Farm Workers union's successful boycotts and organizing in California's agricultural sector in the 1960s and 1970s drew on a network of support among churches, civil rights activists, consumers, students, and other sympathizing strata around the country (Shaw 2008). The success of the 1997 national strike at United Parcel Service (by the Teamsters union, no less, the American union most likely to evoke hostile public reactions) similarly depended on the union's nurturing of widespread support from non-labor allies, including even UPS customers (Witt and Wilson 1999).

A similar need for alliances arises in the legislative arena. Trade unions in the early twentieth century could never have won passage of state-level workers' compensation, pension, and wage and hour laws on their own. They combined with middle-class reformers and other allies to gain legislative protection (Katz 1986). They replicated these movements at the national level in the 1930s to achieve passage of the Fair Labor Standards Act, the Social Security Act, and other important worker safety nets (Downey 2009). Public health professionals played a key role in winning passage of the Occupational Safety and Health Act (OSHA) of 1970 (Leopold 2007).

The U.S. labor movement's main legislative campaign after the election of Barack Obama to the presidency sought passage of a bill titled the Employee Free Choice Act (EFCA). EFCA was meant to improve chances of successful organizing in non-union workplaces, and thus reverse the steady decline of trade union "density," the percentage of the labor force represented by unions. Labor strategists and allies in the human rights and other communities engaged in a sharp debate on how to construct an overarching issue frame for labor law reform, and the extent to which it gave priority to a "restore the middle class" economic appeal rather than make a claim for workers' rights as human rights.

Labor's efforts to muster public support for EFCA, and the extent to which it both used and foreswore human rights arguments, provide important lessons in framing, diffusion, discourse-steering, and resonance-creating strategies on behalf of working-class interests in a middle-class society. However, understanding labor's frame-shifting strategy for EFCA requires historical context, in both the labor field and the human rights field, to see how lessons from the past carry into today's workers' rights advocacy.

HISTORICAL CONTEXT FOR LABOR AND HUMAN RIGHTS ADVOCACY

The Wagner Act's Economic Foundation

For most of the twentieth century, labor activists focused their demands on improving the wages and working conditions of American workers (Brody 1980; Dubofsky 1994; Lichtenstein 2002). The concept of human rights rarely entered labor discourse. Meanwhile, the human rights movement sought to prevent genocide, end repressive dictatorships and death squads, and protect political prisoners across the globe (Claude and Weston 2006; Hopgood 2006).

They rarely took up labor struggles, which they viewed as economic in nature, not human rights-related (Neier 2002).

Trade unions and their allies made a fundamentally economic argument for workers' organizing and collective bargaining rights – a Keynesian case, even if they did not label it as such. If workers could organize and bargain, they could win higher wages. Higher wages would create a larger middle class, whose greater purchasing power would stimulate economic demand and growth.

Strikes, factory occupations, and other conflicts marked American industrial relations in the 1930s (Bernstein 1969). Congress responded by passing the National Labor Relations Act (NLRA) of 1935. The act, also known as the Wagner Act, gave workers the right to form unions and bargain collectively. The law had a congenital defect, however: Its constitutional basis was the Commerce Clause, not the Bill of Rights – that is, workers had the right to organize and bargain to promote the economy, not because organizing and bargaining were fundamental rights (Pope 2002).

For decades following passage of the NLRA, Congress, the courts, and successive administrations and labor boards made decisions based on the act's economic premises. One Supreme Court decision put it bluntly: the right to organize and bargain "are not protected for their own sake but as an instrument of the national labor policy of minimizing industrial strife."[1]

The problem with an economic raison d'être for workers' organizing and collective bargaining is that these efforts become vulnerable to shifting economic (and thus political) winds. When politicians and judges saw organizing and bargaining as good for the economy, they expanded workers' rights. When they saw organizing and bargaining as inimical to the smooth functioning of enterprise, they cut back on workers' rights.

The NLRA's declared policy, in the words of its Section 1, is "encouraging the practice and procedure of collective bargaining." But over more than seven decades since the act's adoption, the trade union density in the United States fell from one-third in the 1950s to 12.3 percent in 2009 (Bureau of Labor Statistics 2010).

The reasons for this decline are varied. They include structural changes in the economy, such as the shift from manufacturing to services, demographic and geographic moves within the United States from the Rust Belt to the Sun Belt, job relocation abroad (once called "runaway shops," now more often "outsourcing"), and more.

Scholars argue about their relative weight, but there is general agreement that employers' aggressive interference with workers' organizing rights under the American labor law system has significantly affected union density (Freeman and Rogers 1999). As one labor scholar noted, "No other country in the world has spawned a thriving 'union avoidance' industry, whose mission is to crush workplace organizing campaigns through employer harassment, intimidation, and reprisals" (Logan 2006).

[1] See *Emporium Capwell Co. v. Western Addition Community Organization*, 420 U.S. 50 (1975).

Taft-Hartley Cutbacks

Many analysts see the Taft-Hartley Act of 1947 as the embodiment of such a shift in economic and political winds. A Republican-controlled Congress passed the Taft-Hartley Act in reaction to a wave of labor militancy in 1946 that saw national strikes in auto, steel, electrical equipment, and other industries.

Taft-Hartley allowed individual states to adopt right-to-work laws prohibiting required dues payments from all represented workers, thus dividing and weakening unions. It outlawed all forms of solidarity action by workers under the rubric of "secondary boycotts." It excluded supervisors and independent contractors from coverage. Citing the need for "employer free speech," the 1947 act allowed companies to campaign aggressively against workers' organizing efforts, using such techniques as captive-audience meetings and supervisors' one-on-one pressure on employees under them.

Captive-audience meetings are mandatory sessions in the workplace held during working hours. Employers require employees to sit through anti-union speeches, videos, role-playing, and other methods of haranguing workers to "vote no" in forthcoming representation elections.

Usually scripted by anti-union consultants who specialize in waging employers' campaigns to break workers' organizing drives, captive-audience speeches often take advantage of a legal distinction between "predictions" of workplace closure, which are allowed under U.S. law, and "threats" of closure, which are unlawful.[2] For example, an employer cannot say, "If you bring in the union, I will close the workplace." But the employer could say, "If you bring in the union and the contract makes us uncompetitive, I might have to close the workplace." Not mentioning that the employer need not agree to such a contract, the message and impression conveyed to employees is that union formation equals workplace closure.

The "one-on-one" tactic is one in which employers require supervisors to hold pressure-filled meetings with individual employees under them, again scripted by consultants for striking maximum fear into subordinate employees. For example, supervisors tell employees especially concerned about health insurance, "If the union comes in, management is going to bargain hard to cut back on health benefits." Supervisors who would rather not apply such pressure are subject to immediate dismissal, as they are excluded from coverage of the NLRA.

Judicial Retreats

In the absence of a rights-based labor law, federal courts had already started undermining the Wagner Act long before Taft-Hartley. The Supreme Court had upheld the act in a 1937 decision based on Commerce Clause arguments

---

[2] See *NLRB v. Gissel Packing Co.*, 395 U.S. 575 (1969), which articulated (without defining) the distinction between unlawful threats and lawful predictions.

that it reduced strikes, not that it advanced workers' rights.[3] A year later, in
the 1938 *Mackay Radio* decision, the Court said that employers have a right to
maintain operations during a strike, and to do so they can hire strikebreakers as
permanent replacements, not merely as temporary replacements while a strike
is under way.[4] In 1941, still well in advance of the Taft-Hartley reforms, the
Supreme Court in the *Virginia Electric* decision said that employers have a
First Amendment right to campaign openly and aggressively against workers'
organizing.[5]

In the 1930s, the lack of trade union organizing and collective bargaining
was defined as a "burden on commerce" justifying the Wagner Act. But later,
trade unions and collective bargaining came to be seen as burdens on a market-
driven economy. Without a human rights foundation, employers could argue
that workers' organizing and bargaining were themselves "burdens" on the
free flow of commerce while they, the employers, enjoyed speech and property
rights to frustrate employees' collective action.

In landmark labor law decisions, the U.S. Supreme Court made further cut-
backs on workers' freedom of association, always with an underlying economic
argument that spurned rights claims or that attached "rights" to employers,
not workers. In the 1981 *First National Maintenance* case, the Court decided
that workers have no right to bargain over an employer's decision to close their
workplace because employers need "unencumbered" power to make decisions
speedily and in secret.[6] As the Court explained:

Congress had no expectation that the elected union representative would become an
equal partner in the running of the business enterprise in which the union's members are
employed.... Management must be free from the constraints of the bargaining process
to the extent essential for the running of a profitable business.... Management may
have great need for speed, flexibility, and secrecy in meeting business opportunities and
exigencies.... [Bargaining] could afford a union a powerful tool for achieving delay, a
power that might be used to thwart management's intentions.

The Supreme Court could hardly have been more frank in asserting that the
smooth functioning of capitalism is more important than workers' rights.

The Court's privileging of economic policy is equally apparent in *Lechmere*,
a case decided a decade after *First National Maintenance*. Here, the Court
ruled that workers have no right to receive written information from trade
union organizers in a publicly accessible shopping mall parking lot, let alone
at the workplace proper.[7] The Court justified this ruling on the grounds that
employer's private property rights outweigh workers' freedom of association.

In both *First National Maintenance* and *Lechmere*, the National Labor Relations Board (NLRB) decisions had been favorable to unions, but the Supreme

---

[3] See *NLRB v. Jones & Laughlin Steel Corp.*, 301 U.S. 1 (1937).
[4] See *NLRB v. Mackay Radio & Telegraph Corp.*, 304 U.S. 333 (1938).
[5] See *NLRB v. Virginia Electric & Power Corp.*, 314 U.S. 469 (1941).
[6] See *First National Maintenance Corp. v. NLRB*, 452 U.S. 666 (1981).
[7] See *Lechmere, Inc. v. NLRB*, 502 U.S. 527 (1992).

Court overruled them. Doctrinally, courts are supposed to defer to the administrative expertise of the NLRB. In practice, however, federal circuit appeals courts and the Supreme Court often make their own judgment on the merits of a case to overrule the NLRB. Professor Julius Getman has described the dynamic thus:

> The reason for the courts' retreat from collective bargaining is difficult to identify, but it seems to rest on a shift in contemporary judicial thinking about economic issues. The NLRA, when originally passed, had a Keynesian justification. Collective bargaining, it was believed, would increase the wealth of employees, thereby stimulating the economy and reducing the likelihood of depression and recession. Today, courts are more likely to see collective bargaining as an interference with the benevolent working of the market, and, thus, inconsistent with economic efficiency most likely to be achieved by unencumbered management decision making. (Getman 2003)

REFRAMING WORKERS' RIGHTS AS HUMAN RIGHTS

Two Communities Converge

Without a human rights foundation, workers' collective activity was vulnerable to perception as impeding economic growth, not promoting it. When the great mid-century organizing waves subsided, trade unions fell into a more bureaucratic, business-union role in society. Both the general public and elite opinion makers came to see union activity simply as labor versus management – two big institutional entities with competing self-interests contrary to the public good. Human rights advocates mostly accepted this labor-versus-management frame of workers' collective action. Responding to widespread abuses around the globe, they had scant connection to organizing and bargaining difficulties of American workers (Leary 2003).

The two movements did share some common terrain. Earlier generations of trade unionists and their supporters had argued during the 1930s that organizing workers and collective bargaining provided "the only road to civil rights, civil liberties, and real citizenship" (Lichtenstein 2002). These unionists explicitly linked workers' rights to notions of "industrial democracy" and an "Americanism" that extended to immigrants who helped build the labor movement (Fink 1983; McCartin 1997).

Although the human rights movement rarely took up labor struggles, the drafters of the 1948 Universal Declaration of Human Rights included workers' freedom of association and the right to decent wages – even the right to paid vacations – as fundamental human rights. And although rights groups' leaders and activists may not have seen labor advocacy as part of their mission, many personally sympathized with workers and trade unions.

At the turn of the new century, labor and human rights advocates holding key staff positions in trade unions and human rights organizations, along with labor and human rights-oriented academics, came together to restrategize and reframe workers' collective action as a human rights mission rather than "pure and simple" syndical action for economic gain. A new labor–human rights alliance took shape, with a wide-ranging discourse and agenda to frame and diffuse workers' organizing and bargaining not as a matter of labor versus management, but as a matter of people exercising basic human rights.

Union-side and human rights-side advocates and their counterparts in the academy did not just bump into each other in the dark. The emergence of a "workers' rights are human rights" theme flowed from preexisting networks and personal relationships among actors going as far back as civil rights and anti–Vietnam War activism in the 1960s, continuing through United Farm Workers union grape and lettuce boycotts and opposition to military dictatorships in Brazil, Chile, and Argentina in the 1970s, then to Central America solidarity work in the 1980s. This community of actors also shared experience contesting policies of the AFL-CIO's international affairs apparatus in the period before a reform leadership took control of the labor federation in 1995, especially activities of the American Institute for Free Labor Development in Central and South America (Buchanan 1990).

In the 1990s, the same labor and human rights activists and academics became involved in efforts to insert labor rights provisions into trade agreements, then initiated complaints, cases, and campaigns under such clauses (Weiss 2003). In similar fashion, they brought complaints under the labor rights clause of the Generalized System of Preferences, a U.S. trade program granting tariff relief to imports from developing countries that respected workers' rights (Compa and Vogt 2001). Although they were not all attorneys, lawyers among them played important facilitating and brokering roles in building networks and advancing the diffusion project.

Many of the advocates who shaped a human rights frame for labor activism had worked together in social justice coalitions. Some had worked together in the same organizations before moving on. Some had even married, divorced, and remarried each other. In short, it is impossible to gainsay the importance of personal histories, personal relationships, and interpersonal networks among actors who crafted and diffused a new labor rights–human rights interpretive frame to, as the editors formulate in the introduction to this volume, "define the issues, codify problems and solutions, target responsible parties, and mobilize political claims."[8]

Labor's Human Rights Initiatives

A variety of new campaigns and organizations took shape with a labor–human rights mission. The AFL-CIO launched a broad-based "Voice@Work" project characterized as a "campaign to help U.S. workers regain the basic human right to form unions to improve their lives." In 2005, the labor federation held more than one hundred demonstrations in cities throughout the United States,

---

[8] The author is the source for this proposition, having been intimately involved in the labor–human rights network described here.

and enlisted signatures from eleven Nobel Peace Prize winners, including the Dalai Lama, Lech Walesa, Jimmy Carter, and Archbishop Desmond Tutu of South Africa, supporting workers' human rights in full-page advertisements in national newspapers (Greenhouse 2005).

In 2004, trade unions and allied labor support groups created a new nongovernmental organization (NGO) called American Rights at Work (ARAW). ARAW launched an ambitious program to make human rights the centerpiece of a new civil society movement for American workers' organizing and bargaining rights. ARAW's twenty-member board of directors includes prominent civil rights leaders, former elected officials, environmentalists, religious leaders, business leaders, writers, scholars, an actor, and one labor leader, the president of the AFL-CIO, the main American labor federation. The convergence of the labor and human rights movements is aptly reflected in the figure of the group's international advisor, Mary Robinson, who is the former United Nations High Commissioner for Human Rights.

Rights Groups Enter Labor Discourse

Among human rights organizations, Amnesty International USA created a Business and Human Rights division with extensive focus on workers' rights. Oxfam International broadened its development agenda to include labor rights and standards, and its Oxfam America group created a Workers' Rights program to take up these causes inside the United States. In 2003, Oxfam launched a "national workers' rights campaign" on conditions in the American agricultural sector. In 2004 the group published a major report titled *Like Machines in the Fields: Workers Without Rights in American Agriculture* (Oxfam America 2004).

Perhaps most notably, Human Rights Watch published a series of reports on workers' rights in the United States under international human rights standards. These reports covered child labor in American agriculture, conditions of immigrant household domestic workers, American workers' organizing and bargaining rights, conditions in the meatpacking industry, Walmart workers, and more.

In *Fingers to the Bone*, Human Rights Watch criticized the United States for its violation of international law on child labor (Human Rights Watch 2001a). According to the organization, American law and practice "contravene various international law prohibitions on exploitative and harmful work by children." The report noted that the United States had violated the Convention on the Rights of the Child and "appears to be headed toward noncompliance with the 1999 ILO [International Labour Organization] Worst Forms of Child Labor Convention." Human Rights Watch expressed further concern that the United States had claimed that no change to law or practice was necessary to comply with the ILO standard.

Hidden in the Home documented abuses against household domestic workers in the United States (often by wealthy diplomats and business executives), citing document confiscation, physical punishment, and conditions tantamount to imprisonment (Human Rights Watch 2001b). The report also pointed out the failure of U.S. law to include domestic workers in labor and employment legislation protecting workers' rights.

In 2000, Human Rights Watch released *Unfair Advantage: Workers' Freedom of Association in the United States under International Human Rights Standards*, a report that catalogued a "sustained attack" on workers' organizing and bargaining rights. The report highlighted failure of the U.S. government to meet its responsibility under international human rights law to deter such attacks and protect workers' rights (Human Rights Watch 2000).

The report contained case studies showing that many workers who try to form and join trade unions to bargain with their employers are spied on, harassed, pressured, threatened, suspended, fired, deported, or otherwise victimized in reprisal for their exercise of the right to freedom of association. The report drew explicit links between human rights law and labor rights, emphasizing that "international human rights law makes governments responsible for protecting vulnerable persons and groups from patterns of abuse by private actors."

Human Rights Watch accompanied the release of *Unfair Advantage* with a carefully crafted diffusion plan targeting news media, policy, governmental, NGOs, and intellectual communities. The report garnered significant attention in local, national, and international media outlets, which repeatedly cited findings that the United States failed to meet international standards on workers' organizing and bargaining rights (Borger 2000; Glascock 2000; Greenhouse 2000; McNatt 2000; Panagariya 2000).

In the wake of this response, *Unfair Advantage* became an authoritative reference point in U.S. labor law and human rights discourse. Labor advocates embraced the report as a standard source for reaching out to new constituencies in a language of human rights, not just labor–management relations. As an example of the Human Rights Watch report reaching new audiences, *Scientific American*, the largest-circulation general science magazine in the country, published a feature on *Unfair Advantage* for its million-plus readership one year after the report came out (Doyle 2001).

Unfair Advantage also became a point of reference in the scholarly community. The American Political Science Association (APSA), for example, gave a "best paper" award at the 2001 APSA Annual Meeting to "From the Wagner Act to the Human Rights Watch Report: Labor and Freedom of Expression and Association, 1935–2000" (Swidorski 2003).

The *British Journal of Industrial Relations* devoted two issues of a symposium to the Human Rights Watch report. Symposium editors Sheldon Friedman and Stephen Wood attracted contributions from leading labor law, labor history, and industrial relations scholars in the United States, Canada, and Britain (Friedman and Wood 2001).

Professor Hoyt N. Wheeler said, "It is by explicitly taking a human rights approach that the Human Rights Watch report makes its most important contribution to the understanding and evaluation of American labor policy"

(Wheeler 2001). Labor law scholar Julius Getman called the report "a powerful indictment of the way in which U.S. labor law deals with basic rights of workers" (Getman 2001). Canadian industrial relations expert Roy J. Adams described its publication as "an important event because of the new perspective that it brings to bear on American labor policy" (Adams 2002).

British human rights law professor Sheldon Leader saw the report as "an important document . . . that should help us see what difference it makes to connect up the corpus of principles in labor law with the wider considerations of human rights law" (Leader 2002). The leading historian of the NLRB, Professor James Gross, noted, "Human rights talk without action is hypocrisy. This report could be an important first step toward action" (Gross 2002).

In 2005, Human Rights Watch continued its program on workers' rights in the United States with a major report on human rights violations in the meat and poultry industry, titled *Blood, Sweat, and Fear* (Human Rights Watch 2005). A central case study in the report described mistreatment of workers at Smithfield Foods' giant hog-slaughtering plant in Tar Heel, North Carolina, including firings, beatings, and false arrests of union supporters. The United Food and Commercial Workers (UFCW) Justice@Smithfield organizing campaign at the Tar Heel plant made extensive use of the Human Rights Watch report in its outreach to civil rights, human rights, and consumer allies, featuring it in a campaign video and on its website. The UFCW ultimately won an NLRB election at the plant (Greenhouse 2008b).

In 2007 Human Rights Watch released *Discounting Rights*, a report on workplace rights violations of Walmart employees in the United States (Human Rights Watch 2007). *Discounting Rights* recounted Walmart management's crushing of employees' union organizing efforts at stores around the United States. The company's tactics included both moves that violated U.S. labor law and moves that were allowed under U.S. labor law but violated international human rights standards.

The report concluded that "Wal-Mart has translated its hostility toward union formation into an unabashed, sophisticated, and aggressive strategy to derail worker organizing at its US stores that violates workers' internationally recognized right to freedom of association." Similar to use of the meatpacking report, advocates targeting Walmart's allegedly harmful impact in various social and economic arenas seized on Human Rights Watch's report to support their calls for reform of company practices (Democracy Now 2007). In general, human rights advocates' new focus on workers' rights gave powerful impetus to the promotion of a joined agenda.

UNIONS' DIFFUSION OF A HUMAN RIGHTS MESSAGE

Trade Union Human Rights Reports

Trade unions' turn to human rights framing does not involve diffusion of militant protest activity. It is not a social movement and does not involve mass action. It mostly takes the form of intellectual diffusion more than social diffusion, aimed at leaders and activists in the labor movement and allied groups, as well as opinion shapers, political officeholders, and other elites. But the evocation of human rights also aims to foster rights consciousness among rank-and-file workers, injecting a human rights core into the trade union mission and encouraging workers to see themselves as fighting for justice, not only for higher wages and benefits.

Workers' rights violations at the largest Catholic hospital chain in Chicago, Resurrection Health Care (RHC), led the American Federation of State, County, and Municipal Employees (AFSCME) to commission a report on how the employer's actions violated principles of Catholic social doctrine and international human rights standards (AFSCME 2004). The union's report insisted that "RHC workers have the right under international human rights law to freedom of association and organization by forming and joining a trade union to seek collective representation before management. RHC has a corresponding obligation to honor this right and respect its exercise. Instead, RHC has responded with an aggressive campaign against workers' organizing rights in violation of rights recognized under international human rights law."

The report served as a tool for union organizing in the workplace and for organizing support in local political, religious, and human rights communities. It prompted the International Trade Union Confederation to feature RHC's violations in its annual report on violations of trade union rights around the world (Hospital Business Week 2007).

In 2004, the Teamsters Union issued a human rights critique of Maersk-Sealand, the giant Denmark-based international shipping company, for violating rights of association among truck drivers who carry cargo containers from ports to inland distribution centers. The company had fired workers who protested low pay and dangerous conditions, and threatened retaliation against others if they continued their organizing effort. These company abuses were putatively legal because the drivers were defined as independent contractors, not as employees. Independent contractor status means that they are excluded from protections of the NLRA and can be fired and threatened with impunity.

Invoking human rights standards to counter this technicality of U.S. labor law, the union charged that company actions "violate international human rights and labor rights norms for workers" and emphasized that "the responsibility of multinational corporations to recognize international human rights is becoming an important facet of international law." The report contained detailed case studies of Maersk's labor rights violations, and recommended that "Maersk should declare publicly its commitment to respect international human rights and labor rights standards, including a policy of non-reprisals against any workers who exercise rights of assembly, association and speech in connection with their employment" (Teamsters 2004).

The Teamsters used the report for action, not just as a research project. The union distributed thousands of copies to affiliates of the International Transport Federation, the global trade union for workers in the transport sector. Workers held protests and distributed copies of the report at the Danish embassy in Washington, D.C. and at consulates around the United States (Joshi and Draper 2004). In 2005 and 2006, Teamsters and Danish union allies distributed the report at Maersk's annual shareholders meeting in Copenhagen. They championed a shareholders' resolution, common at American companies' annual meetings but a novelty for Maersk, calling on the company to adopt international labor rights standards as official company policy (Mongelluzzo 2005, 2006). As a result, Maersk ordered its American managers to halt adverse action against union supporters and moved toward dialogue with union representatives.[9]

In similar fashion, the Teamsters' use of international human rights and labor rights arguments brought a breakthrough in organizing among private school bus drivers employed by First Student, Inc. in locations around the United States. First Student is the U.S. subsidiary of UK-based FirstGroup, Ltd., a multinational transportation company.

The International Brotherhood of Teamsters (IBT) brought a human rights critique of First Student's anti-union campaign tactics – captive-audience meetings, one-on-one meetings by supervisors with employees, implicit threats, and the like – to UK union and NGO counterparts, the British media, the House of Commons, FirstGroup's annual shareholders meeting, and other audiences (Clement 2006). Their combined pressure moved top management to issue a "Freedom of Association" policy requiring neutrality toward worker organizing. First Student management backed away from its aggressive interference. The IBT has scored a series of NLRB election victories in 2008 and 2009, bringing thousands of new workers into the union (Teamsters 2009).

Using International Instruments

Trade unionists are also turning to international human rights instruments and mechanisms to support organizing and bargaining struggles. In recent years the ILO's Committee on Freedom of Association has responded to unions' complaints about violations of workers' organizing and bargaining rights in cases involving immigrant workers, airport security screeners, North Carolina public employees, and low-level supervisors, among others.

Immigrant Workers. In 2002, the AFL-CIO filed a complaint to the ILO Committee on Freedom of Association (CFA) challenging the Supreme Court's *Hoffman Plastic* decision.[10] In *Hoffman*, the Supreme Court had held, in a 5–4 decision, that an undocumented worker, because of his immigration status, was not entitled to back pay for lost wages after he was illegally fired for union organizing. The majority said that enforcing immigration law takes precedence over enforcing labor law. The four dissenting justices said there was no such conflict and that a "backpay order will *not* interfere with the

---

[9] Author interview with Teamster port drivers campaign representative, March 22, 2009.
[10] See *Hoffman Plastic Compounds, Inc. v. NLRB*, 535 U.S. 137 (2002).

implementation of immigration policy. Rather, it reasonably helps to deter unlawful activity that *both* labor laws *and* immigration laws seek to prevent."

The union federations' ILO complaint argued that eliminating the back pay remedy for undocumented workers annuls protection of workers' right to organize, contrary to the requirement in Convention 87 to provide adequate protection against acts of anti-union discrimination. In November 2003, the CFA agreed, declaring that the *Hoffman* doctrine violates international legal obligations to protect workers' organizing rights.

The Committee concluded that "the remedial measures left to the NLRB in cases of illegal dismissals of undocumented workers are inadequate to ensure effective protection against acts of anti-union discrimination." The ILO Committee recommended congressional action to bring U.S. law "into conformity with freedom of association principles, in full consultation with the social partners concerned, with the aim of ensuring effective protection for all workers against acts of anti-union discrimination in the wake of the Hoffman decision" (ILO Committee on Freedom of Association 2003).

TSA Airport Screeners Case. In November 2006, the ILO Committee on Freedom of Association issued a decision in a complaint filed by the AFL-CIO and the American Federation of Government Employees (AFGE) against the Bush administration's denial of collective bargaining rights to airport security screeners. The administration argued that events of September 11, 2001 and related security concerns made it necessary to strip Transportation Security Administration (TSA) employees of trade union rights accorded to other federal employees.

The Committee said that it "is concerned that the extension of the notion of national security concerns for persons who are clearly not making national policy that may affect security, but only exercising specific tasks within clearly defined parameters, may impede unduly upon the rights of these federal employees." It recommended that "priority should be given to collective bargaining as the means to settle disputes arising in connection with the determination of terms and conditions of employment in the public service" and urged the government "to carefully review, in consultation with the workers' organizations concerned, the matters covered within the overall terms and conditions of employment of federal airport screeners which are not directly related to national security issues and to engage in collective bargaining on these matters with the screeners' freely chosen representative" (ILO Committee on Freedom of Association 2006).

North Carolina Public Employees Case. In 2006, the United Electrical, Radio, and Machine Workers of America (UE) filed a complaint with the ILO Committee on Freedom of Association on behalf of North Carolina public employees. The UE is an independent union known for its progressive politics, internal democracy, and willingness to engage in militant struggle, as evidenced by the union's widely publicized occupation of a Chicago factory in November 2008 and their subsequent victory in having the plant reopened (Cullotta 2009).

The union's complaint charged that North Carolina's ban on public worker bargaining, and the failure of the United States to take steps to protect workers' bargaining rights, violated Convention No. 87's principle that "all workers, without distinction" should enjoy organizing and bargaining rights, and Convention No. 98's rule that only public employees who are high-level policy makers, not rank-and-file workers, should not have the right to bargain.

In April 2007, the Committee ruled in the union's favor and urged the U.S. government "to promote the establishment of a collective bargaining framework in the public sector in North Carolina... and to take steps aimed at bringing the state legislation, in particular through the repeal of NCGS §95–98 [the statute prohibiting collective bargaining by public employees], into conformity with the freedom of association principles" (ILO Committee on Freedom of Association 2007).

This decision prompted North Carolina state legislators to introduce, for the first time in decades, legislation that would grant collective bargaining rights to state and local employees.[11] The legislation is pending and advocates recognize that achieving it is difficult, but they count getting such a bill onto the legislative agenda as an important policy advance, and credit the international attention through the ILO case and other international mechanisms for reaching this point.[12]

Supervisory Exclusion Case. In October 2006, the AFL-CIO filed another CFA complaint, this time against the NLRB's decision in the so-called *Oakwood* trilogy. In *Oakwood* and companion decisions, the NLRB announced an expanded interpretation of the definition of "supervisor" under the National Labor Relations Act.[13] Under the new ruling, employers can classify as "supervisors" employees with incidental oversight over coworkers even when such oversight is far short of genuine managerial or supervisory authority.

In its complaint to the ILO, the AFL-CIO relied on the ILO Conventions, arguing that the NRLB's decision contravened Convention No. 87's affirmation that "[w]orkers and employers, without distinction whatsoever, shall have the right to establish and... to join organizations of their own choosing without previous authorization." In a March 2008 decision, the Committee found that the criteria for supervisory status laid out in the *Oakwood* trilogy "appear to give rise to an overly wide definition of supervisory staff that would go beyond freedom of association principles" and urged the U.S. government "to

---

[11] See North Carolina General Assembly, House Bill No. 1583 (April 2007).

[12] Author interview with Robin Alexander, Director of International Affairs, United Electrical Workers, March 20, 2008.

[13] See *Oakwood Healthcare, Inc.*, 348 NLRB No. 37; *Croft Metal, Inc.*, 348 NLRB No. 38; *Golden Crest Healthcare Center*, 348 NLRB No. 39 (October 2, 2006), called the *Oakwood* trilogy.

take all necessary steps, in consultation with the social partners, to ensure that the exclusion that may be made of supervisory staff under the NLRA is limited to those workers genuinely representing the interests of employers" (ILO Committee on Freedom of Association 2008).

A Europe Card

Advocates understand that issuing human rights reports and taking rights claims to the ILO or other international human rights bodies does not yield enforceable rulings within the American legal system. Most international law is "soft law," in which decisions are hortatory, not binding. Projecting American labor's human rights frame to an international scale is part of a broader framing and diffusion project to change labor policy discourse in the United States, in part by convincing potential allies around the world that American workers face human rights abuses too.

Many European actors, including labor groups, NGOs, investors, and governments, look at labor relations in the United States through a human rights lens, eager to know how American labor law and practice compare with ILO standards. "The freedom to form or join a union of one's choice and to bargain collectively for the terms of employment are fundamental human rights enshrined in the U.N. Universal Declaration of Human Rights and the core conventions of the ILO," a coalition of socially responsible investment funds, many based in Europe, said in a May 2009 letter to Congress (Rosenkrantz 2009). Norway's national pension fund, with billions of dollars in holdings, cited Walmart as a firm in which it would not invest based on the company's labor practices (Landler 2007).

European representatives of the American union Service Employees International Union (SEIU) held a webinar in July 2008 with thirty European "socially responsible investment" (SRI) managers. The SEIU wanted to convey the reality of American management's anti-union tactics to a European investor audience, hoping they would put pressure on European companies to respect workers' rights in their U.S. operations. During the webinar, the European SRI specialists did not care about the NLRA or the technicalities of labor law violations under U.S. law. They wanted to know how management abuses and labor law failures compared with ILO standards and international human rights standards, with a keen interest in decisions of the Committee on Freedom of Association.[14]

CRITIQUES OF THE HUMAN RIGHTS FRAME

Rights versus Solidarity

Labor's reframing of syndical struggles as a human rights mission has not gone without criticism from natural allies as well as natural enemies. In the latter

---

[14] The author is the source for this proposition, having participated in the webinar.

camp, the National Right to Work Committee, a leading anti-union force in American labor affairs, warned that human rights arguments and decisions by international bodies such as the ILO Committee on Freedom of Association might influence American court decisions. The Right to Work Committee suggested that the United States withdraw from the ILO because its processes "are a lobbying tool for organized labor and a potential embarrassment for the United States" (Muggeridge 2008).

For their part, some labor-sympathizing scholars and activists counsel against a human rights argument for workers' organizing and bargaining in the United States. They maintain that a rights-based approach plays into individualistic, atomizing dynamics that undermine solidarity and industrial democracy as principles for labor action. For example, historian Nelson Lichtenstein argues that "a discourse of rights has also subverted the very idea . . . of union solidarity. . . . Without a bold and society-shaping political and social program, human rights can devolve into something approximating libertarian individualism" (Lichtenstein 2003). Another historian, Joseph McCartin, warns that "rights talk tends to foster a libertarian dialogue, where capital's liberty of movement and employers' 'rights to manage' are tacitly affirmed rather than challenged" (McCartin 2005).

Labor lawyer Jay Youngdahl maintains:

> [T]he reliance on a reframing of labor struggles as first and foremost human rights struggles is misplaced. It is not hyperbole to say that the replacement of solidarity and unity as the anchor for labor justice with "individual human rights" will mean the end to the union movement as we know it. . . . Rights discourse individualizes the struggle at work. The union movement, however, was built on and nourished by solidarity and community. . . . A complete turn towards the individual rights approach by the labor movement will signal the surrender of the fight for workplace solidarity and with it the unique and crucial position that our movement has occupied over the last one hundred years in the permanent struggle for justice for those at work.   (Youngdahl 2009)

The Rights Case

These cautions contribute to a needed debate about the role and effectiveness of human rights activism and human rights arguments in support of workers' rights. But they are not convincing arguments for jettisoning the human rights frame. They are an argument for using a human rights frame carefully and strategically.

The human rights reframing of labor action is not meant to supplant discourse on worker solidarity, industrial democracy, economic security, and the like. The human rights frame reinforces such discourse with a rights-based case for solidarity.

The phrase "individual human rights" does not appear in the 2000 Human Rights Watch *Unfair Advantage* report. Contemporary human rights analysis does not concede a sharp dichotomy between individual rights and collective rights. Workers live in an intricate web of relationships – personal, economic, cultural, juridical, institutional, and more – in which the exercise of individual rights takes place. Individual rights can be fulfilled only in this social framework.

Human rights experts bring authority to labor discourse that trade unionists cannot achieve on their own. If the AFL-CIO had published Human Rights Watch's *Unfair Advantage* word for word, the broader public would have discounted it as self-interested partisanship. But the report carried with it Human Rights Watch's independence and expertise in the human rights arena, giving its critique of workers' rights violations in the United States an authoritativeness that could not be matched by trade union actors making the same claims.

THE BATTLE FOR EFCA

The Employee Free Choice Act – What Is It?

Debates over whether or how to integrate human rights arguments into a labor rights frame were put to a test in the 2009 legislative battle over EFCA, the trade unions' top priority following the election of Barack Obama. Union leaders presented EFCA as a do-or-die battle for the very existence of the labor movement (Dreier and Candaele 2008). The U.S. Chamber of Commerce called it "Armageddon" (Greenhouse 2008a).

To counter employers' power to wage aggressive, threat-filled campaigns to destroy employees' organizing efforts, EFCA would require companies to recognize and bargain with unions if a majority of workers signed cards joining the union and authorizing the union to negotiate on their behalf. Issues such as the life span of valid cards, workers' right to revoke a card, how and when the cards will be examined, and so on, would be left to the NLRB to decide in a future rulemaking procedure.

EFCA also would institute first-contract arbitration if no collective agreement was reached within ninety days. Employers often frustrate workers' organizing success by dragging out negotiations or refusing to bargain in good faith. Current labor law sets no penalties other than an order to return to the bargaining table, where the same cycle can repeat itself. Only 56 percent of newly-organized bargaining units certified by the NLRB after an election were successful in reaching a first contract. Only 38 percent of such units reached a contract within one year (Ferguson and Kochan 2008).

Under EFCA, ninety days of bargaining without reaching an agreement would lead to thirty days of mediation with assistance from the Federal Mediation and Conciliation Service (FMCS). If mediation does not succeed in bringing parties to an agreement, the FMCS would move to mandatory arbitration and a contract. The FMCS would formulate rules and regulations of the arbitration system after passage of the bill.

In addition to card-check and first-contract arbitration, EFCA also calls for stronger penalties on employers that violate the law, including triple back pay for unlawfully fired workers and monetary penalties in the form of fines up to $20,000 against employers that are repeat violators.

Damages and fines have never been a part of the American labor law system. Sanctions can be only "remedial, not punitive" under the NLRA. The "remedial, not punitive" principle was fashioned by the Supreme Court in the 1940 *Republic Steel* case, in which the Court decided that the NLRB is not empowered to penalize labor law violators, but only to "make whole" victims of violations.[15]

Employers who unlawfully fire workers for union activity are liable only for back pay *minus* interim earnings – any salary the worker obtains from another job during the period of unlawful dismissal. Workers have a legal obligation to seek another job to "mitigate" the employer's liability.

For many employers, it is an easy calculation to fire organizing leaders and pay them a token back pay years later when their case is finally resolved (employers can delay resolution for years by filing appeals to the courts). Very few workers opt for reinstatement because they have gotten on with their lives and they do not want to return to a hostile atmosphere.

To address the delay problem, EFCA also would require the NLRB to seek a court injunction to reinstate fired workers immediately when the board finds "merit" in an unfair labor practice charge, before it is fully litigated. The goal here is to get the workers back into the workplace quickly so that the organizing effort does not falter.

The last time trade unions and their allies made a serious run at labor law reform was in 1977–78, when Jimmy Carter took office and Democrats similarly had control of Congress. A drop in union density from 25 percent to 20 percent in that decade triggered trade unions' sense of crisis. The focus then was on quick representation elections, elections within fifteen days of a petition. That bill passed the House of Representatives handily, but failed in the Senate by falling two votes short of the sixty needed to halt debate – to end a filibuster, as it is called – and move to a final vote.

The legislative struggle in 2009 was almost exactly the same. EFCA had solid majority support in the House and majority support in the Senate, but advocates could not reach sixty votes in the Senate to end a filibuster and move to a final vote on the bill as it was originally proposed.

Unions Flinch on Human Rights

Human Rights Watch and other NGOs rallied to labor's side in the struggle over EFCA. Calling EFCA "a human rights imperative," Human Rights Watch called for passage of the bill "to help remedy glaring deficiencies in current U.S. labor law that significantly impair the right of workers to freely choose

---

[15] The "remedial, not punitive" principle was fashioned by the Supreme Court in *Republic Steel Corp. v. NLRB*, 311 U.S. 7 (1940), in which the Court decided that the NLRB is not empowered to penalize labor law violators, but only to "make whole" victims of violations.

whether to form a union" (Human Rights Watch 2009a). Human Rights Campaign, Interfaith Worker Justice, International Labor Rights Forum, Leadership Conference on Civil Rights, National Workrights Institute, and other rights-advocating groups added their voices to calls for EFCA's passage (American Rights at Work 2009).

Trade union strategists flinched. They decided to back away from a human rights frame and to downplay human rights arguments in labor's push for passage of EFCA. At a time of economic crisis following the financial crisis that began in late 2008, unionists thought that the human rights frame was too abstract and too "soft" to sway public opinion and Congress.

Analogizing to the civil rights movement and success in winning new antidiscrimination laws in the 1960s, human rights advocates warned, "We didn't win the Civil Rights Act of 1964 by saying it would help the economy." But hoping to strike while the economic iron was hot, trade union strategists replicated the "original sin" of the Wagner Act, setting workers' organizing and bargaining on an economic foundation, not a human rights foundation. They highlighted the same Keynesian-style "restore the middle class" theme that animated the Wagner Act: Congress should make it easier for workers to organize not because organizing is a fundamental right, but because organizing will result in higher wages, greater purchasing power, and economic recovery.[16]

The AFL-CIO's core EFCA briefing message for members of Congress was titled "What the Freedom to Join Unions Means to America's Workers and the Middle Class" and is quoted here in some detail to indicate the weight of the economic theme:

America cannot be a successful low-wage consumer society. The Bush administration tried to make up for stagnant wages with consumer debt – a choice that has proven disastrous. Our country needs more money to go to America's workers and less to Wall Street speculators and CEOs. That is why a key element of our nation's economic recovery must be to restore workers' freedom to form unions, speak for themselves and negotiate a fair share of the wealth they create. Rising income, not more debt, is the only way out of the economic crisis.

Denying Americans the freedom to form unions at their place of work is not just unfair, it is destructive economic policy. Taking away workers' rights on the job has hurt the American middle class, increased economic inequality and destabilized our economy. With deunionization, we have set off a long-term downward spiral of lower wages and fewer benefits. Pockets of workers with good jobs try to hold on to a middle class standard of living, even as more and more people suffer lower wages, less health care and no retirement security. As companies fight to cut costs, consumer demand falls, breeding recession and instability.

When workers have the right to come together and form unions, their lives improve and the larger economy is healthier: Productivity rises, product and service quality improves, economic inequality is reduced and wages are boosted substantially for all

---

[16] The author is the source for this proposition, having participated in strategy debates with union officials and labor law experts that resulted in the decision to subordinate a human rights argument to an economic case for EFCA.

workers – but especially for low-wage workers and workers of color. Unions and collective bargaining have been especially important in giving workers access to health insurance and defined-benefit pensions.

(AFL-CIO 2009)

Management Takes Up Rights

The management community suddenly became pseudo-human rights champions in the EFCA campaign. Employers developed and promoted a human rights frame to defeat EFCA as it was originally proposed. They formed ad hoc coalitions called the Coalition for a Democratic Workplace and the Employee Freedom Action Committee, spending tens of millions of dollars in opposition to EFCA.

Employers characterized as "free speech" their ability under current law to aggressively campaign against workers' organizing efforts. They stressed "the importance of protecting secret ballot rights for American workers" (Raudabaugh 2008). They enlisted former Democratic presidential candidate George McGovern to publish an anti-EFCA declaration saying, "We cannot be a party that strips working Americans of the right to a secret-ballot election" (McGovern 2008).

Employers called EFCA's first-contract arbitration provision an assault on employers' collective bargaining rights. A letter to Congress insisted, "Compulsory interest arbitration is the antithesis of free collective bargaining" (Chamber of Commerce 2009). Another anti-EFCA thrust said, "With just a few lines of legislative language, Congress would revoke for newly-organized firms the principle of free collective bargaining – that employers and unions may walk away from a contract they find unsatisfactory" (Furchtgott-Roth 2009).

Employers and unions mobilized equally impressive grassroots and Washington-based lobbying efforts on EFCA (Acuff 2009; States News Service 2009). But employers overwhelmed trade unions' economic case for EFCA with a rights-based frame opposing it. One commentator noted, "The nation's labor unions, which organized so effectively last year to help elect President Obama, have been outmaneuvered so far on their top priority by their opponents in the business community.... Before labor groups had fully engaged this winter, the allied business groups successfully cast the legislation as undemocratic: How could Congress oppose secret-ballot elections" (Hamburger 2009)?

Analyzing EFCA's falter, a widely read and respected web reporter wrote:

The problem seems to be, rather, that the debate is mostly being engaged in on the right's terms. The phrase "secret ballot" occurs in conjunction with 34% of Google News hits on EFCA; by contrast, the phrase "right to organize" occurs in conjunction with just 2%.

EFCA's advocates, in other words, may be too busy playing defense. They also may also overestimate the extent to which most Americans tend to feel sympathetic toward unions. Although most of the public supports the right to unionize, the public feels far more ambivalent about unions themselves.

While a certain amount of anti-corporate populism can probably be productive in this environment, I don't know that the unions fundamentally want to make this a narrative about class conflict. Many working-class Americans are in industries that – EFCA or not – are not especially conducive to union formation, and others may see unions as advancing the particular objectives of their members, but not those of the working class as a whole. Polling has generally revealed that more Americans support the right to union formation than would want to form a union themselves.

The more effective framing, rather, might be in normative rather than economic terms. That is, don't focus on the *benefits of unionization*, but rather on *the right to union formation*. For example: the ability to form a union is a fundamental American right, companies are routinely infringing upon that right, and EFCA is necessary to protect that right. This would also provide for a stronger rebuttal to the "secret ballot" talking point ("EFCA would deprive employees of their right to a secret ballot"), which is oriented precisely along these lines.

(Silver 2009)

CONCLUSION

Trade unionists made a strategic choice to stress economics in the EFCA campaign in the heat of the economic crisis of 2008–2009. They judged that a populist mood gave economic arguments more sway in moving voters and legislators. One problem, though, was that economic uncertainty gave the unions' argument a double edge. One cut in favor of their Keynesian case, but another cut against it, suggesting that a growth in unions and collective bargaining would add new costs and new burdens on employers, leading to even more layoffs and lack of competitiveness.

Although the management side still gave priority to a rights-based argument against EFCA, employers welcomed the economic argument. Management groups blanketed Washington and the national news media with a bought-and-paid-for March 2009 study predicting huge job losses if EFCA became law (Layne-Farrar 2009). They said that now, in the midst of a severe economic crisis, is not the time to saddle businesses with greater costs from union bargaining. The head of the U.S. Chamber of Commerce said:

In response to declining interest in this bill, its supporters ramped up the rhetoric surrounding it, offering it as the solution to everything from the financial crisis to providing more employees with health care, and even improving workplace safety. EFCA suddenly became economic pixie dust which when sprinkled by benevolent union leaders would raise wages, create jobs, and rebuild the middle class. Trust me, if rapidly increasing union membership was the key for recovery and shared prosperity I would be out there organizing. But this bill will make it more difficult for businesses to adapt and innovate. Increasing unemployment and stifling job growth is exactly the wrong prescription for our ailing economy.

(Donohue 2009)

Unions failed to win EFCA as originally proposed, and the bill remained stalled in the U.S. Senate in early 2010. Although it was disappointing for human rights advocates, labor's retreat from a rights-based frame in the 2008–2009 EFCA campaign did not signal abandonment of the human rights diffusion project under way in the past decade.

Labor and human rights advocates acknowledge that convincing a broad public that workers' rights are human rights does not succeed or fail in a single legislative thrust. Labor law reform depends on relative political power of workers and employers, not on human rights and labor rights arguments, however compelling they might be. But these arguments add moral and ideological force to the workers' side in their long-term struggle for political space in a market-hegemonic economic system.

5

Framing the GMO

*Epistemic Brokers, Authoritative Knowledge,
and Diffusion of Opposition to Biotechnology*

Ronald J. Herring

> I blame GM crops for farmers' suicides.
>
> His Royal Highness Charles, Prince of Wales, October 5, 2008

CONTENTIOUS KNOWLEDGE CLAIMS: MIRACLE SEEDS
AND SUICIDE SEEDS

Why would Prince Charles famously declare that farmers commit suicide because of "GM crops"? At first blush, the declaration seems counterintuitive: Farmers have adopted transgenic crops rapidly and widely over the past twelve years where they are affordable and available. Why would people whose livelihoods depend on planting the right seeds select ones that are driving their neighbors to suicide? Does global diffusion of agricultural biotechnology indicate false consciousness on the part of farmers? Are they duped or innumerate? Prince Charles did not concoct his conclusion from whole cloth, nor is he alone in his outrage over the continuing holocaust of poor farmers at the hands of genetically modified organisms (GMOs). Widespread anxiety and outrage derive from authoritative knowledge claims diffused within transnational advocacy networks. Of particular importance are epistemic brokers, who occupy critical nodes at the intersection of local and global networks. Epistemic brokers select, contextualize, authenticate, sometimes theorize, and always disseminate knowledge about transgenic crops. Both networks and brokers are enabled by the historical framing of agricultural biotechnology: the lumping and splitting of recombinant DNA technologies that made the GMO.

With rapid diffusion of biotechnology has come reciprocal diffusion of frames, knowledge, and tactics to block transgenic crops. Unlike control of international air traffic or infectious diseases, no authoritative knowledge provides consensual norms for products of genetic engineering (Jasanoff 2005). Some nations have approved or promoted biotech crops; many others prohibit them. "GMO-free zones" continue to expand; moratoria on the technology are contested from India to California. Contention around the GMO diffuses through international institutions: the World Trade Organization, the *Codex Alimentarius*, the Cartagena Protocol, the United Nations Development Program, the European Commission, and the Food Safety Authority. Although much of the political discourse poses a North-South architecture of contention, the axis exhibits neither income nor areal clustering. The top five nations using transgenic crops after the United States are Argentina, Brazil, India, Canada, and China (James 2008).

Diffusion of transgenic crops poses little puzzle; the material interests of firms and farmers have been evident in their behavior. In much of the world, farmers have purchased new seeds at premium prices, mobilized politically for access to biotechnology, and frequently planted illegal "stealth" seeds even at risk of prosecution (James 2008; Jayaraman 2001; Joshi 2003; Herring 2007b). Few, if any, innovations in agriculture have spread so rapidly. Nevertheless, whole areas of the world – Africa and West Asia stand out – have low levels of adoption, and most subsistence crops have not received new traits through genetic engineering. Although there are complex reasons for differential diffusion of the technology, politics is fundamental: In many nations GMOs are illegal.

Networks opposing biotechnology have succeeded in much of the world, in part through diffusion of powerful knowledge claims; rival networks promote diffusion of biotechnology with similar appeals to authoritative knowledge. AgBioWorld, for example, introduces its website text with: "More than 3400 scientists support the use of biotechnology to improve agriculture in the developing world, including 25 Nobel Prize winners" (www.agbioworld. org). Corporate claims diffuse through these networks and supported public forums. Because farmers and firms have material interests in transgenic crops, and clearly outnumber activists in oppositional networks, the puzzle is how the opposition has been so successful. This chapter will therefore analyze oppositional, not promotional, tactics and knowledge. Nevertheless, the diffusion dynamic must be conceptualized as dialectical: oppositional politics confronts organized promotion and official sanction. These political forces reflexively form one another. Much of the dialectic is precisely mirrored: The pro-biotech narrative perfectly inverts, for example, the opposition's framing of authoritative knowledge from "GMOs: Unsafe and Untested" to "GMOs: Tested and Safe."

MASTER FRAMING: THE PECULIAR CASE OF THE GMO

Reciprocal diffusion of GMO crops and GMO-free zones developed from specific framing that proved powerful in a path-dependent way. The GMO frame was constructed at a particular point in history, not from science, but as a vector-sum of complex politics, including powerful influences of transnational social movements. The construction of the GMO as a special object of governance altered political interests and proved generative of tactics, knowledge, and organizational identities. Even pro-biotech activists and institutions have acceded to this frame: They have largely been reduced to changing the valence sign on the GMO from negative to positive.

Developments that culminated in the GMO began in 1973. Molecular biology, through recombinant DNA (rDNA) techniques, developed new capacity to move genes across species, creating new entities. As with all novel technologies, alternative frames were both available and arguably necessary to provide meaning and valence. Transgenic techniques might be framed either as radically unnatural or as a continuation of plant genetic modification with more efficient tools (McHughen 2000; Winston 2002). However natural or unnatural, property in these biological inventions became possible in 1980 in the United States, the global promulgator of strong property rights, raising the specter of corporate monopoly and control – and enhanced American hegemony on a global scale. New capacities and entities together raised new anxieties around regulation and ownership; these discourses came to be globally contested as *biosafety* and *bioproperty* (Herring 2007a).

With the new field of genetic engineering came new political interests. Some were straightforward: potential profits for commercial firms, higher incomes for farmers, new pharmaceuticals for consumers. For citizens more generally, interests in genetic engineering required processing through a cognitive screen to make sense of a daunting complexity. Contestation for framing that screen around rDNA technology in agriculture pitted novel threats against technological promise: FrankenFoods versus a solution to the Malthusian dilemma of global hunger (Pinstrup-Andersen and Schiøler 2000).

Opponents of biotechnology argued that transgenic plants produced novel threats in comparison to existing plants, necessitating at least surveillance and regulation, perhaps prohibition. This frame of unique threat is now so thoroughly naturalized that it is easy to miss its fundamental dependence on a prior framing: the invention of a special category of plants called GMOs. The GMO frame was constructed through both lumping and splitting of rDNA technologies. Most important, the frame excluded transgenic organisms in fields other than agriculture, both plants and animals, as in increasingly important pharmaceutical and industrial applications. In agricultural crops, products of rDNA technology were lumped together into one ominous category, regardless of trait, genetic event, or species (Herring 2008a). Without this framing, there could be no targeting – and torching – of GMO test plots; campaigns against GM food; or mobilization for GMO-free zones.

The GMO frame is now dominant in political discourse, media usage, and law. Alternative framing is equally plausible biologically. Genetic modification of plants has always involved putting new traits into existing cultivars (McHughen 2000: 80–84, passim). Some of these techniques – prior to rDNA technology – are quite radical, invasive, and "unnatural" by the standards of Gregor Mendel; all involve genetic modification (Miller and Conko 2000). The GMO frame splits some forms of genetic modification from others, and classifies plants by how traits got into the organism, not by characteristics of the plant itself. Process trumps product. An alternative schema would ask how traits, once incorporated, would affect food safety or environmental integrity. Because there are risks from introduction of all new cultivars into agricultural systems, plausible policy concerns would, in this alternative schema, center on specific risks of particular traits, in particular plants, in particular ecologies, regardless of how the trait got into the plant. In the Agbios database of 2008 (www.agbios.com/main.php), for example, fourteen traits from transgenes had been commercialized globally – insect resistance, virus resistance, fatty acid composition, and pro-vitamin A production, for example. In total, forty-five different transgenes representing 117 unique genetic events had been inserted into twenty-two crops. Permutations of these variables are huge.

Lumping and splitting in framing alter regulatory and political responses; we would, for example, usually disaggregate "chemicals" into useful, poisonous, inert, unknown, and safe categories and act accordingly. Likewise, disaggregation of transgenic plants would yield a different set of political possibilities. The "sustainable development" frame, for example, is globally authoritative, well funded, and widely shared in advocacy networks concerned with human welfare. Insecticides are the iconic unsustainable treadmill technology. Synthetic insecticides increase farmers' costs, drive development of pest resistance, and have especially deadly effects on field laborers in poor countries and in fragile agro-ecologies generally (Shelton 2007; Jeyaratnam 1990; Pray et al. 2002).The second most prominent transgenic trait is insect resistance. Specifically, Bt technology claims to reduce pesticide applications and externalities by enabling plants to manufacture insecticidal proteins in their own tissues, targeted on specific pests. Would Bt technology work? Would insect resistance develop quickly? Would its ecological effects be better or worse than existing synthetic sprays? These were big questions, difficult to answer without extensive field testing.

Before there was systematic evidence on actual results in cropping systems, Bt crops were opposed in coalitions for which sustainable agriculture and development are primary goals. Because introduction of the insect-resistant trait into Bt plants involved genetic engineering, the plants were coded as GMOs. Even field trials to determine environmental effects were opposed, and sometimes destroyed (Boal 2001). The cognitive motivation for this behavior reflects the power of framing: GMO threats are so obvious that tests are both pointless and dangerous (Shiva et al. 1999). The global Pesticide Action Network pursues sustainability specifically through reductions in pesticide use, but rejects Bt crops (Pesticide Action Network International 2007). The utility of the trait – insect resistance – was eclipsed by how the trait was introduced. Exclusion of Bt technology from a sustainable-development frame depended on this decisive framing and its centrality to oppositional networks: One technique for modifying plants was unacceptable, whatever its utility to the farmer or environment.

To illustrate the political nature of the GMO frame, one might compare a parallel means of genetic modification of plants that escapes the GM stigma: mutagenesis. Mutagenesis employs harsh chemicals or radiation to scramble plant DNA, to induce more mutations with which breeders can work; disruption of plant genetic material is more extensive than with transgenesis, which typically involves insertion of limited quantities of DNA (Batista et al. 2008; Herring 2008a). Mutagenic cultivars receive no special regulation or political attention; they are unlabeled, acceptable in global commodity trade, thoroughly naturalized. Ironically, mutagenic agricultural plants escape special notice and regulation much like transgenic pharmaceuticals. Moreover, mutagenesis is used by the same multinational life science firms as transgenesis. The initial lumping and splitting of technologies that produced the GMO was only one among many possible outcomes.

Invention of the GMO as an object of special suspicion and regulation coincided with and enabled a decisive shift in European law and policy, which in turn influenced farmers and nations having trade relations with Europe.[1] Initial enthusiasm for transgenic technology in Europe was replaced by increasingly restrictive practice in the late 1990s and early 2000s. This outcome was in no sense inevitable – indeed, it is the obverse of regulatory practice in the United States. Authoritative framing of transgenics evolved over time in Europe, reflecting interactions among firms, social movements, industries, public perceptions of risk, and institutions of governance in a specific historical context (Tait 2001; Chataway et al. 2006; Bonny 2003; Jasanoff 2005). Biotech firms, for example, walk a fine line in coproduction of the frame: To claim intellectual property, they must claim novelty; to avoid anxiety, they must claim continuity with six thousand years of plant breeding. Moreover, history matters. The European U-turn on molecular plant breeding in 1999 was a conjunctural lucky hit for opponents of genetic engineering. The Bhopal gas disaster (1984) in India, the Chernobyl nuclear accident (1986) in Ukraine, coupled with "mad cow" disease (bovine spongiform encephalopathy, 1986) in Britain, along with other instances of regulatory failure, eroded trust in government, science, and assurances of safety from the state.

Nevertheless, even in this period, skepticism about official science and corporate control did not apply to all genetic engineering. Pharmaceuticals produced by rDNA techniques – beginning with human insulin in 1978 – were split from the GMO frame. There was no mass mobilization for banning genetically engineered pharmaceuticals. As a consequence, global trade has not been segmented around "GM drugs"; that category, that object of governance, does not exist, although the use of rDNA technology is common in pharmaceuticals, and indeed much supported by public opinion in Europe (Gaskell et al. 2006: 15–22). There are no "FrankenPills" on posters. Indeed, an anticoagulant protein derived from the milk of transgenic goats with a human gene in its mammary glands – ATryn – was approved in Europe three years before the FDA approved it in the United States in 2009 (Kling 2009). Only transgenic seeds carry the stigmata of the GMO.

---

[1] The European Parliament and the Council. *Off. J. Eur. Commun.* L106, 1–38 (2001); Barboza 2003; Paarlberg 2001.

FOOD, RISK, AND UTILITY IN EUROPE

Opposition activists in Europe began with and found special resonance for the construct of "GM-foods." Anxiety around food is easily aroused, with good reason. Lives depend on keeping *Amanita verna* separate from supermarket mushrooms. Once introduced into international trade in the 1990s, food products relying in whole or in part on plants bred with molecular techniques were branded GMOs by activists. GM-foods were targeted by preexisting coalitions of American and European groups opposed to corporate power and irresponsibility, particularly in environmental issues (Schurman 2004; Schurman and Munro 2006). Mobilizational success depended in part on the structure of the food industry in the UK in particular, and Europe generally, and, as critically, recognition of this structure by activists (Lezaun 2004). Once major distributors claimed to have GM-free food, competitors felt compelled to follow suit. Both the state and farmers in France, for example, originally considered biotechnology to be essential for maintaining global economic competitiveness; erosion set in with reframing of agricultural transgenics in terms of environmental risks, corporate (especially American) power, and threats to culturally validated food norms.[2] European policy was profoundly affected, although the shifts in public opinion were not dramatic; mass-public knowledge of genetic engineering had neither depth nor complexity (Gaskell et al. 2006).

States universally seek to assure mass publics of food safety through deployment of institutionalized expertise; biosafety regulations are state responses to hypothetical risks created by the frame itself. "GM-food" triggered regulatory oversight in Europe, but the category does not exist in the U.S. regulatory schema. The Food and Drug Administration asks instead whether or not foods from transgenic crops are "substantially equivalent" to non-transgenic equivalents (Council for Biotechnology Information 2001; Miller 1999). It is the product, and its effect on human biological processes, that matter. If one finds the same range of variance by gross measurement in foods from transgenic and non-transgenic crops, there is no need for a special category of food. If the food is safe, it is safe, regardless of the process by which the cultivar was bred. Are foods from transgenic crops "substantially equivalent" to other sources, or sufficiently different to warrant extra caution, labels, and a separate regulatory schema? Or does the EU threshold for triggering the GMO designation of 0.9 percent transgenic content in food make foods safer?[3] Regulatory institutions themselves become focal points for mobilization; are they adequate? Who chooses regulators? Are there too many scientists and too few citizens on panels? Why should results be trusted? The answer for all of us

---

[2] Bonny 2003; Sato 2007: 47–78; Gaskell et al. 2006: 51, passim; Fukuda-Parr 2007: 27–28. The regulatory and conceptual splitting of biotechnologies also coincided with the political economy of powerful corporate interests in Europe (Graff et al. 2009).

[3] See Weighardt 2006 for an argument that the EU standard is incoherent in a scientific sense, as well as arbitrary and unenforceable.

depends on whom we trust, hence our common dependence on authoritative knowledge.

Splitting food products from other recombinant products was politically prudent. No rational activist mobilizes against drugs that the medical profession claims to be lifesaving. Physicians are authoritative figures; from state regulation and elaborate socialization, people tend to trust their prescriptions. Ironically, pharmaceuticals constitute a sector in which risks are quite high; authoritative knowledge has often proved inadequate or worse (thalidomide, Vioxx). But consumers expect drugs, like surgery or air travel, to come with risks. European public opinion on novel and potentially risky technologies has been similarly pragmatic rather than ideological. A major report commissioned by the EU concluded:

Europeans support the development of nanotechnology, pharmacogenetics and gene therapy. All three technologies are perceived as useful to society and morally acceptable. Neither nanotechnology nor pharmacogenetics are perceived to be risky. While gene therapy is seen as a risk for society, Europeans are prepared to discount this risk as they perceive the technology to be both useful and morally acceptable.

(Gaskell et al. 2006: 27–8)

The so-called "white" (industrial) biotechnologies, like the "red" (medical) biotech applications, are widely supported in Europe. There is broad support for industrial applications in degradable bioplastics and biofuels, even to the extent of supporting government subsidies for development. Even "pharming," whereby pharmaceutical products with mammalian activity are produced by genetically engineered plants, is supported by more Europeans than those opposing it, in every country except Austria (ibid.: 24–26; figures 8, 9). GM-food is unpopular, but of the possible benefits recognized in sample surveys, three reasons for purchasing it are all plausibly related to utility: less pesticide residue, nutritional benefits, and general environmental protection (ibid.: 69–71; figure 32).

This cost-benefit logic was eclipsed in global diffusion of the GMO frame. A decisive step came with global soft law governing transgenic crops, supported by the EU's collaboration with transnational advocacy networks and low-income countries (Tiberghien 2007: 60–63; Falkner 2000). The Cartagena Biosafety Protocol was passed in 2000, and brought into force September 11, 2003. The protocol slightly modified Europe's "Genetically Modified Organism" into the "Living Modified Organism [LMO]," but followed the same lumping frame, as opposed to the splitting logic of the United States (which opposed the protocol). The core assumption of the protocol – indeed, its raison d'être – is that rDNA techniques in agriculture pose more potential risk than other means of transforming cultivars. That a biosafety protocol is needed for some plants and not others reinforced the threat scenario of the GMO. By producing an authoritative segregation of transgenic plants from all others globally, Cartagena generated nodes for mobilization and institutional development across national boundaries. Its very existence links regulation to environmentalism, as Cartagena is formally a protocol under the Convention on Biological Diversity. Though there is no evidence of environmental damage to date (Thies and Devare 2007), Cartagena expanded the ambit of anxiety and globalized special status for surveillance and governance.

The institutional map remade by Cartagena creates highly specialized regulatory nodes, producing administrative choke points.[4] These nodes enable relatively small numbers with appropriate knowledge and skills to have disproportionately large political effects. Biosafety institutions must be created, but every step of establishing them can be challenged in the courts, which provide choke points in all institutionalized political systems. Regulatory institutions are difficult to construct, especially in countries with little expertise in this still-esoteric field. Inertia works against approval. If a nation "lacks capacity" to create mandated institutions, biotechnology cannot proceed, at least openly. The absence of biosafety laws and institutions has meant delays in official authorization of transgenics in many countries (although farmers are not always so legalistic). Intra-governmental differences in interest have likewise delayed or blocked institutional development; because of their constituencies, ministries of the environment typically offered more resistance to GMOs than did ministries of agriculture.[5] Ironically, the legal hurdles created by biosafety regulations dramatically increase the cost of deploying new seeds, and thus become functional equivalents of property; only large firms with deep pockets and testing expertise – multinational life science corporations – can surmount hurdles that block small and local seed companies. Biosafety regulation functionally substitutes for bioproperty (Herring and Kandlikar 2009).

Moreover, difficulties in creating these institutions – whether for lack of capacity or political opposition – not only slow diffusion by directing interests of firms toward other sectors and places, but also, ironically, offer resources to oppositional networks. The World Bank, the EU, bilateral aid programs, the United Nations Environment Programme (UNEP), and other international funders have programs for building biosafety capacity. Capacity building may well mean foreign training for activists in mechanisms for tightening regulations to block approval of transgenics (Paarlberg 2008: 117–134, passim). Cartagena logic created niches for salaried employees and consultants in global regulation, education, and testing activities. These are material consequences of framing; beneficiaries are sharply differentiated by class and cultural capital from average citizens.

With Cartagena the GMO frame became authoritative, but also significantly broader and more threatening. Choke points are especially effective under

---

[4] Choke points derive from the same structural metaphor as "bottlenecks," but with stronger connotations. Military strategy has employed choke points to defeat superior forces with few soldiers; Thermopylae is a classic case.

[5] Consider the institutional struggle in Brazil over who exactly could be experts on the choke point of biosafety approval – and the subsequent battle between Lula's Agriculture and Environment ministries (Herring 2007b: 140–145; more generally, Pray and Naseem 2007; Paarlberg 2001).

the "precautionary principle." Articles 10.6 and 11.8 of Cartagena explicitly privilege precautionary logic:

Lack of scientific certainty due to insufficient relevant scientific information and knowledge regarding the extent of the potential adverse effects of an LMO on biodiversity, taking into account risks to human health, shall not prevent a Party of import from taking a decision, as appropriate, with regard to the import of the LMO in question, in order to avoid or minimize such potential adverse effects.

(Convention on Biological Diversity 1992)

Not only is authoritative evidence for these hazards lacking, but disproving the negative is also logically impossible; the GMO became guilty unless proven innocent. Like the feared release of a transgene that cannot be recalled, the GMO entered world politics and took on a life of its own. Cartagena legitimized precaution concerning unspecified risks to human health, food safety, biodiversity, and ecological integrity. This frame – and not that of regulators in the United States – became prominent among advocacy professionals in many low-income countries. In jointly adopting, theorizing, and adapting the frame, epistemic brokers in global networks legitimized and spread its central risk message; their diffusion of disturbing empirical accounts subsequently reinforced and magnified the construction of unique threat posed by GMOs.

EPISTEMIC BROKERAGE AND DIFFUSION: MUTUAL DEPENDENCE IN NETWORKS

Receptivity of the GMO narrative of anxieties around biosafety and bioproperty was conditioned by fears of neocolonialism. Intellectuals in the ex-colonial world made critical contributions to theorizing genetic engineering as especially catastrophic for development (Shiva 1997). The nascent threat construction was specified concretely: threats to national independence, in the form of dominance of agriculture by multinational corporations (MNCs); threats to farmers, in the form of bondage to monopoly seed corporations ("bio-serfs," "neo-feudalism"); threats to nature, in the form of "biological pollution" (gene flow); and threats to human health, in the form of undiscovered allergens.[6]

Threatening constructions of agricultural biotechnology joined opponents of corporate globalization from rich and poor countries in transnational advocacy networks (TANs). These networks were led by international nongovernmental organizations (INGOs) such as Greenpeace International and Friends of the Earth International. INGOs carry considerable authority; their imprimatur ratifies authoritative knowledge about little-known science to brokers in the periphery. But what science diffuses? Mae-Wan Ho's book *Genetic Engineering* (2000) posited "serious hazards inherent in the technology." The author is

---

[6] On global framing, see Tarrow 2005: 59–76, 203; on intellectual work in theorizing the GMO, Schurman and Munro 2006. For examples of this narrative, see Friends of the Earth International 2006; Greenpeace International 2007; Madsen 2001; Assayag 2005; Herring 2005; Reddy and Bhaskar 2005; Heins 2008; Shiva et al. 2000; Scoones 2008.

identified as a British scientist and Fellow of the U.S. National Genetics Foundation. Her book's subtitle query – "Dream or Nightmare?" – was answered decisively on the nightmare side. The sub-subtitle is *Turning the Tide on the Brave New World of Bad Science and Big Business*. The book's appendix contains two calls to action: Global Moratorium on GE Biotechnology and No to Patents on Life. As a cover endorsement, the publication *Earth Matters*, from Friends of the Earth, states:

The battle to stop genetic engineering is nothing less than a struggle for human freedom itself. Mae-Wan Ho's book provides excellent ammunition for us all.

The "ammunition" in Ho's book claims the authority of science. The appendix contains the text of a World Scientists' Statement "signed by more than 100 scientists from twenty-four countries" (Ho 2000: 299). Included in this statement is reference to transgenic potatoes that had deleterious biological effects on rats that ate them. These potatoes were included in Alan McHughen's explanation of "scary myths" about transgenic crops (2000: 114–121, 258). The experiment that produced the scare was not scientifically credible. Nevertheless, few of us read peer-reviewed journals of plant science. Much of the world reads about these poisonous potatoes, along with fish genes in tomatoes and the grave threats of FrankenFoods. The threat construction often came to ex-colonies from sources in former colonial powers, and carried thereby a kind of ironic authority. Refutations, or counter-narratives, were missing from networks opposing GMOs. When mentioned, refutations were dismissed as self-serving because of corporate interests in biotechnology. Because transgenics were produced and owned by MNCs, effective regulation – or even objective assessment – was widely discounted (Friends of the Earth International 2006). MNC science was held to be suspect; MNC political power rendered government science untrustworthy as well. Permissive regulation in the United States – the source and political supporter of GMOs – was seen as a predictable reflection of corporate power under neoliberalism.

Global diffusion of authoritative disaster stories prompted activists to globalize campaigns for moratoria or outright bans on transgenic crops. If one believed the narratives – that is, trusted the epistemic brokers – this outcome is consonant with widely shared values. To carry out these campaigns, INGOs needed credibility in domestic politics and civil society in rich countries, and the resources that follow. Credibility of INGOs derived in part from their claim to speak for the interests of poor people in poor places, who cannot speak for themselves. Advocacy professionals needed partners, both for projects on the ground and for authenticated local knowledge about the effects of transgenics in poor places. These locales stand at considerable cognitive and spatial distance from headquarters. "The field" cannot be accessed directly for reasons of geography, language, skills, culture, or lifestyle. Reciprocally, diffusion of claims from local activists necessitated connection to compatriots with the linguistic and technical skills necessary for operating in global networks (e.g.,

Madsen 2001). Hinges between the local and cosmopolitan networks create brokerage niches.

Dependence in networks is mutual. Local and national NGOs need resources from international development agencies and bilateral donors: projects, salaries, and materiel. Global networks provide livelihoods and potential mobility for individuals as well as the means of dissemination: websites, computers, conferences, press releases, and forums for studies and reports. The sums of money involved are reportedly large (Byrne 2003). In many settings, it seems likely that the small and urban opposition to GMOs would collapse without these external resources. Volker Heins (2008: 121) concluded from his study of NGOs in international politics:

> Both these cases reveal a curious irony: for international donors, being grassroots and close to local communities is a prerequisite for any group that seeks foreign funds; at the same time, these groups apply for funds only because the project of going grassroots and building a basis of supporters in their own country has failed.

Whatever the financial flows, knowledge diffusion in TANs is bidirectional, if often asymmetric. Local activists depend on their networks for extra-local authoritative knowledge about esoteric and complex issues: gene flow, terminator technology, allergenicity, and intellectual property. What they learn has political consequences. If local activists stand for poor farmers and sustainable development, and GMOs destroy both farmers and their environment, campaigns against GMOs are imperative.

"Monsanto's terminator gene" provides an archetypal example of the critical role of epistemic brokers in networks. The bioproperty and biosafety subnarratives of the GMO were connected globally through dissemination of reports of "terminator technology" – so named by a Canadian NGO (Rural Foundation International, now ETC Group) through web communications (ETC 2007). The terminator summarized, in one construct, the multiple threats of biotechnology. The biocultural abomination of seeds that could not reproduce resonated with a narrative of corporate greed and acts against nature (Gold 2003). Although demonstrably untrue on the ground, the threat diffused widely. "Monsanto's terminator gene" came to India through epistemic brokers located in international networks, such as Vandana Shiva and Navdanya (Herring 2006). Monsanto, as creator and owner of terminator technology, then provided a condensation symbol for the narrative: multinational, American, owner of an unnatural and exploitative technology. Monsanto, as target, diffused as well, along with the tactic of peoples' tribunals. In public trials, the corporation was tried in absentia and convicted, preceded by press releases and enacted with extensive media coverage.[7] Even today, people all over the

---

7 See Pimbert and Wakeford 2002 for an explanation of "citizen juries" as a mechanism to counterbalance established "experts" with knowledge of the people. For an example, see "Monsanto on trial before the Permanent Peoples' Tribunal in Rome," www.grisnet.it/filb, accessed June 15, 2009, report published June 21, 2001 in the *Law, Social Justice & Global Development* Electronic Law Journal.

world firmly believe that farmers cannot save and replant GMO seeds, despite extensive evidence to the contrary (Herring and Kandlikar 2009).

Campaigning works against empirical tethering of knowledge claims. Nuanced findings and conditional conclusions do not work in advocacy politics that depend on clear messages for media releases and campaign slogans (Bob 2005). Some claims against GMOs seem bizarre in retrospect but have persisted and diffused. Vandana Shiva, for example, claimed that Bt cotton seeds in India were not only "suicidal," but also "homicidal" and finally "genocidal." Transgenic cotton caused the suicides of tens of thousands of Indian farmers (Shiva 2006a, 2006b). Diffusion of this narrative was a necessary condition for Prince Charles' pronouncements on farmer suicides that gained international press attention, and thus reinforced the urgency of opposition. A more recent article appeared in the *Huffington Post*,[8] raising the death toll significantly and stating flatly that organic farmers "are earning 10 times more than the farmers growing Monsanto's Bt-cotton." The article contains egregious errors of fact and interpretation, but Dr. Shiva has achieved the status of epistemic broker for all things Indian in much of the Western media. Fact-based refutations (e.g., www.geneticmaize.com/2009/06/shameful-shiv) have appeared in what the Bush administration sometimes dismissed as the "reality-based community," but nothing has had the prominence of Dr. Shiva's original. Few *Huffington* readers will search out Narayanamoorthy and Kalamkar (2006) or Gruère et al. (2008). Information costs are so high that few of us cross networks and compare sources. And though there is strong media selection for extreme events, it is also important that the GMO frame itself provides resonance for extreme claims: These plants are fundamentally different from all other plants, and carry special risks.

The hinged-brokerage dynamic can be illustrated with one example. The Warangal district in the state of Andhra Pradesh, South India, is the most widely cited location of catastrophic effects of GMOs (Bt cotton) on local people.[9] From a ground view, Warangal also seems very densely populated by agricultural NGOs, although comparative data are not available. The Centre for Sustainable Agriculture (CSA) in the regionally cosmopolitan city of Secunderabad, for example, funds four local NGOs in Warangal district, including the Centre for Rural Operations and Programmes Society (CROPS), which oversees the "GMO-free zone" of Eenabavi – a hamlet of thirty families sustained distally by Oxfam Trust, HIVOS-Netherlands, and AEI Luxembourg. The Deccan Development Society (DDS) of Secunderabad, also active in study and work in the district, lists eighteen international funders, all in Europe or Canada, and six Indian government agencies. Both CSA and DDS reports figure prominently in critical assessments of Bt cotton in India in a major publication by Friends of the Earth International (2006), *Who Benefits from GM Crops?*

---

[8] www.huffingtonpost.com/vandana-shiva/from-seeds-of-suicide-to_b_192419.html, accessed June 4, 2009. For sources contrary to the extreme claims in the article, see Herring 2008b.
[9] See Shiva et al. 2000; Stone 2002, 2007; Herring 2008b.

From Warangal emerged internationally circulated stories of "failure of Bt cotton," followed by sheep dying from ingestion of Bt cotton leaves. Sheep-death reports were attributed to mobile shepherds and publicized by state-level NGOs; they entered the global political and policy stream via INGOs that fund national and state-level organizations in the area. A press release from Dr. Mae-Wan Ho, leader of the Independent Science Panel in London (www.i-sis.org.uk/MDSGBTC.php) and the author of *Genetic Engineering: Dream or Nightmare* (2000), was titled "Mass Deaths in Sheep Grazing on Bt Cotton." A week later, the *Guardian* published John Vidal's "Outcrop of Deaths," citing 1,600 sheep killed by Bt cotton leaves on May 10, 2006. Sheep deaths came back to metropolitan and English-reading India via the GM Watch report: "Mortality in Sheep Flocks after grazing on Bt Cotton fields – Warangal District, Andhra Pradesh." Americans read the account via the Organic Consumers Association of Finland, Minnesota, which campaigns for "Health, Justice, Sustainability, Peace and Democracy." Their coverage was titled "More on Mass Death of Sheep in India After Grazing in Genetically Engineered Cotton Fields," accompanied by a line, "Straight to the Source." The source was the Centre for Sustainable Agriculture, Secunderabad. The link was dead when an attempt to access was made in 2008, although the story itself remained online. In direct interviews, leadership at CSA Secunderabad backed away from published claims: the number 1,600, the certainty of diagnosis, the evidentiary base.[10]

The Bt-dead-sheep story is biologically impossible, as recognized by Delhi's Genetic Engineering Approval Committee, the chief regulatory institution in India (Venkateshwarlu 2007). There is no biological mechanism for the Bt insecticidal protein to kill sheep, nor any evidence that it has done so; there are many reasons sheep may die, but Bt cotton is not one of them. The story did, however, resonate with the GMO frame in activist networks and their media contacts. The following year, reports from the same area escalated to deaths of cattle from eating Bt cotton leaves.[11]

Although vertical diffusion is more important to scale shift (Tarrow, Chapter 11 in this book), horizontal diffusion contributes to network strength and expands GMO-free space. In neighboring Pakistan, Najma Sadeque, in the *Financial Post*, May 12, 2008, wrote a piece titled "After a disastrous track record in 40 countries, *Bt* cotton is 'welcomed' in Pakistan." Sadeque's article illustrates the coherent and compelling narrative of disaster from GMOs (Herring 2009b). She wrote that in 2002 farmers in Madhya Pradesh (India) planted Bt seeds and "ended up with 100 per cent failure." The article asked: "How could farmers fail to see the figures that showed it really didn't make sense to grow Bt cotton? – They were deceived by false claims." The authority is indigenous: "Deccan Development Society (DDS), an Indian grassroots NGO . . . found [that] those who grew non-BT cotton made six times more

---

[10] For team members, methods and findings, see Herring 2008b, 2009b; Rao 2007a,b.
[11] *Deccan Herald*, February 7, 2007; *The Hindu*, March 2, 2007; *GM Watch*, March 4, 2007.

profits than the BT cotton farmers!" Agro-economic failure was accompanied by alarming externalities: After grazing on Bt cotton leaves, "In just four villages in Andhra Pradesh, 1800 sheep died horrible, agonising deaths within 2–3 days from severe toxicity." The Teeth Maestro Internet posting of Sadeque's article was accompanied by an article repeating a version of the terminator hoax long discredited in India: "Monsanto – genetically modified BT Cotton 'terminator' seeds being introduced in Pakistan." Ironically, Pakistan already had Bt cotton, smuggled in from stocks of farmer-bred hybrids in India, which would have laid this claim to rest had anyone checked with farmers.

The Internet was a necessary condition for this diffusion of alarming claims. Web communities of knowledge and action are readily identifiable and can be mobilized quickly (see Earl and Kimport, Chapter 7, this volume). Some "civil society organizations" are essentially a few individuals with access to a server; it is difficult to discern this fact distally. Without the web, there would be no counterweight to international science panels and peer-reviewed journal publications that find no empirical support for GMO disaster narratives on the farm or in the stomach. Websites also become products to convince funders and donors that good works are being done: Diffusion itself is a product. Press releases permit crossfertilization of media in different sites, multiplying incidents as they go; media reports from local press then feed international coverage, lending an air of authenticity to the knowledge thus displayed.

Authoritative and widely accessible reports from NGOs reinforce major themes of the oppositional narrative: supine peasants, unequal power, co-opted states. Local NGOs have credibility, partly from indigeneity, partly from the eyewitness nature of their reporting. They also have concrete interests in the failure of biotechnology; failures legitimate continuing oppositional campaigns, and new campaigns for alternatives: organic farming, sustainable agriculture, and "GMO-free zones." These alternatives are popular and well-funded through European networks and official aid programs in India (Bownas 2008). NGOs not only carry an aura of civil action (nongovernmental), but in the contemporary international political opportunity structure, they also have a legitimate place at the table, and a means of acting.[12]

Extreme claims get both the instant dissemination and authoritative standing enabled by more and more distal circulation. If overwhelming farmer adoption has in effect settled the agroeconomic questions around Bt cotton in India, new claims are needed to justify continuing the struggle. Reports of dead sheep are notoriously difficult to disconfirm – the animals are mortal – and frightening. Shepherds are among the most vulnerable of the poor, and often marginalized by ethnicity. Tethering reports to distal and obscure sources prevents any decisive confrontation with facts. Ironically, Bt-dead-sheep knowledge became authoritative precisely because it was unverifiable. Extreme claims depend on

---

[12] Chapter 27 of Agenda 21 authorized the role of NGOs and other "stakeholders" around sustainable development. Article 71 of Chapter 10 of the UN Charter granted consultative status in global representation.

the common folk wisdom (present in fifty-five languages) that "where there is smoke there must be fire" (Heath and Heath 2007: 11–12). This aphorism recognizes the salience of smoke over other forms of evidence – such as a thermometer. Accounts of extreme events diffused through consonant networks attempt to unsettle an emergent scientific consensus with difficult-to-assess evidence from "the field." Keeping uncertainty alive is in the interest of all brokers in global coalitions against biotechnology, as the empirical evidence on development and poverty is settling on the other side of the cognitive rift (Herring 2007c).

Global and distal narratives of bioproperty are less dramatic than mass die-offs of livestock, but exhibit similar dynamics. The narrative of a global tyranny of monopoly and patent control globalized by Vandana Shiva (1997) and adopted by TANs has proved inconsistent with facts on the ground, institutional evolution, farmer ingenuity, and state institutional capacity. Monsanto had no patent in India for the Bt seeds that were to crush "bio-serfs," nor did it have any "terminator technology." These facts are largely unknown outside specialized knowledge communities; reports of epistemic brokers in oppositional networks substituted for knowledge that incurs very high information costs. Who can track patent law in numerous countries? Who can assess terminator claims? Empirically, intellectual property in seeds has generally proved difficult to claim or enforce (Jayaraman 2001, 2004). In the field, opportunistic appropriation of technology has been common, as with films, pharmaceuticals, music, and software (Herring 2007b; Naim 2005). In some countries – most notably China – public-sector research and firms have been important in biotechnology (Cohen 2005). Public-sector universities have produced important breakthroughs, such as the virus-resistant papaya (Gonsalves et al. 2007; Davidson 2008). Humanitarian-use transfers offer an institutional alternative to private property, as developed in pro-vitamin A "golden rice" (Lybbert 2003). Epistemic brokerage within networks shields partisans from these contradictions in the narrative, just as cognitive and physical distance shields reports of dead sheep in Warangal from disconfirmation.

From this illustration, we can pose some tentative conclusions about diffusion of knowledge in GMO networks. Opposition depends on Janus-faced brokerage influenced by characteristics of local advocacy groups and international coalition dynamics.[13]

Advocacy Network Characteristics and Knowledge Flow

Advocacy networks in India are often markedly hierarchical, both in terms of traditional social relations (class and standing, or caste) and modern stratifications (education, language). Subordinates hesitate to disagree with leaders; leaders want to hear confirmation of broader mobilization narratives (agroeconomic catastrophes from GMOs; suicides; dead sheep). This communicative

---

[13] This section closely follows the section of Herring 2009b titled "Interests in Contentious Narratives," which expands on the ideas in the text.

incapacity prevents confrontation with the empirical even within local networks, but reinforces diffusion of a consistent narrative to international advocacy networks. Communicative incapacity is reinforced by the distance of middle-class activists from agriculture and agriculturalists. The extralocal nature of consumption and validation demotes empirical concerns; it actually matters little what local farmers think of the narrative. Extreme claims gain a hearing in the global cacophony.

Moreover, urban cultural bias resists crediting farmer skill and agency. In India, the rural cottage-industry production and diffusion of dozens of illegal transgenic cotton varieties under the radar of Delhi and Monsanto was incongruent with narratives of peasant passivity and victimization (Jayaraman 2004; Gupta and Chandak 2005). The stealth tactics and agency of actual farmers do not resonate with "bioserfs" crushed by patent power of multinationals. Class matters; the radical freedom of movement leaders from the dull compulsion of economic facts means there is no penalty for getting it wrong.

International Coalition Dynamics

Coalitions seek to broaden support by weaving seemingly incongruent strands together: "Code Pink Says No to GMO," but so does the Pesticide Action Network (and, not unimportantly, the pesticide industry). International networks facilitate flows of reciprocal but asymmetric authoritative knowledge. The very successful hoax of "Monsanto's terminator gene" came to India from a Canadian website, from which it bounced to much of the world via transnational networks authenticated by Indian intelligentsia (Herring 2006). Reciprocally, farmer suicides and dead sheep moved from periphery to center, then back to periphery with added credibility. A reciprocal authenticity dynamic develops: Ex-colonial powers and their press authenticate global narratives for local networks, and local narratives with authenticity based on indigeneity provide confirmation for global narratives. Brokerage is not class-neutral; brokers need skill sets and cultural capital sufficient to act as Janus-faced hinges in a cosmopolitan world. There are authenticity rents to be garnered – some large, some meager – for brokers of contentious knowledge. Authenticity rents are enhanced by the celebration of local knowledge that dovetails with the skepticism about science in contemporary critiques of modernity (Nanda 2003: 125–159).

Reports of extreme events from India – GMO-driven mass suicides, livestock deaths, crushing patents – have resonance and credibility for the reasons suggested above, but lack empirical validity.[14] Nevertheless, these outcomes

---

[14] The farmer-suicide narrative is contradicted by authoritative evidence on the economics of Bt cotton, beginning decisively with high rates of adoption. See Gruère et al. 2008; Naik et al. 2005; Gupta and Chandak 2005; Bambawale et al. 2004; Herring 2008b, 2009b; Bennett et al. 2006; Narayanamoorthy and Kalamkar 2006. The dead-sheep narrative misunderstands the mechanism for the Cry1Ac insecticidal protein's effect on Lepidopterans – a mechanism that cannot function in mammalian guts (Thies and Devare 2007; Shelton 2007; Rao 2007a,b).

attributed to GMOs violate universal values embedded in numerous global agreements – sustainability, development, equity – and thus motivate global collective action. The normative structure is largely consensual: No one wants poor farmers or their livestock to die. It is not normative dissensus, but dissonant knowledge claims that drive opposition to GMOs. The urgency generated by these reports from the field quite reasonably motivates remedial actions: mandatory labeling, moratoria, GMO-free zones, and financial contributions to NGOs furthering these objectives.

THE GMO AS GENERATIVE FRAME

Genetically engineered crops have diffused rapidly across the globe, despite vigorous opposition in civil society, restrictive intellectual property claims, and adverse regulation by many states (James 2008; Herring 2008a). Simultaneously, successful political opposition has kept much of the world GMO-free, at least formally. Opposition has been effective not at the farm level, where material interests dominate, but in formal-legal institutions. Success in these arenas resulted from (1) a fundamental framing success in lumping and splitting transgenic technologies to create a contentious object of governance: the GMO, and (2) diffusion of authoritative knowledge in advocacy networks. In knowledge diffusion, epistemic brokers at the intersection of cosmopolitan and local advocacy networks play critical roles. They have reinforced the original frame's privileging of unique risks in agricultural transgenics, but also transformed the narrative through deployment of local knowledge.

The GMO frame bundles all the uncertainty involved in rDNA technology, minus the widely recognized potential. It collects anxieties but excludes utilities: FrankenFoods but not FrankenPills. This framing facilitated diffusion of knowledge claims, targets, and tactics within global networks. The GMO framing created a cognitive opportunity structure through which a wide variety of political activists could define their struggles. Global soft law inimical to the diffusion of transgenic plants depended on European framing. The Cartagena Protocol on Biosafety, in turn, created national-level choke points that leveraged the power of small numbers with appropriate skills and network connections to contest diffusion of transgenic plants. Embedded in new institutions, the frame proved powerful through restructuring interests, particularly in poor food-exporting countries with ties to Europe.

Once incorporated into European and global law, the GMO framing proved generative – of targets, subnarratives, and institutions. There is insufficient space to discuss all generative effects, but some recapitulate themes from this chapter. The frame itself provides *objectives*, as in "GMO-free zones" that proliferate globally; *targets* or *focal points* provided by field testing sites, themselves enabled by the frame's reification of special risk; *organizational identities* such as GM Watch; *segregation in international trade* mandated by special regulations for "GM crops"; *choke points* created for transgenic plants alone, and no others; a *market-premium niche* (GMO-free food); and, of increasing importance, an *appropriable antithesis* for mobilization and funding: organic agriculture.

Without widespread diffusion and acceptance of this biologically problematic frame, there could be no "GM-food," no "GMO-free zones," no GM field trials, no global and national biosafety institutions that target only transgenic crops. There could be no "living modified organisms" to generate transaction costs and targets under the Cartagena Protocol. The framing also restructured interests of farmers and nations, and thus affected patterns of diffusion of transgenic technology. Much diffusion was driven underground to evade biosafety and bioproperty norms embedded in the GMO frame; networks of farmers spread transgenics under the radar of firm and state (Herring 2007b).

Framing success depended on historically specific politics. Transgenic technologies entered world history at a point when transnational networks opposed to corporate power and environmental irresponsibility were connected and active (Schurman 2004; Schurman and Munro 2006). Such networks offered skills, personnel, finances, and legitimacy – and authoritative knowledge. By partnering with selected brokers in national and local networks in the poorer world, the transnational coalition against transgenics enhanced its claims to authority and legitimacy through dissemination – and celebration – of knowledge "from below" (Assayag 2005). Despite the importance of Europe in this global dynamic, the GMO narrative has been a truly global production. It has been remade by diffusion through transnational networks of solidarity and trust. GMOs came to India authoritatively coded as a threat of corporate monopoly imposed through a terminator technology; epistemic brokers legitimated by their command of this new and esoteric knowledge incorporated this modular component into existing networks seeking farmer welfare and autonomy (Bownas 2008).

Incorporation was facilitated by the fact that genetic engineering is cognitively distal; it requires interpretation and mediation by expertise: people who understand gene networks, gene flow, and gene-use restriction technology (i.e., the terminator). The distance of this discourse from ordinary experience necessitates epistemic brokerage; if nothing else, information costs for most of us are very high. Certain brokers command trust because of their position in networks united by ideological commitments. Fox News viewers received very different knowledge about weapons of mass destruction in Iraq than did readers of TomDispatchBlogspot.com. All members of our species depend on trusting the right brokers on global warming. Yet GMO brokerage seems different from that in other networks. Human Rights Watch and Amnesty International, for example, rest their credibility on factual accounts that face intense scrutiny and refutation by governments. They strongly resist diffusion of erroneous claims, even to the distress of their supporters. INGOs involved with biotechnology work in a field in which cognitive distance of supporters from the science and from agriculture are significant, and the possibility of decisive refutation is remote. Torture, we intuitively understand; how insecticidal proteins kill sheep is inaccessible.

New technologies are especially susceptible to both framing and epistemic brokerage. The great cognitive divide often settles on risk: Is risk to be balanced against benefit, as with surgery or air travel, or is the very presence of risk a cause for resistance? European consumers split rDNA foods from rDNA applications in industry and medicine on grounds of utility. Indian farmers exhibited the same utility orientation of European consumers; they quickly adopted Bt cotton to reduce pesticide costs and improve profits. When faced with regulatory obstacles, they stood up against the state and simultaneously took local control of the technology in a transgenic cottage industry (Jayaraman 2004; Herring 2005; Gupta and Chandak 2005). This information did not diffuse widely, in large part because the story Prince Charles believed and promulgated took center stage. A small number of thin networks succeeded in making global disaster stories of Bt cotton authoritative. GMOs returned to Europe from India as not only "suicidal" but also "homicidal," and finally "genocidal," killing off a hapless and supine third world peasantry and their livestock as well. This return flow of local knowledge was legitimated by the indigeneity of local activists and by brokers of global stature in trusted networks. Disaster stories reinforced the master narrative's core of risk, and confirmed with hard numbers, names, and places the devastating effects of the GMO, effects not even imagined at the time of Europe's U-turn on agricultural biotechnology.

PART II

MECHANISMS OF DIFFUSION

6

Dialogue Matters

Beyond the Transmission Model of Transnational Diffusion between Social Movements

Sean Chabot

On February 21, 1936, after traveling for nearly six months, Dr. Howard Thurman and his delegation finally arrived in Bardoli for a meeting with Gandhi. They exchanged warm greetings with the Indian leader and sat down on the floor of a large tent. Then Gandhi started asking Thurman (accompanied by his wife Sue, Edward Carroll, and Phenola Carroll) a series of probing questions about the experiences and social conditions of African Americans in their home country. Thurman (1979: 132) later wrote in his autobiography, "He wanted to know about voting rights, lynching, discrimination, public school education, the churches and how they functioned. His questions covered the entire sweep of our experience in American society." After several hours of intense discussion, Thurman and the others finally had a chance to ask Gandhi some burning questions:

Thurman: Is non-violence from your point of view a form of direct action?
Gandhi: It is not one form, it is the only form.... It is the greatest and the activest force in the world. One cannot be passively non-violent.... It is a force which is more positive than electricity and more powerful than even ether. At the center of non-violence is a force which is self-acting....
Thurman: Forgive the weakness, but may I ask how are we to train individuals or communities in this difficult art?
Gandhi: There is no royal road, except through living the creed in your life which must be a living sermon. Of course the expression in one's own life presupposes great study, tremendous perseverance, and thorough cleansing of one's self of all the impurities. If for mastering of the physical sciences you have to devote a whole lifetime, how many lifetimes may be needed for mastering the greatest spiritual force that mankind has known? But why worry even if it means several lifetimes? For if this is the only permanent thing in life, if this is the only thing that counts, then whatever effort you bestow on mastering it is well spent.
　　　　　("Interview to American Negro Delegation," *CWMG* 68: 235–237)

The time reserved for their meeting had passed quickly and the visitors hurried to catch their train. But as they departed, Gandhi remarked, "Well, if it comes true it may be through the Negroes that the unadulterated message of non-violence will be delivered to the world" (*CWMG* 68: 237–238; see also Tendulkar 1960–1963, Vol. IV: 61; Fischer 1962: 322; Thurman 1979: 132; Kapur 1992: 88–90).

What is the significance of interpersonal discussions – such as the one between Thurman and Gandhi – for our understanding of transnational diffusion between social movements? I argue that, as contentious politics scholars, we need to focus more of our theoretical and empirical efforts on making sense of such communication. We must pay more attention to how people actually interact and relate to each other if we want to gain deeper insight into the complexities and agency involved in this process. The purpose of this chapter is to explore new ways of doing so. The first section suggests that the dominant framework for analyzing transnational diffusion among social movements relies on a transmission model of communication. It highlights recent work on the subject by Sidney Tarrow (2005), who incorporates prominent developments in the field. Extending Tarrow's model, the next section defines dialogue and proposes a dialogical framework for examining how transnational diffusion among social movements occurs. Although transmission often applies to the spread of catchy symbols and technical information, intensive dialogue is necessary for the spread of innovative and multidimensional strategies. The third, and most important, section applies my framework to the case of the Gandhian repertoire's journey from the Indian independence movement to the American civil rights movement. It highlights what the editors call the "multidimensionality" of transnational diffusion and specifies its impact on African American liberation struggles over several decades. The conclusion reviews my key arguments and considers their relevance for contemporary scholars as well as activists.

THE TRANSMISSION MODEL OF COMMUNICATION AND TRANSNATIONAL DIFFUSION

In *The New Transnational Activism*, Tarrow synthesizes nearly all relevant scholarship in our field into his own approach to studying transnational diffusion among social movements.[1] Figure 6.1 (Tarrow 2005: figure 6.2, 105) depicts the model he has developed for analyzing the pathways of transnational diffusion.

Alternative Pathways of Transnational Diffusion

Tarrow starts with a *localized action* – such as a strike or a sit-in – embedded in a national context and shaped by an existing repertoire of contention

---

[1] See also C. Walsh-Russo, May 2004, "Diffusion and Social Movements: A Review of the Literature."

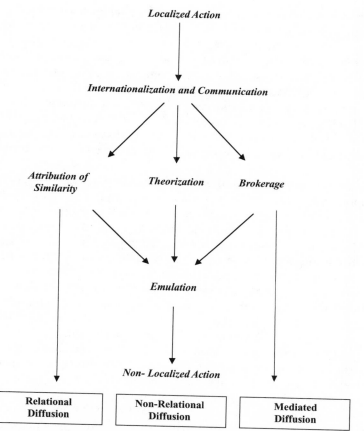

FIGURE 6.1. Alternative Pathways of Transnational Diffusion between Social Movements (Reproduced from Tarrow 2005: 105)

(Tilly 1986, 1995b). If perceived as successful, the localized action might spread across geographical borders because of the growing *internationalization* of political actors, networks, and structures, which promotes *communication* of institutional similarities and differences among contentious actors in various places. Particularly in a world with new and widely available technologies such as the Internet, activists can easily and quickly exchange information across great distances. As a result, internationalization and communication are now "the large impersonal processes that lie in the background of all forms of transnational diffusion" (Tarrow 2005: 103). After the transnational diffusion process is set in motion, it evolves along one or more of the three major pathways. *Attribution of similarity* refers to the construction of social bonds and personal networks that allow people who identify with each other to receive information along established lines of interaction and adopt one another's forms of action. *Theorization*, in contrast, captures how people in one country develop simplified interpretations of protest by unfamiliar people in another country, enabling specific tactics (such as suicide bombing) to spread along indirect channels such as the mass media, Internet, or word of mouth. Finally, *brokerage* focuses on how bridging individuals and institutions forge linkages among previously unconnected social sites, spurring transfers of information and methods among them. As Tarrow emphasizes in the conclusion, these three mechanisms lead to *relational, nonrelational,* and *mediated* diffusion processes, respectively. All pathways, moreover, produce *emulation* (i.e., the adoption of transmitters' ideas and practices by receivers) and *nonlocalized action* (i.e., the spread of strategies and campaigns beyond initial settings) (Tarrow 2005: 103–106).

Tarrow's model is certainly useful for scholars interested in identifying particular social mechanisms and analyzing diverse cases. But it does not help us explore in depth how actual people, facing concrete social situations, interact with and learn from each other. More specifically, by asserting that communication is a "large impersonal process," Tarrow excludes what activists involved in struggles for social justice feel, think, say, and do when they form interpersonal and social relationships across borders. Like many other contentious politics scholars, he assumes that communication primarily involves *transmission* of information from transmitters (who have successfully applied an unfamiliar idea or practice in one context) to receivers (who try to adopt basically the same idea or practice in another context). He does not pay sufficient attention to the more intense and enduring communication that needs to occur for receivers to learn how to apply transmitters' contentious strategies in their own social contexts and struggles. Like most scholars in the field, Tarrow's approach underestimates the role of political and creative agency.

First, Tarrow argues that *structural similarities* facilitate the transfer of new forms of contention. With capitalism and the modern state now dominant throughout the world, the strategies for challenging social injustices emerging from these structures are also more likely to spread. To use Tarrow's terms, "Countering the specificity and locality of the repertoire of contention was its modularity and transferability across space and into different sectors of movement activity. With globalization and internationalization, both the speed and the modularity of diffusion of forms of contention have increased" (Tarrow 2005: 102–103). Although this might explain the transmission of abstract information, however, it does not say much about how the people involved make sense of such information and reinvent it for practical application in their own social movements.

Second, as do many other diffusion scholars, Tarrow focuses on the *availability of communication channels* to account for how actors become aware of institutional similarities and differences across national contexts. Because new technologies such as cell phones and the Internet are common in most parts of the world, many activists can easily and quickly share information without confronting geographical barriers (Tarrow 2005: 103). Again, though, the fact that the majority of activists have access to these technologies might make the transmission of technical facts easier, but this does not necessarily enable the spread of emancipatory knowledge and practices. Moreover, activists in one country might become aware of an innovative action in another country without recognizing its broader relevance, and without learning how to apply its strategy to their own situation.

Next, as highlighted in his contribution to this volume, Tarrow distinguishes among distinct *pathways* for the transnational diffusion of contentious ideas and practices. Although he demonstrates that knowledge flows within existing social networks (relational diffusion), via impersonal media (nonrelational diffusion), or with the help of brokers (mediated diffusion), however, he still evades the question of how and what exactly people learn from each other when they communicate. How do activists translate awareness of foreign actions into strategies that are relevant to their own situations? How do they apply such reinvented strategies in practice? How do they incorporate these strategies into their broader political cultures of opposition? These are challenges that require not just the straightforward transmission of information from transmitters to receivers, but a great deal of reflection, interaction, discussion, and experimentation by all participants in the transnational diffusion process.

Finally, Tarrow suggests that communication promotes transnational diffusion to the extent that it leads to *emulation*. When structural conditions (internationalization and communication), social mechanisms (attribution of similarity, theorization, and/or brokerage), and pathways (relational, nonrelational, and/or mediated diffusion) are favorable, a particular set of protest ideas and practices is more likely to spread far and wide. Each adopter will modify these protest ideas and practices "at the margins" to suit its specific social context, but the personal and collective learning process primarily involves imitation of the innovator. The more adopters emulate certain protest ideas and practices, the more modular (i.e., widely available and influential) they become. In short, communication achieves its purpose when the transmission process is complete (Tarrow 2005: 104–105). Although common among social movement scholars, this view is problematic: Communication does not always flow smoothly and in one direction (from one actor or social setting to another), and learning can involve creativity as well as emulation. Do receivers learn most by absorbing and reproducing the knowledge provided by transmitters? Or does meaningful learning imply active participation by receivers as well as transmitters in a joint process of discovery and transformation? These questions are particularly important for thinking about the transnational diffusion of unfamiliar, complex protest tactics and repertoires.

THE SIGNIFICANCE OF DIALOGUE FOR TRANSNATIONAL DIFFUSION

Tarrow is correct when he argues that in the modern world, communication often means transmission of abstract information from one actor to another.

But such exchanges do not promote the kind of political agency, learning, and collaboration that allow for successful transnational diffusion among social movements. For complex tactics and repertoires to travel across vast distances without losing their substance requires meaningful dialogue – not just impersonal communication – among the people involved. Activists who are interested in adopting foreign protest methods need opportunities to interact with innovators so they can ask relevant questions, forge trusting relationships, and decide for themselves whether these new methods are applicable in their particular situations. After activists decide to adopt, moreover, they need to continue talking among one another about how to translate unfamiliar strategies into familiar language, and about how to use these strategies to engage in transformative collective action.[2]

The meaning of dialogue and its relevance for studying contentious politics is a broad subject that I hope to explore further in future work. For our purposes, it is sufficient to distinguish dialogue from various forms of monologue and to highlight its pedagogical, communicative, and relational aspects. *Monologue* (like transmission) basically refers to one-way communication between speakers with knowledge about particular subjects and listeners without such knowledge. In monological classrooms, for example, teachers would do nearly all the talking about academic topics that they consider important, while students passively absorb what they hear with the purpose of reproducing abstract facts on various tests. By memorizing and regurgitating what teachers tell them is significant, students in such classrooms gain technical knowledge. However, because teachers would control students' minds as well as relationships, students would not learn how to think critically or act creatively. Everyday conversations also tend to be monological in the sense that participants tell stories and share feelings without trying to contribute to a joint process of discovery. Moreover, debates are generally monological because participants offer personal viewpoints to win arguments, not to gain new insights by listening to alternative viewpoints.

In contrast, *dialogue* involves two or more active participants who are willing and able to contribute their viewpoints and to engage in rounds of questions and responses aimed at learning from others and expanding horizons. It is an ongoing and joint discovery process that leads to new questions rather than conclusive answers. Inclusive communication across different social groups is more dialogical than exclusive communication within one social group, whereas communication that enables reconciliation is more dialogical than is communication with destructive purposes. Although dialogue is never perfect or complete, some communicative interactions and social settings are clearly more dialogical than others (Burbules 1993: 7–8). In dialogical classrooms, for example, teachers and students are equally active learners who seek to increase

---

[2] "Success" here refers to the ability of activists in one social setting to benefit from new protest methods from another social setting in their struggles against structures of oppression and for social justice – not just to the transfer of those protest methods across borders.

their understanding of each other, their social worlds, and the subject matter at hand by addressing urgent problems, interrogating conventional knowledge, and proposing alternative forms of thinking as well as acting (Freire 2000: 87–124). From this perspective, dialogue is, by definition, controversial and oppositional: Participants aim at challenging ideologies, power relations, and institutions that were previously taken for granted. At the same time, though, dialogue can also be constructive: By committing to an open-ended and collective learning process, participants may seek new ways to improve their knowledge, ways of life, and social environments. Such inclusive and intergroup dialogue is particularly important for the development of agency among activists and social movements challenging social injustice.

Dialogue has distinct pedagogical, communicative, and relational implications. First, unlike other forms of communication, it is directed toward exploration and new understanding of subjects that are relevant to the lives and social worlds of everyone involved. Besides gaining knowledge about specific subjects, moreover, participants learn to take turns expressing their own experiences and perspectives and listening to the voices of others, in a collaborative process of investigation. In these pedagogical interactions, participants change themselves – by revising previous beliefs and behaviors – rather than each other. Second, dialogue implies a particular approach to the various dimensions of communication, including language, reason, morality, and social organization. It treats language as both a means for engaging in dialogue and a product of previous statements. As Bakhtin (1981) argued, the language that allows a particular group of people to make sense of what they are saying to each other is always related – whether directly or indirectly – to discussions among other groups of people, in other social settings and historical periods (see also Steinberg 1999). Language, in turn, shapes our capacity for reason as well as the social influences on our thinking. Dialogue promotes a kind of "interpersonal reasoning" that enables and relies on open-minded, responsive, and caring relationships among its participants (Noddings 1991: 158). It requires that participants see themselves as moral beings who struggle to live up to values such as respect, equality, concern, and love for the good of fellow human beings, social welfare, and self. Furthermore, fruitful dialogue encourages individual action as well as social organization toward the inclusion of previously silenced voices and the emancipation of marginalized social groups (Collins 2000: 273–290). Finally, dialogue is relational in the sense that it depends on not only the time and energy contributed by individual participants, but also on the quality and authenticity of relationships *among* them. Thus, dialogue is especially successful and liberating when participants develop ever-growing commitment to one another, to the dialogical process (both within and beyond their social groups), and to struggles for social justice (Burbules 1993: 8–16).

These attributes of dialogue are relevant for understanding and analyzing how transnational diffusion among social movements occurs. They highlight, for example, that communication across borders (at least initially) tends to be monological, because meaningful dialogue is controversial and labor-intensive,

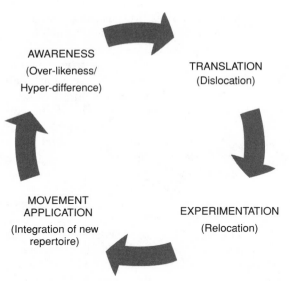

AWARENESS
(Over-likeness/
Hyper-difference)

TRANSLATION
(Dislocation)

MOVEMENT
APPLICATION
(Integration of new
repertoire)

EXPERIMENTATION
(Relocation)

FIGURE 6.2. Dialogical Framework of Transnational Diffusion between Social Movements

particularly in social settings based on competition rather than cooperation. Thus, activists' first impressions of a foreign tactic or repertoire are often superficial and stereotypical.[3] For deeper learning to occur, however, activists need to engage in genuine dialogue with experienced practitioners, so they can gain insights from applications in the original social context and start imagining whether – and if so, how – this foreign tactic or repertoire might work in their own social contexts. They then need to discuss how to translate their knowledge of this protest method into familiar terms, how to experiment with it in practice, and how to expand and intensify preliminary collective actions. Although dialogue with innovators remains important, much of their communication will now focus on building coalitions for larger and broader applications within their own country to ensure that their efforts have a positive impact on oppressed people and communities. For transnational diffusion among social movements to succeed – in the sense of expanding the transformative power of receiving social movements – the foreign tactic or repertoire must be embedded in a fertile political culture of opposition in the new social context.

Drawing on the definition of dialogue sketched earlier, my dialogical framework for studying transnational diffusion between social movements consists of four interrelated and reinforcing forms of communication. As Figure 6.2 indicates, dialogue is crucial for the transitions from one form of communication to the next, and for the continuation of the diffusion process. The

---

[3] Tarrow and other diffusion scholars in our field focus primarily on this kind of communication.

first form, *awareness*, refers to potential receivers' initial responses to a tactic or repertoire applied by contentious actors in another country. These initial responses, often influenced by coverage in the mass media, are usually monological and stereotypical rather than dialogical: they either overstate similarities ("over-likeness") or exaggerate distinctions ("hyper-difference") with transmitters and their social contexts (Fox 1997). Transnational diffusion remains superficial or ends prematurely unless potential receivers learn to move beyond these limited interpretations.

The second process, *translation*, involves meaningful dialogue between potential transmitters and potential receivers about the relevance of the contentious tactic or repertoire outside of its original setting. Through various forms and channels of communication, the two sides create more intimate transnational relationships and learn about the possibilities for "dislocation" of the diffusion item. Again, though, transnational diffusion ceases unless potential receivers engage in the third process, *experimentation*, which requires learning to put intellectual knowledge about the foreign tactic or repertoire into collective practice in their own social contexts. Generally, such "relocation" begins with implementation in the form of small-scale direct action campaigns and implies intensive dialogue among adoption pioneers (Fox 1997). The final (and most demanding) process, *movement application*, entails the expansion of small-scale applications into a sustained and massive social movement. Transnational diffusion of extensive repertoires is particularly demanding and only occurs when receivers are able to integrate new repertoires through dialogue and coalition-building with a wide variety of actors (Foran 2005: 21–22; Chabot and Vinthagen 2007). The spread of single tactics across borders is more common, but also less consequential for the liberation struggles of receiving activists and social movements.

As Figure 6.2 indicates, these four forms of communication feed into and rely on each other, producing a circular process. Transnational diffusion succeeds to the extent that dialogue enables the transition from awareness to translation, from translation to experimentation, from experimentation to movement application, and so forth. It fails (or is incomplete) when one or more of these linkages falters – that is, when awareness no longer leads to translation, translation no longer stimulates experimentation, experimentation no longer encourages transformation, and so forth.

The purpose of my framework is not to offer a new set of causal mechanisms for explaining a wide variety of historical or contemporary cases. My aim is not to replace Tarrow's model, but to provide more precise conceptual tools for specifying how activists in different parts of the world can become better at communicating with and learning from each other. Unlike Tarrow and others, I argue that successful transnational diffusion between social movements is actually very rare and difficult, no matter how eager the participants or how favorable the circumstances. Progressing from initial awareness to translation, experimentation, and movement application is never certain or easy for the individuals and groups involved; it requires high levels of political agency and endless collective struggle. But, as the Gandhian repertoire's journey from the Indian independence movement to the U.S. civil rights movement indicates, history shows that it is not impossible. In my view, a deeper understanding of the dynamics and implications of this case of transnational diffusion between social movements would benefit scholars as well as activists.

This chapter contributes to the aims of *The Diffusion of Social Movements* in several ways. First, by examining communication and interaction between vastly different social movements – different in terms of strategic purpose, historical period, geographical area, cultural tradition, social context, economic climate, political setting, and so forth – I hope to show that meaningful dialogue does not necessarily require similarity and proximity of the participants. Second, by paying attention to some of the actual people involved, I want to stress the significance of human reflection, emotion, expression, action, and learning in analyzing contentious politics and the spread of knowledge claims. Third, by studying connections between two influential social movements across continents and four decades, I aim to expand the scope of diffusion studies in our field. But my main purpose is to conceptualize how exactly dialogue evolves and shapes transnational diffusion among social movements. In particular, I want to address the question: How did African American intellectuals and activists become aware of the Gandhian repertoire, translate it into familiar terms, experiment with it in local settings, and integrate it into their own social movement?

APPLYING THE DIALOGICAL FRAMEWORK OF TRANSNATIONAL DIFFUSION TO THE INDIAN INDEPENDENCE MOVEMENT AND THE U.S. CIVIL RIGHTS MOVEMENT

The main subject of dialogue in my case of transnational diffusion between social movements was the relevance of the Gandhian repertoire of nonviolent contention. As Howard Thurman's discussion with Gandhi illustrates, African American leaders and activists were primarily interested in whether (and, if so, how) Gandhi's strategies for challenging British rule in India were applicable for their own struggle against racial segregation in the United States. Without going into too much detail, the Gandhian repertoire was founded on the concept of *satyagraha*, an innovative theory and practice for engaging in nonviolent action as part of a mass social movement. Satyagraha, which literally means "clinging to Truth," was both a practical technique and a spiritual principle for waging political struggles with nonviolence as the means and Truth as the end. According to Gandhi, violence perpetuates chaos, domination, war, and oppression, whereas nonviolence seeks to avoid injuring living beings (whether symbolically, emotionally, or physically) and promote social justice and harmony. Although nonviolence can overcome violence in particular situations, however, each victory sets the stage for yet another struggle. For Gandhi, the purpose of nonviolent action was to seek Truth, which he interpreted as a moral (or religious) vision of an ideal society without social injustice, suffering, and selfishness. Although absolute Truth was inaccessible and unattainable for human beings, practitioners of satyagraha could follow their incomplete and imperfect "glimpses of truth" in seeking it (Terchek 1998: 33–36).

Gandhi's views on means and ends not only shaped people's daily lives, but also guided the contentious repertoire of the Indian independence movement. The Gandhian repertoire included a wide range of claim-making routines that protest groups in India learned, shared, and implemented in their interactions with authorities and the public at large. These familiar ways of engaging in collective action in Indian society were not the result of abstract thinking or structural determination, but evolved in response to previous experiences, existing social conditions, and ever-changing plans for the future (Tilly 1995b: 26–27). More specifically, the Gandhian repertoire was a unique blend of action, discursive, and organizational strategies.[4] First of all, it involved various grassroots efforts in everyday life as well as nonviolent direct action campaigns in the public limelight. Thus, Gandhi stressed the importance of ashrams (self-sufficient communities) and the constructive program as well as nationwide protest events. Second, the Gandhian repertoire implied forms of communication that challenged dichotomies separating religion from politics, morality from interests, private from public life, head from heart, nationalism from cosmopolitanism, and friend from foe. Its language and symbols emphasized that nonviolence was an active force for bringing people together in the name of peace and social justice, not a method for submission or separatism. Third, the Gandhian repertoire called for organizational structures and coalitions that were inclusive, egalitarian, open to inspection, and popular rather than elitist. Indian movement leaders paid special attention to involving members of Congress as well as poor peasants, Hindus as well as Muslims, men as well as women, young as well as old, intellectuals as well as workers – although not always successfully.

To apply the action, discursive, and organizational components of the Gandhian repertoire in a satyagraha campaign, leaders and participants had to follow specific rules, disciplinary guidelines, and steps. *Gandhian rules* focused on self-reliance, initiative, openness concerning goals and methods, demands aimed at social justice rather than short-term interests, internal examination of weaknesses, efforts toward honorable cooperation with opponents, moral legitimacy, and preventing coopting by the authorities. The *Gandhian code of discipline* urged participants to harbor no anger, ignore orders given in anger, avoid insults or attacks, protect opponents from insults or attacks, accept arrest and go to jail voluntarily, never surrender property held in trust, behave with dignity as prisoners, and obey leaders' orders or resign from their units in case of fundamental disagreement. Finally, the *Gandhian steps* before starting mass protest campaigns consisted of (1) negotiation and arbitration,

---

[4] For action repertoires, see Tilly (1995b) and Traugott (1995); for discursive repertoires, see Steinberg (1999); for organizational repertoires, see Clemens (1996). See also Chabot (2003: 5, 25–28).

(2) group preparation, (3) agitation and public demonstration, and (4) issuing of an ultimatum to the targeted authorities. When authorities failed to respond, satyagraha activists engaged in one or more of the following non-violent direct action methods: economic boycotts or strikes, non-cooperation with power holders, and civil disobedience of immoral laws. The eventual goal of the Gandhian repertoire and the Indian independence movement was not only national autonomy from the British Empire, but also transformation of oppressive social and political structures and liberation from all forms of tyranny (Bondurant 1971; Chabot 2003: 37–69).

From the beginning, civil rights and peace advocates in the United States were intrigued by what they read about the Indian independence movement led by Gandhi. But they also recognized that satyagraha was not just a single tactic that they could imitate without changing their general approach to activism. They soon realized that importing the Gandhian repertoire as a whole would require an intensive process of rethinking and revising familiar ways of fighting social injustice in the United States. Although the challenges of translating the Gandhian repertoire and experimenting with it in American settings were daunting, the potential transformative impact of doing so made such efforts seem worthwhile.[5] The remainder of this section will use my dialogical framework (see Figure 6.2) to gain more specific insight into how American intellectuals and activists contributed to the transnational diffusion of the Gandhian repertoire from the moment they first became aware of Gandhi to the years when they applied Americanized forms of satyagraha in their own struggle for racial desegregation. I hope my discussion of this case will encourage us to consider its relevance for analyzing other cases of tactical diffusion.[6]

INITIAL AWARENESS OF THE GANDHIAN REPERTOIRE: OVER-LIKENESS AND HYPER-DIFFERENCE

American opinion leaders and media started paying regular attention to the Indian independence movement after the Rowlatt campaign of 1919 and the Non-Cooperation Movement of 1920–1921, which firmly established Gandhi as a national leader.[7] The conservative press in the United States emphasized the threatening implications of Indian nationalism and Gandhi's strategy, for

---

[5] Thus, although I distinguish between the diffusion of single tactics and whole repertoires – and focus on the latter – I suggest that my dialogical framework also applies to single tactics. I would expect that overcoming initial stereotypes, dislocation, relocation, and transformation of political cultures of opposition contribute positively to the success and impact of single tactics as well as whole repertoires. I call for more comparative case studies to evaluate the validity of this argument.

[6] For a more extensive and detailed case study, see my unpublished dissertation (Chabot 2003).

[7] For detailed discussions of the U.S. media's responses to Gandhi and the Indian struggle, see Singh (1962), Seshachari (1969), Jha (1973), Chatfield (1976), Kapur (1992), Fox (1997), and Chabot (2003).

both the British Empire and social unrest at home. In the *New York Times Current History Magazine* (July 1922: 649), for example, journalist Maurice Joachim wrote:

There has always been an undercurrent of ruthless criminality in the Indian masses. This is kept under control in normal times, but Gandhi's doctrines have caused it to the surface and he has received a ready response because the majority of Indians experience an abnormal pleasurable excitement in defying the law.

Joachim expressed a common view among conservative commentators, invoking "hyper-difference" between Indian and American society to make derogatory claims about Indian nationalists and justify British attempts to repress them through propaganda and military action (Israel 1994). The relatively moderate press was generally more sympathetic toward Gandhi and his cause. Similar to other liberal journals, an editorial in *The New Republic* (July 27, 1921: 232) noted that:

When Mr. Gandhi calls on his followers to renounce the social order which the British *raj* has imposed on India, to give up titles and offices, to refrain from Courts, to withdraw their children from Government schools, and all to abstain from violence... [h]e is following more closely the methods of Jesus than any leader since Saint Francis.

But by describing Gandhi as following in the footsteps of Jesus, and Gandhian methods as similar to those of Christian saints, such interpretations perpetuated "over-likeness" stereotypes without saying much about the actual situation in India. Thus, both critics and supporters of Gandhi in the mainstream media failed to move beyond existing biases and consider the relevance of the Gandhian repertoire for the United States (Fox 1997).

Meanwhile, prominent Christian pacifists in the United States expressed special interest in Gandhi and Indian nationalism, which they saw as important for preventing another world war. John Haynes Holmes, a founder of the Fellowship of Reconciliation (FOR) and arguably its most influential spokesperson, sparked a heated debate in 1921 with a sermon titled "Who Is the Greatest Man in the World Today?" After considering men such as French novelist Romain Rolland and Russian premier Lenin, Holmes chose the relatively unknown Gandhi. He told his audience about Gandhi's achievements in South Africa and India, and concluded:

In his political endeavors, he is as stern a realist as Lenin, working steadfastly toward a far goal of liberation which must be won. At the same time, however, is he an idealist, like Romain Rolland, living ever in the pure radiance of the spirit.... [W]hen I think of Gandhi, I think of Jesus Christ. He lives his life; he speaks his word; he suffers, strives and will some day nobly die, for his kingdom upon earth.   (in Chatfield 1976: 620).

On one hand, Christian pacifists like Holmes played an essential role by introducing and popularizing Gandhi's ideas among diverse audiences in the United States (Chatfield 1976: 587–621). On the other hand, however, they reproduced the "over-likeness" barrier by using Western symbolic figures – such as

Rolland, Lenin, and Jesus – to make sense of the Indian independence movement and its leader.

African Americans fighting for racial equality also paid close attention to what was happening in India after World War I. Members of the National Association for the Advancement of Colored People (NAACP), the leading civil rights organization at the time, recognized early on that the Indian struggle against the worldwide color line was related to their own. Through *The Crisis*, the NAACP's journal, and numerous black newspapers (including the *Pittsburgh Courier*, New York's *Amsterdam News*, *Baltimore Afro-American*, *Atlanta Daily World*, *Chicago Defender*, and *Norfolk Journal and Guide*), they stayed informed about the latest events and developments in India. Although most contributors to *The Crisis* expressed support for the Indian independence movement, however, none suggested that the Gandhian repertoire was directly relevant to their cause. Like the journal's editor, famous sociologist W. E. B. Du Bois, African American intellectuals and leaders generally favored reformist strategies – such as court action, public appeals, legislative pressure, and inter-racial contact – rather than mass civil disobedience or nonviolent direct action. They believed that although satyagraha might work in a spiritualist culture like India and with a civilized opponent like the British Empire, applying it in a brutal environment such as the American South would be deadly. Despite widespread admiration for Gandhi and Indian nationalism during these years, therefore, African American civil rights advocates generally fell in the "hyper-difference" trap when they responded to the Gandhian repertoire (Kapur 1992: 24–40; Fox 1997).

INTELLECTUAL TRANSLATION OF THE GANDHIAN REPERTOIRE:
DISLOCATION FROM INDIA

Most American opinion leaders had heard about Gandhi by the end of the 1920s. But it was the Salt March campaign in 1930 and 1931 that really caught the imagination of a wider American public, especially when *Time* magazine declared the Indian leader "Man of the Year" and put his face on the cover. Although media coverage was often favorable during the 1930s, it perpetuated existing hyper-difference and over-likeness stereotypes. The translation and dislocation of the Gandhian repertoire did not occur until Christian pacifists and African American intellectuals started engaging in serious (and often contentious) dialogue about the specific dynamics and practical implications of nonviolent contention.

The issue of nonviolence caused internal division among Christian pacifists, particularly in FOR. Some felt that absolute devotion to pacifism in the face of tyranny was unrealistic, if not unethical. Others believed that the FOR should continue to focus on nonviolent means as the best way to achieve peace and justice as ends. Richard Gregg, who had moved to India in 1925 and become a close friend of Gandhi, played a particularly important role in this debate.

In 1929, he returned to the United States to write a book on why satyagraha was so successful in India and how it could guide American activists. Initially published in 1934, *The Power of Nonviolence* made three key points. First, it clarified in familiar psychological terms why using moral means was crucial for achieving just ends:

> In a [nonviolent] struggle...the retention of moral balance seems to depend on the qualities of one's relationship to moral truth.... He must have primarily the disposition best known as love – an interest in people so deep, and determined, and lasting as to be creative; a profound knowledge of or faith in the ultimate possibilities of human nature; a courage based upon a conscious or subconscious realization of the underlying unity of all life and eternal values or eternal life of the human spirit; a strong and deep desire for and love of truth; and a humility that is not cringing or self-deprecatory or timid but is rather a true sense of proportion in regard to people, things, qualities and ultimate values. These human traits of love, faith, courage, honesty, and humility exist in greater or less strength in *every* person.
>
> (Gregg 1959: 44, 49)

Second, it stressed that the main prerequisite for mass nonviolent direct action was group discipline rather than saintly leaders. Everyone was capable of the rigorous training and thorough preparation enabling such group discipline (ibid.: 143). Finally, it explicitly argued that the Gandhian repertoire was applicable in other countries and outlined a concrete program for building a nonviolent social movement in the United States (ibid.: 143–175). The book's influence was immediate and widespread, especially because Gregg frequently gave speeches and published articles on its central arguments. Moreover, it set the stage for the publication in 1939 of *War Without Violence* by Krishnalal Shridharani, an Indian student at Columbia University and Salt March veteran, whose careful analysis of satyagraha and concrete strategies for its application beyond India further stimulated translation and dislocation (and would later guide CORE's first experiments with Gandhian sit-ins).

Gandhi's dialogue with Thurman and his colleagues in 1936 also contributed significantly to translation and dislocation of the Gandhian repertoire. When Thurman asked Gandhi, "Is non-violence from your point of view a form of direct action?" he was raising an issue that emerged from earlier debates with fellow black theologians, preachers, and scholars at home. But Gandhi's response, highlighting the active and universal force of nonviolence, was relatively new to his visitors. Whereas African American intellectuals generally focused on either the strategic or the moral dimension of satyagraha, Gandhi emphasized both at the same time. And when Thurman wanted advice on how to "train individuals or communities in this difficult art," the Indian leader refused to offer a definite program, implying that they had to experiment with their own forms of nonviolent direct action, suitable for their own causes and circumstances. Gandhi made abundantly clear, though, that satyagraha was not exclusively Indian and, after talking with the African American delegation for three hours, even suggested that members of their community might be the first to deliver "the unadulterated message of nonviolence...to the world" ("Interview to American Negro Delegation," CWMG 68: 235–237).

After Thurman and the others returned to the United States, they shared what they learned and experienced during the trip with students, congregations, readers, audiences, and fellow religious leaders. The next year, Benjamin Mays and Channing Tobias, both Thurman's colleagues at Howard University, also traveled to India and met with Gandhi. In their dialogue, Gandhi noted that nonviolent resistance is actually much more active than violent resistance: "It is direct, ceaseless, but three-fourths invisible and only one-fourth visible.... A violent man's activity is most visible while it lasts. But it is always transitory.... Non-violence is the most invisible and the most effective [force]" (CWMG 70: 261). He also emphasized that "a minority can do much more in the way of non-violence than a majority.... I had less diffidence in handling my minority in South Africa than I had here in handling a majority" (ibid.: 263–264). These journeys across the Pacific Ocean, and the communication within African American communities that followed, added new impetus to the translation and dislocation of the Gandhian repertoire, especially for young and ambitious black students such as James Farmer.

PRACTICAL EXPERIMENTATION WITH THE GANDHIAN REPERTOIRE: RELOCATION IN THE UNITED STATES

After World War II broke out in September 1939, the mainstream media shifted much of their focus to events in Europe, dramatically reducing its coverage of the Indian independence movement. But despite a lack of media attention, Christian pacifists and African American civil rights advocates continued to think and talk about how to initiate nonviolent action in the United States. Led by A. J. Muste, a militant pacifist and founder of the American Workers Party, FOR activists started laying the institutional foundation for a Gandhian revolution. Jay Holmes Smith, who had lived in India as a missionary, set up the Harlem Ashram and helped form the Committee for Non-Violent Direct Action, which organized numerous anti-war demonstrations in New York and Washington, D.C. (Anderson 1997: 70–71). And in the wake of World War II, Smith and other radical pacifists created the Committee for Non-Violent Revolution (CNVR) and the Peacemakers, explicitly calling for the application of "the method of non-violent direct action...developed by Mahatma Gandhi, to such areas of injustice and consequent conflict as race discrimination, denial of civil liberties...[and] any other entrenched social evil" (Wittner 1969: 63–64).

Around the same time, African American labor leader Asa Philip Randolph founded the March on Washington Movement (MOWM) to force President Roosevelt to address racial discrimination in the armed services and defense industries (Pfeffer 1990: 53). At the MOWM's first conference, in September 1942, Randolph proposed the adoption of a Gandhian strategy:

[T]he Negro needs more than organization. He needs mass organization with an action program, aggressive, bold and challenging in spirit. . . . Witness the strategy and maneuver of the people of India with mass civil disobedience and non-cooperation and the marches to the sea to make salt. . . . Numbers in mass formation is our key, directed, of course, by the collective intelligence of the people. . . . India is now waging a world shaking, history making fight for independence. India's fight is the Negro's fight.

(in Broderick and Meier 1965: 201–210)

The MOWM never grew into the mass Gandhian movement that Randolph had in mind. But along with the FOR, NVDA, CNVR, and Peacemakers, it was an initial attempt at relocating and experimenting with the Gandhian repertoire in American society.

In retrospect, though, the Congress of Racial Equality (CORE) was the most groundbreaking organization involved in the relocation of the Gandhian repertoire. The original founder of CORE, James Farmer, had been a student of Mays and Thurman at Howard University and, in September 1941, accepted the position of race relations secretary at FOR. After working at FOR's office in Chicago for several months, Farmer became convinced that current strategies were inadequate. He drafted a memo, titled "Provisional Plan for Brotherhood Mobilization" and addressed to FOR chairman A. J. Muste, arguing for the formation of a Gandhian social movement to fight racial injustice:

We must withhold our support and participation from the institution of segregation in every area of American life – not an individual witness to purity of conscience, as Thoreau used it, but a coordinated movement of mass noncooperation as with Gandhi. And civil disobedience when laws are involved. And jail where necessary. More than the elegant cadre of generals we now have, we also must have an army of ground troops. Like Gandhi's army, it must be nonviolent. Guns would be suicidal for us. Yes, Gandhi has the key for me to unlock the door to the American dream. (Farmer 1985: 74)

Mailed on February 19, 1942, the final version of this memo credited recent efforts of Jay Holmes Smith and the book by Shridharani as sources of inspiration, and outlined a specific strategy for applying the Gandhian repertoire in American society. Farmer's plan recognized social and cultural differences between the United States and India and warned against blind imitation of satyagraha: "The American race problem is in many ways distinctive, and must to that extent be dealt with in a distinctive manner. Using Gandhism as a base, our approach must be creative in order to be effectual" (Farmer 1985: 356). It also emphasized the need for mass mobilization beyond existing pacifist and civil rights groups, the importance of preventing violence and chaos, and the role of religion in multiracial and multiethnic recruitment. And finally, it called for small-scale experiments with nonviolent direct action before organizing a mass movement: "This, of course, is following the Gandhian and commonsense procedure of launching vital campaigns only when satisfactory discipline and unity is arrived at" (ibid.).

The FOR's National Council decided that Farmer's plan was too radical, but it authorized him (along with George Houser, the youth secretary) to launch an affiliated organization. In April 1942, Farmer, Houser, and six others founded CORE and initiated their first Gandhian campaigns in Chicago. FOR members throughout the country soon heard about CORE's actions and set up additional chapters in Seattle, Denver, New York, Philadelphia, and Evanston (Meier and Rudwick 1973: 9). To ensure unity of purpose and method, each member and group had to follow CORE's "Action Discipline," which closely followed Shridharani's steps for applying Gandhian strategy: "Gather facts. Negotiate. Rouse public opinion, and then, if absolutely necessary, and only as a last resort, Take Direct Action" (ibid.: 13).

One day, when Farmer and another CORE member entered Jack Spratt Coffee House, the manager refused to serve them and ordered them to leave. The next day, Farmer wrote a letter to the manager, asking for a meeting to negotiate a settlement. Two months later, however, the manager still had not replied, so he and fellow CORE members decided that the time for nonviolent direct action had come. First, they informed the police chief of their plans, reminding him of the civil rights law prohibiting discriminatory practices. Then, a group of twenty-eight CORE activists entered the establishment in parties of two, three, and four – each with one African American man or woman. In his autobiography, Farmer (1985: 106–107) wrote:

With the discipline of peacefulness strictly observed, we occupied all available seating spaces at the counter and in booths. . . . Waitresses looked at each other and shrugged. Then they looked at the woman in charge for a cue, but none was forthcoming. . . . After making a phone call, the woman in charge swept past me and spoke to Jimmy Robinson [a white CORE member].

"If the colored people in your group will go to the basement, I'll have them served there."

I responded: "No, ma'am. We will not eat in the basement." . . .

"I'll call the police," she said, and now she was looking directly at me with a triumphant expression on her face. . . .

Within minutes, two of Chicago's finest walked in. . . .

[O]ne of them asked, "What did you call us for, lady? I don't see anybody disturbing the peace. What do you want us to do?"

"I want you to throw these people out, of course," she replied.

"Lady, we can't do that. What're they doing wrong? You're open for business, aren't you? They're not trespassing. . . . You must either serve them or solve the problem yourself the best way you can."

The woman in charge ordered the waitresses to serve everyone.

Everyone ate their meal and paid their bill, leaving good tips for the waitresses. That same evening, Robinson wrote a letter to Jack Spratt, expressing gratitude for the service and his establishment's change in policy. Over the next few weeks, CORE observers confirmed that racial practices at the coffee shop had improved and that their "sit-in" was successful (Farmer 1985: 107–108; Raines 1977: 29–32).

Although small campaigns like these received little media attention, they became legendary among more radical FOR members, many of whom started or joined CORE chapters in their own home towns. And in January 1943, inspired by alumnus Farmer and CORE's struggle, several female students at Howard University initiated their own sit-in at a local cafeteria, organized workshops, and motivated seventeen students to sign a nonviolent action pledge and join their Gandhian campaign. Within forty-eight hours, the owner capitulated and began serving African American customers (Murray 1987: 207–208). As Farmer had envisioned in his memo to Muste, small-scale and local experimentation with the Gandhian repertoire was taking place across the country during the early 1940s. To the pioneers of nonviolent sit-ins in the United States, the emergence of a Gandhian social movement for racial equality seemed like a matter of time.

MOVEMENT APPLICATION: INTEGRATION OF THE GANDHIAN REPERTOIRE

Transnational diffusion between social movements, however, is not a smooth and linear process, but more like a bumpy and winding road. Following a few minor victories, participants in FOR, MOWM, and CORE hoped for the emergence of a broad and sustained Gandhian movement during the late-1940s and early-1950s. Unexpectedly, though, the Cold War, Gandhi's death, and McCarthyism contributed to an unfavorable social and political climate for any form of protest, let alone mass nonviolent direct action. Yet behind the scenes, several individuals and institutions continued to lay the groundwork for a Gandhian political culture of opposition, incorporating nonviolent emotions, ideologies, cultural idioms, and organizational strategies into their political strategies and ways of life (Foran 2005: 21; Chabot and Vinthagen 2007).

At the Highlander Folk School, for example, director Myles Horton and his associates brought together Gandhian activists from a wide variety of protest organizations to engage in dialogue about key issues, participate in workshops on nonviolent action, build solidarity networks, and prepare for more favorable circumstances (Morris 1984: 145; Adams 1975; Egerton 1994). Bayard Rustin, a former leader of FOR and CORE, visited India in 1949, forging ties with Gandhians in independent India. From the other side of the ocean, Indian nationalist Ram Manohar Lohia came to the United States in the summer of 1951 for a lecture tour and talked to young activists about engaging in civil disobedience despite the dangers. And in 1953, FOR's James Lawson went to India as a missionary, where he taught at Hislop College and joined the activities of Serva Seva Sangh, the leading Gandhian organization in the country. These domestic and transnational networking activities did not produce major campaigns at the time. But they transformed the political and cultural infrastructure, paving the road for a Gandhian social movement at a more opportune moment.

Although scholars in our field commonly acknowledge that Gandhi influenced Martin Luther King, Jr. and the U.S. civil rights movement, we rarely consider the broader historical and geographical processes involved in the Gandhian repertoire's diffusion from India to the United States. If we look carefully, though, we see that the dislocation and relocation efforts between 1930 and 1954 significantly shaped all the major events of the African American freedom struggle. For now, I will just focus on three such events: the Montgomery bus boycott (1955–1956), the student sit-ins (1960–1961), and the Birmingham campaign (1963).

Sociological and historical studies on the Montgomery bus boycott generally emphasize the role of local leaders, organizations, and circumstances, but the best ones consider these factors in the context of domestic political opportunities and past boycotts (e.g., McAdam 1982; Morris 1984; Garrow 1986; Robinson 1987; Branch 1988; Burns 1997). They highlight the contributions of leaders such as Martin Luther King Jr. and E. D. Nixon, activists such as Rosa Parks and Jo Ann Robinson, and organizations such as the NAACP and Montgomery Improvement Association (MIA). They examine the influence of power elites in Montgomery, Alabama and Washington, D.C. and compare the campaign in Montgomery to similar ones in previous years. But these studies rarely shed light on how the transnational diffusion processes that evolved between 1920 and 1955 shaped this protest event. In contrast, King was very explicit about his debt to Gandhi's approach:

> As the days unfolded . . . the inspiration of Mahatma Gandhi began to exert its influence. I had come to see early that the Christian doctrine of love operating through the Gandhian method of nonviolence was one of the most potent weapons available to the Negro in his struggle for freedom. . . . In other words, Christ furnished the spirit and motivation, while Gandhi furnished the method.   (King 1958: 84–85)

After this passage, moreover, King gives credit to African American mentors such as Howard Thurman and Benjamin Mays – key figures in the dislocation of the Gandhian repertoire – for his own "pilgrimage to nonviolence." Like Farmer and CORE in the early-1940s, therefore, King and other participants in the Montgomery bus boycott contributed to the relocation of the Gandhian repertoire. This time, though, their application helped transform the political culture of opposition and create a Gandhian social movement in the United States. In other words, King's references to Gandhi were not just "exotic intellectual patina," as Doug McAdam (1996: 347) asserts. They expressed his recognition of much deeper historical and transnational connections with the Indian independence movement.[8]

King was certainly not the only link with Gandhi and India. A few months after the Montgomery bus boycott started, for example, the MIA invited two prominent Christian pacifists, Bayard Rustin and Glenn Smiley, to help organize the campaign. Since his return from India in 1949, Rustin had probably been the most militant Gandhian activist in the country, whereas Smiley was a well-known white minister and FOR member. Both led educational dialogues

---

[8] King decided to visit India in 1959, following in the footsteps of his mentors as well as other Gandhians in the United States (Chabot 2004).

on the practical implications of nonviolent direct action and, after forcing local authorities to meet the MIA's demands, Smiley drafted a code of conduct for reentering the buses that was clearly Gandhian. Among other things, it urged black bus riders to "Remember that this is not a victory for Negroes alone, but for all Montgomery and the South" and "Be loving enough to absorb evil and understanding enough to turn an enemy into a friend" (Burns 1997: 326–327). And after the Montgomery bus boycott, Rustin initiated efforts to form a new civil rights organization – the Southern Christian Leadership Conference (SCLC) – and firmly establish the Gandhian repertoire as the bedrock of the emerging civil rights movement's political culture. The SCLC's founding document read, in part: "The basic tenets of Hebraic-Christian tradition coupled with the Gandhian concept of *satyagraha* – truth force – is at the heart of SCLC's philosophy" (in Broderick and Meier 1965: 269–273). Thus, the origins of SCLC were not only Southern, but also partly transnational.

After the Montgomery bus boycott, the African American freedom struggle submerged for a few years, as civil rights activists and organizations considered their next move. Then, on February 1, 1960, the student sit-ins started in Greensboro, North Carolina and soon expanded across the South. The diffusion of the 1960 sit-ins is a popular topic among contentious politics scholars. However, writings on the subject tend to focus on communication channels (rather than the actual content and form of communication) and short-term processes within the South (e.g., Tilly and Tarrow 2006: 183–192; Polletta 1998; Killian 1984; McAdam 1982, 1983; Morris 1981). A recent article by Kenneth Andrews and Michael Biggs (2006), for example, uses quantitative analysis to argue that the number of black college students, size of activist cadres, information provided by news media, resources in the black community, and local political opportunities within the first few months explain how the sit-ins spread. They say very little, though, about how and what student activists actually communicated with one another. I suggest that, among other things, sit-in participants learned (both from the media and by talking with others) how to apply the Gandhian repertoire in their own circumstances. In doing so, they tapped into the practical knowledge on nonviolent direct action gained during previous civil rights campaigns, including the Montgomery bus boycott and especially CORE's sit-ins during the early 1940s. By revitalizing the U.S. civil rights movement, moreover, the 1960 sit-ins further stimulated the Gandhian repertoire's journey across the Pacific Ocean.

Contrary to most studies on the 1960 sit-ins, I propose that what happened in Nashville, Tennessee contributed more to diffusion than did the trigger event in Greensboro, North Carolina (Wolff 1970; Carson 1981; McAdam 1983; Oppenheimer 1989; Polletta 1998). Months before four black students sat down at a Woolworth's lunch counter on February 1, black students in Nashville had already started attending weekly workshops on nonviolence by James Lawson – the FOR secretary who had lived in India – and had participated in educational activities at Highlander Folk School as well as the SCLC's Institute of Nonviolent Resistance to Segregation. During these educational dialogues, they learned how to respond to verbal and physical assaults by participating in role-plays and staging sociodramas. They also set up an institution, the Nashville Student Movement, and initiated several preliminary sit-ins at the lunch counters of Nashville's downtown stores in November and December 1959 (Lewis 1998: 86). After Christmas break, attendance at Lawson's workshops swelled and the activists were confident that they could maintain the collective discipline and moral commitment required of Gandhian direct action. So when a friend phoned Lawson on February 3 and told him about what had just happened in Greensboro, he immediately called a meeting. That evening, the Nashville students decided to initiate their own sit-in campaign on Saturday, February 13 (Lewis 1998: 92; Halberstam 1998: 90–92).[9]

Although the four students in Greensboro knew about Gandhi, they had not studied the main principles and strategies of satyagraha.[10] In contrast, with the guidance of Lawson, the students in Nashville had learned how to apply the Gandhian repertoire from leading American Gandhians. However, they did not blindly imitate their predecessors and mentors. Based on what they had heard, read, discussed, and seen in practice, a few students formulated their own list of "Dos and Don'ts" to ensure that the lunch counter sit-ins would remain nonviolent and constructive:

DO NOT: 1. Strike back nor curse if abused.
2. Laugh out.
3. Hold conversations with floor walker [at the targeted store].
4. Leave your seat until your leader has given you permission to do so.
5. Block entrances to stores outside nor the aisles inside.

DO: 1. Show yourself friendly and courteous at all times.
2. Sit straight; always face the counter.
3. Report all serious incidents to your leader.
4. Refer information seekers to your leader in a polite manner.
5. *Remember the teachings of Jesus Christ, Mahatma Gandhi, and Martin Luther King. Love and nonviolence is the way* (Lewis 1998: 98; italics mine).

These guidelines, reinvented for their specific purposes, helped prevent violence and chaos among the activists, whose campaign ended when Nashville's mayor announced the racial integration of lunch counters in the city. Unlike the Greensboro four, though, the leaders of the Nashville sit-ins – including Bernard Lafayette, Marion Barry, James Bevel, Diane Nash, and John Lewis – were committed to Gandhian opposition for the long haul. When, in April 1961, SCLC's Ella Baker and Lawson organized a conference at Shaw University to form a student-led civil rights organization – the Student Nonviolent Coordinating Committee (SNCC) – Lafayette, Barry, Bevel, Nash, Lewis, and

---

9 For wonderful footage of the Nashville sit-ins, see *A Force More Powerful*, episode 1.
10 Ezell Blair, Jr., one of the initial students, told a reporter that he had seen a television program on Gandhi and the Indian struggle, but had never read any of his writings (Wolff 1970: 156–157).

some other Nashville leaders agreed to take charge.[11] Thus, through various forms of dialogue, the students in Nashville not only tapped into the legacy of past experiments with satyagraha in the United States, but also added new momentum to the transnational diffusion process. In the civil rights campaigns that followed, including the Birmingham struggle of 1963, these young SNCC activists would serve as the most creative, courageous, and militant participants in the Gandhian movement for African American freedom (Halberstam 1998).

The Birmingham campaign in many ways represented the peak of the Gandhian repertoire's transnational diffusion process. From the moment that movement leaders started discussing and planning massive nonviolent direct action in May 1962, they complied with the Gandhian repertoire's guidelines in all facets of their work. Like CORE in the 1940s, they started by gathering facts about the social context. At the time, Birmingham was the most segregated city in the United States and "the country's chief symbol of racial intolerance," as King (1963: 54) put it. It had segregated hospitals, facilities, schools, parks, and lunch counters, while most of its black residents lived in ghettos, suffered exploitation in factories, and lacked voting rights. And "Bull" Connor, its commissioner of public safety, was a proud racist who regularly coerced and threatened the black population. Next, the Alabama Christian Movement for Human Rights (ACMHR), a local affiliation of the SCLC, initiated negotiations with Birmingham's authorities, but the latter failed to keep promises or improve racist policies. Finally, following CORE's third step, movement leaders prepared the local community by recruiting and training volunteers, mobilizing various civil rights groups, raising funds, holding meetings, and galvanizing public opinion. They also instituted a Leadership Training Committee led by Lawson, Nash, and Bevel to make sure that all participants took classes on nonviolent resistance and signed a commitment card to ensure adherence to Gandhian principles and strategies.[12]

When local power elites refused to respond, the SCLC announced the campaign's starting date and its four concrete demands:

1. The desegregation of lunch counters, restrooms, fitting rooms, and drinking fountains in variety and department stores.
2. The upgrading and hiring of Negroes on a nondiscriminatory basis throughout the business and industrial community of Birmingham.
3. The dropping of all charges against jailed demonstrators.
4. The creation of a biracial committee to work out a timetable for desegregation in other areas of Birmingham life (King 1963: 102–103).

---

[11] James Lawson drafted the SNCC's original statement of purpose, stating in the first sentence: "We affirm the philosophical or religious ideal of nonviolence as the foundation of our purpose, the presupposition of our faith, and the manner of our action" (in Broderick and Meier 1965: 273–274).

[12] The commitment card was remarkably similar to the pledge signed by Salt March participants (Bondurant 1971: 92). It started with: "I hereby pledge myself – my person and body – to the nonviolent movement. Therefore I will keep the following ten commitments." The commitments stressed Christian love, reconciliation, prayer, self-sacrifice, courtesy, social service, healthy habits, obedience to leaders, and nonviolence in word and deed (King 1963: 63–64).

After the struggle started on April 3, 1963, civil rights activists applied the Gandhian repertoire's action forms and strategies that had proven most successful in the past: They started with sit-ins at downtown lunch counters, then engaged in mass marches to city hall, an economic boycott of downtown stores, more sit-ins at local churches and libraries, marches to inaugurate the voter registration drive, and civil disobedience of a court injunction to cease demonstrations. They filled up the jails and when the main leaders were behind bars, young children took their places on the front lines. Faced with such persistent and confrontational civil disobedience, Bull Connor eventually ordered his troops to commit the brutal acts that would capture the imagination of millions of newspaper readers and television viewers (King 1963: 100). In short, the Gandhian repertoire was now an integral part of the U.S. civil rights movement: it shaped not only its political culture of opposition, but also its interactions with political institutions and the public at large. The Birmingham campaign of 1963 also represented the culmination – but not the end – of the transnational diffusion process from the Indian independence movement to the U.S. civil rights movement. As the African American freedom struggle evolved (with shifts from protest to politics, and from Gandhian nonviolence to Black Power), the Gandhian repertoire's journey also changed form and direction.

CONCLUSIONS

Based on my exploratory case study, we can now evaluate the four main components of my dialogical framework in Figure 6.2 and compare it with the model in Figure 6.1. Whereas Tarrow (like other diffusion scholars) assumes that communication is impersonal and primarily involves the exchange of information, I focus on what kind of communication takes place and how this shapes the transnational diffusion process. First, I agree with Tarrow that most communication between social movements is superficial and monological. Although this might lead to initial *awareness* of foreign tactics or repertoires, however, it will produce only limited forms of transnational diffusion because of the perceptual barriers of hyper-difference and over-likeness. As we saw with the American media's reactions during the 1920s, for example, awareness might set Tarrow's three pathways of transnational diffusion (attribution of similarity, theorization, and brokerage) in motion, but the emulation that follows does not enable meaningful learning and application by receiving movement activists and organizations. The resulting nonlocalized action might invoke images of the transmitting social movement, but it will not allow for implementation of the latter's innovative ideas and practices.

Second, my approach goes beyond that of Tarrow and other diffusion scholars in emphasizing the possibility for dialogue across significant differences in social movements, historical periods, and social contexts. As Thurman's discussion with Gandhi indicated, for example, such dialogue usually starts at the intellectual level and involves *translation* into familiar language for the receivers (both for Thurman himself and for his audiences at home) and *dislocation* of the diffusion item from its original setting. This is a slow, ongoing, and uncertain process, with many possible obstacles. Thus, Thurman and his delegation had to travel long distances and spend a great deal of energy to have a three-hour meeting with the Indian leader. When they returned home, moreover, they faced considerable risks in talking about the radical implications of the Gandhian repertoire for the social position of African Americans in their country. I suggest that such dialogue often involves far more than the attribution of similarity and theorization mechanisms highlighted in Tarrow's model. I also argue that brokerage is particularly important if it involves political agency and promotes creative reinvention (not just emulation) of the diffusion item (Chabot 2002; Chabot and Duyvendak 2002).

My third point is that creative reinvention can lead to new forms of dialogue, characterized by practical and collective *experimentation* that builds on intellectual translation and dislocation. This kind of communicative action is required for the *relocation* of foreign tactics or repertoires into new social contexts. The sit-ins organized by CORE during the 1940s, for example, were crucial for transnational diffusion, despite the fact that most of the relocation activities occurred locally and within the United States rather than transnationally. Clearly, therefore, transnational and domestic diffusion are not necessarily separate processes. As diffusion scholars, we need to use a broader historical and geographical perspective to see the complex connections between important events such as CORE's sit-ins during the 1940s and the 1960 student sit-ins in the South, and to understand their relevance for the spread of diffusion items (or what workshop organizers call "knowledge claims") such as the Gandhian repertoire. At the same time, we also need to recognize that emulation is not the best indicator for determining whether diffusion has occurred. Thus, for me, the sit-ins during the 1940s and 1960s are positive signs of collective learning and practical experimentation, even though sit-ins were not part of the original Gandhian repertoire. Again, creative application is more important for transnational diffusion between social movements than blind imitation.

The fourth key argument of my framework is that successful transnational diffusion between social movements is (and always has been) rare, because it requires not only intellectual and action-oriented dialogue, but also *movement application* and *integration* of the new repertoire. In other words, U.S. civil rights groups remained half-hearted about adopting the Gandhian repertoire until it became the strategic and ethical guide of the U.S. civil rights movement. Without denying local and national origins, my discussion of the Montgomery bus boycott, student sit-ins, and the Birmingham campaign showed that transnational diffusion shaped the African American liberation struggle in crucial ways. Instead of merely acknowledging King's intellectual debt to Gandhi, I explored how deep and broad the Gandhian influence actually was. Rustin's visit to India and contribution to SCLC, Lawson's visit to India and contribution to the Nashville sit-ins as well as the SNCC, and the central role of their students are just a few threads in the wide web of connections between the Indian independence movement and the U.S. civil rights movement. Merely examining Tarrow's pathways from localized to nonlocalized action would not have allowed me to capture the meanings and implications of the numerous human relationships shaping the Gandhian repertoire's transnational diffusion. Without a sense of the big picture, I would not have understood why so many pacifists and African American activists were so eager to learn from Gandhi and the Indian independence movement for so long. And without reading life histories of Thurman, Mays, King, Rustin, Farmer, and Lewis, for example, I would not have known what motivated them to work so hard and risk so much to make a Gandhian movement in the United States possible.

To conclude, I hope that my arguments contribute significantly to scholarship on the three questions raised in the introduction: What is being diffused? How does diffusion occur? What is the impact of diffusion? In response to these questions, I focused on the diffusion of a repertoire, on the role of dialogue in transnational diffusion, and on transitions between initial awareness and movement application. But at the same time, I want to ensure that our academic efforts speak to the actual dilemmas faced by oppressed people and activists in today's world. In my view, people fighting for global peace and justice have as much to learn from the Gandhian repertoire's diffusion to the U.S. civil rights movement as scholars. How we (as scholars and activists) respond to promising yet unfamiliar protest strategies will, to a large extent, shape our ability to create new and better worlds. I propose that we will do this more successfully if we critically reflect on our initial stereotypes of foreign ideas and practices, work collectively toward dislocating and relocating them, and learn to integrate them into our struggles against neoliberal capitalism and for the welfare of humanity.

7

The Diffusion of Different Types of Internet Activism

Suggestive Patterns in Website Adoption of Innovations

Jennifer Earl and Katrina Kimport

There has been substantial interest in Internet activism among academics from a wide spectrum of fields over the past decade. Whether studying unlikely Internet phenoms such as the Zapatistas (e.g., Garrido and Halavais 2003), theorizing about the relationship between information technology and social movements (e.g., Tarrow 1998b; Tilly 2004), or examining how specific protest tactics, such as online petitions, have made their way online (Earl 2006a; Earl and Schussman 2007; Earl and Kimport 2008), researchers have been working to understand the impacts of a large array of new digital technologies.

One question that has been raised, but far from sufficiently answered, involves the dynamics of diffusion online. For instance, a number of scholars have argued that Internet usage can lead to changes in the scale of organizing (Foot and Schneider 2002) by increasing the speed of diffusion (Ayres 1999), increasing the size of the audience (Myers 1994), or increasing the global reach of messages (Garrido and Halavais 2003). Other authors have stressed the spread of online activism to new types of participants and to address novel issues (Earl and Kimport 2009). However, little is known thus far about the processes involved and how far different types of diffusion have already progressed (but see Earl 2010 for a theoretical review of potential broad types of diffusion relevant to online protest).

In this chapter, we address these issues by focusing on the online spread of multiple models of Internet activism (which we view as innovations) across twenty different cause areas, using the adoption rate of specific practices associated with these models as empirical markers of their diffusion to date. Although we use cross-sectional data, and hence rely on the reasonable assumption that the adoption rate we empirically find marks the extent to which these online practices have diffused over the roughly two decades since the advent of the

We would like to thank the National Science Foundation for generous support of this research through a NSF CAREER Award (SES-0547990) and thank the many research assistants who worked on this project (see www.soc.ucsb.edu/faculty/earl/earl_lab/earl_lab.htm for a full listing).

World Wide Web, the richness of our data allows us to gain unique leverage over important questions. For instance, beyond mapping the spread of different visions of Internet activism we also document the extent to which adoption rates vary substantially by cause and begin to explore factors that might contribute to these different adoption rates. In doing so, we uncover signs suggestive of the deeper diffusion processes that may be at work, setting up future research to examine these processes in more detail.

DEFINING INTERNET ACTIVISM

Earl, Kimport, Prieto, Rush, and Reynoso's (forthcoming) review of scholarship on online protest finds that four broad categories of Internet activism have been studied in extant research: (1) brochureware; (2) the online facilitation of offline protest; (3) online participation; and (4) online organizing. Although Earl and her collaborators acknowledge that sometimes specific websites or social movement organizations (SMOs) use more than one of these types of Internet activism, these types nonetheless describe the highest order distinctions in uses of the Internet around protest.

In brochureware versions of Internet activism, the Internet is used as an information transmission medium not unlike other broadcast media. Websites adopting this vision of Internet activism contain information on their cause but do not offer ways of becoming involved in that cause through the website (save perhaps by donating to the website itself). Whether discussing brochureware or not, this vision of information as activism fits with many of the existing works discussing diffusion online. For instance, Ayres (1999) discusses the speed of information diffusion online, noting possible dangers from the speedy diffusion of inaccurate information. Meanwhile, Bennett (2005) examines how broadly information can diffuse through hyperlinks, and Tarrow (1998b) reflects on both the speed and scope of information diffusion online.

A second type of Internet activism is the online facilitation of offline protest, which provides information about specific protest events (e.g., advertising the time and place of a rally or march) in which site visitors can become involved, and may sometimes introduce interactive elements in support of the offline event. For instance, in a 2007 United for Peace and Justice (UFPJ) march and rally, UFPJ had ride-share boards that were meant to help coordinate transportation to Washington, D.C. for those planning to attend from out of town. Sites adopting this vision of online activism sometimes also offer other forms of support to protest events, such as downloadable signs in the hope of producing more consistent messaging for participants. To the extent that information about the planning of an event is what is being diffused, one could imagine that Bennett's (2005) and Tarrow's (1998b) claims about broad and fast information diffusion are relevant to this type of protest, too. And given Tarrow's stress on interpersonal trust and network connections as prerequisites for action, this is also likely the relationship between the Internet and contention on which he comments in Chapter 11 of this volume.

Thirdly, Earl et al. (forthcoming) discuss online participation as a form of Internet activism, which involves the use of tactics that can be engaged in while online. Online petitioning, or more disruptive and illegal tactics such as denial of service actions, are examples of online tactics. When websites offer the opportunity to participate in such tactics to site visitors, according to Earl et al. (forthcoming), they are embodying online participation as Internet activism. Although research has documented the growing importance of these forms of activity (e.g., Earl 2006a), research has yet to empirically measure and model diffusion of this type of Internet activism. This is perhaps particularly surprising because these online forms of engagement tend to be very modular, which both the introductory and concluding chapters of this volume note is a key characteristic of innovations that diffuse widely.

Finally, where the fourth type of Internet activism – online organizing – is concerned, whole campaigns or social movements may be coordinated online such that very little of the organizing effort takes place outside of the Internet. For example, Earl and Schussman (2003, 2004) studied the strategic voting movement, which was a campaign in the 2000 and 2004 presidential election cycles to reinvent, through collective practices, how voting takes place in the United States. Fighting the undemocratic aspects of the Electoral College and the practical limitations that winner-take-all elections pose for voters' expression of their electoral preferences, organizers of this campaign hoped to use the Internet to pair individuals with complementary voting preferences within and across state lines. By pairing individuals in strategic ways, coordinated voting by pairs of individuals allowed the voting changes that the campaign sought to be achieved through practice, even though legislative efforts to institutionalize changes had failed. Diffusion dynamics involving this type of Internet activism have not been studied much thus far.

Building on these distinctions, we focus in this chapter on the diffusion of different types of Internet activism, treating each type of activism as an innovation. We empirically document the extent of diffusion for these innovations thus far, using patterns of variation in adoption as clues about possible causal processes driving the spread of these innovations. Specifically, we examine the diffusion of brochureware as Internet activism, given that it represents the most minimal way that a cause could move online, and the diffusion of online organizing and participation, which represent very significant shifts in movement activity into the online world. In part, our interest in these two poles of Internet activism is theoretically oriented: understanding the diffusion of these two opposing ends of a spectrum of Internet usage for social change helps to map, and then hopefully make sense of, the landscape of online social change efforts.

Our focus is also inspired by the relatively high level of contention over the potential impacts of online organizing and online participation as models of Internet activism. Some scholars have argued that, when well done, online organizing and online participation offer opportunities to change the processes involved in protest organizing, opening social movement tactics to a wider array of individuals and causes (Earl and Kimport 2009; Earl et al. forthcoming).

However, other scholars have worried about the drift of activism into an online world. For instance, in observing the size of the digital divide early in the twenty-first century, Tilly (2004) worries that the migration of social change efforts onto the Internet will further disenfranchise people who already have limited access to other communication media and who may also lack any regular access to the Internet. Thus, whether one sees important potential or substantial danger in Internet activism, and online organizing and participation in particular, it is important to study how far these versions of Internet activism have made their way online.

We begin to address these questions by examining the rates at which brochureware and online forms of organizing and participation have been incorporated into organizing on twenty different causes online. As discussed more in the following sections, we use unique data from random samples of websites on twenty causes to provide a population view of Internet activism. This dataset is particularly appropriate for the questions at hand for two primary reasons. First, as a generalizable, population view of Internet activism, the dataset enables us to ask and answer broad questions about the adoption of various kinds of Internet activism. Second, the breadth of the dataset, with data on twenty distinct causes of varying lineages in the offline protest arena, allows us to analyze not only the broader question of the diffusion of activism on the Internet, but also the extent to which various forms of Internet activism have permeated – or failed to permeate – particular causes.

DIFFUSION PROCESSES

Although we begin by trying to establish how far the adoption of different versions of Internet activism has spread online, we do not end our analysis there. Indeed, as Strang and Soule (1998) point out, simply establishing that an innovation has spread does not allow access to important questions about how an innovation spreads and what specific diffusion processes are involved. For instance, understanding whether a diffusion process was fundamentally mimetic or driven by social influence in a tightly networked set of adopters is critical to a broader understanding of the diffusion of online protest forms.

Unfortunately, existing work on Internet activism does not provide a good theoretical guide in terms of what diffusion processes may be at work. Indeed, existing work predominately focuses on information diffusion (Ayres 1999; Tarrow 1998b; Bennett 2005), and even more tangentially on the diffusion of Internet access itself and the impact of the corresponding "digital divide" on political activity online (DiMaggio et al. 2001), not on the diffusion of practice innovations, such as online petitioning, as we examine here. Without many theoretical expectations on which to build, we undertake a relatively open-ended analysis of patterns of spread across the twenty causes we examine, which, as we discuss later, ultimately does allow us to uncover important clues about what diffusion processes may be at work.

Specifically, after descriptively exploring variations in adoption rates of different models of Internet activism, we also model the likelihood that a website includes specific visions of Internet activism based on characteristics of the website. For instance, we examine whether websites that adopt various forms of Internet activism written by multiple authors, operated by social movement organizations, are limited to blogs, or function as directories. We also look at whether websites that are cause specialists (i.e., make claims about a narrow set of issues) adopt different forms of activism from websites that discuss a wide range of causes (i.e., cause generalists; see Earl 2006a), positing that more focused sets of claims evidence strong commitments to particular issues that may be more likely to be mobilized into action. We show that analyzing the impact of these basic structural characteristics of websites on adoption likelihood can lead to greater insight about diffusion processes, particularly when read in juxtaposition to existing research.

DATA AND METHODS

For our analyses, we draw on a unique dataset that provides a population-level view of websites engaged in twenty different causes. Unlike data used in previous studies of Internet activism that have relied largely on case studies (with the notable exceptions of Earl et al. forthcoming, Earl and Kimport 2008, and Earl and Kimport 2009), our dataset is composed of twenty random samples of reachable populations of websites – that is, sites that a user could locate without being given the URL – addressing these twenty causes (i.e., one sample per cause; for a complete list of causes, see Figure 7.1), which are then quantitatively content-coded to produce population-level estimates. Causes were selected to represent issues of perennial interest to social movement scholars (e.g., civil rights), issues that are extremely episodic in terms of mobilization (e.g., immigration), and issues directly tied to the Internet (e.g., the open source software movement). With these data, we cannot only characterize the spread of Internet activism but also offer cross-movement comparisons of the types of Internet activism in which cause-oriented websites are engaged. The entire dataset contains data on 1,387 sites, although, as discussed in further detail later, we restrict our analyses to sites that contain protest content relevant to their targeted search claim.

OVERVIEW OF DATA COLLECTION METHODS

Drawing on Earl's (2006a) work studying random samples of larger populations of various online protest forms, the creation of this dataset began with concatenations of multiple Google searches (each search capturing up to one thousand search results) to approximate reachable populations of websites for each of the twenty causes. Search terms were designed based on keywords paired with an action word (such as "stop" or "protest") and pretested for efficacy. The maximum number of effective search terms was used for each cause to generate the most comprehensive snapshot of webpages engaged in that issue at the time; pages missed in one search were likely to be captured in another, with only very weakly relevant webpages being missed altogether (Earl 2006a). Because the resulting populations were so large, we randomly sampled, archived, and quantitatively content coded 1-percent samples of websites from each cause. The Google searches were run in September 2006 and the subsequent archiving of sampled sites for later quantitative content coding took place over the following month, as hundreds of thousands of webpages were saved using automated software utilities. For a more complete description of the data collection methods, please see Earl et al. (forthcoming).

CONTENT-CODING OF WEBSITES AND TACTICS

All websites and any tactics they hosted or directly linked to in each of the twenty random samples were content-coded. Because the Google searches returned webpages that discussed the twenty issue areas in a variety of ways, coders first evaluated whether a site contained protest content. In the analyses that follow, we consider only those sites that contained protest content. Although many more variables were coded than are relevant here, we report on ten variables used in the analyses here.[1] Sites were coded for five variables describing structural characteristics of the sites: whether the site appeared to be written by multiple authors or expressed a single voice (including an "organizational voice"); whether the site was run, or sponsored, by an organization (not necessarily an SMO specifically); whether the site was exclusively a blog; whether the site was a directory of other websites; and whether the site explicitly affiliated itself with a social movement.

In addition, each site was assessed for the presence of 382 different issues and coded for its position on *any* issues named on the site, regardless of which of the twenty samples the site was captured in, along with any news, educational, or informational material it provided on issues. Although we did not restrict coding to issues related to the sampling cause, we did restrict the cases included in the analyses to sites that contain claims or news, informational, or educational material relevant to the sampling cause to more accurately speak to the characteristics of each cause area. For instance, if a site was part of the abortion sample and discussed both abortion access and universal health care, both these issues would be coded and the case would be included in our analysis. However, if the same site did not discuss abortion, it would be excluded from our analysis because it was part of the abortion sample but did not ultimately discuss abortion as expected.

Finally, we coded three protest action-related variables. Protest actions (i.e., tactics) were coded for whether they were explicitly labeled as past or archived. Nonarchived actions were coded for whether they took place offline, such as a

---

[1] In the analyses that follow, we focus on characteristics observable to a user of the website; we do not include any back-end data on how the sites were produced.

vigil in front of the Supreme Court, or online, such as an online petition. Online actions were further distinguished as either hosted on the coded website or directly linked to from the website. Regular intercoder reliability tests yielded a 93 percent reliability rate.

DATA ANALYSIS

In the following sections we conduct logistic regressions to predict the log-odds of including hosted online tactics on a website and of including no tactics, but still containing protest content (i.e., brochureware). In both cases, the independent variables are multiple authors, organizational sponsorship, whether the site is exclusively a blog, whether the site is a directory, movement affiliation, cause breadth, and news breadth. In a second model for each dependent variable, we also include dummy variables for the cause areas that created the individual samples (using homelessness as the reference category because it is the least frequent adopter of only online tactics). These dummy variables were included to determine whether movements were significantly different from one another in adoption patterns after the other variables in the model were controlled for. The regressions were run in Stata 9SE.

FINDINGS

As Wejnert (2002) argues, the characteristics of a technology may affect diffusion. Of the types of Internet activism described previously, brochureware is the most easily accomplished from a technical perspective, as making claims on a website requires only basic HTML skills. Organizing and facilitating participation in online tactics, on the other hand, demands more sophisticated website production, suggesting that the presence of online tactics represents the diffusion of more complex uses of the Internet for activism. Moreover, online tactics suggest a different kind of diffusion: the diffusion of protest into uniquely online arenas of contention. Online tactics are not tethered to traditional protest forms as are brochureware sites that broadcast a claim but do not enable mobilization around it. Thus the initial question we address is the extent to which different forms of Internet activism, particularly brochureware and online protest opportunities, have diffused online.

As Figure 7.1 shows, brochureware has spread the most across the twenty causes we examine, representing 50 percent or more of the sites in eight of the twenty causes. With these cause-specific data, we can further note that the rate of brochureware varies by cause, from a high of 70 percent in sites about homelessness to a low of 22 percent in websites about women's rights advocacy.

Sites with at least one online action are also present in each of the twenty causes, representing the opposite pole of Internet activism and signaling the diffusion of an online field of contention. Some causes showed very low levels of online protest, with homelessness-related advocacy and education being

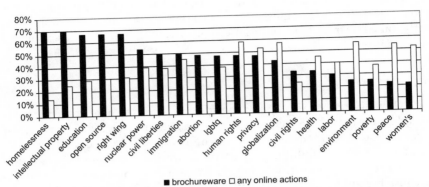

■ brochureware □ any online actions

FIGURE 7.1. Brochureware and Online Protest Opportunities by Cause (ordered by percent "brochureware")

among the lowest and human rights and environmental websites among the highest levels.

Although Figure 7.1 provides a broad overview of different patterns of spread across these twenty issue areas, it does not provide a strong sense of any particular cause's overall shape, nor does it distinguish between whether online actions are hosted on the site itself (a more technically challenging option) or connected to the site via a hyperlink to another website (a less technically challenging option). Thus, to provide a richer view and to distinguish between hosted versus linked online tactics, we examine Figure 7.2.

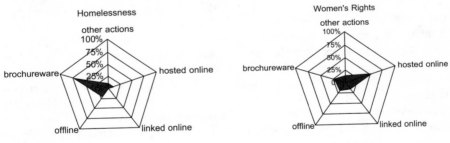

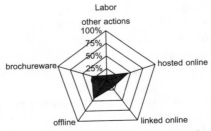

FIGURE 7.2. Distribution of Types of Internet Activism in Three Causes

Figure 7.2 provides Internet activism "footprints" (Witte 2008) of three example causes: homelessness, women's rights, and labor, which were selected because of the valuable analytic contrasts they provide. Each footprint is constructed by plotting the relative frequency of websites in the listed cause field that are brochureware sites or offer offline actions, hosted online actions, linked online actions, or other actions. The area created provides a richer visual understanding of the different online signatures of the three causes shown.

The homelessness footprint represents the brochureware extreme, in which most of the sites engaged in this cause contained no actions (70%) and only a small percentage of the sites hosted any online actions (10%). In this cause, the rate of hosted online tactics is low and the frequency of linked online tactics is zero.[2]

The women's rights cause, on the other hand, showcases the opposite pole, with high levels of hosted online tactics (52%). The women's movement cause also had a number of sites linking to online tactics (14%). Only 22 percent of sites had no tactics at all. In comparing the mirror images represented by homelessness and women's rights, it is apparent how diverse the adoption of different models of Internet activism is among the causes examined.

Still other causes were more evenly distributed in their range of tactical forms. Websites from the labor sample, for instance, contained similar percentages of sites containing hosted online actions (44%) and offline actions (44%), along with a smaller but still substantial percentage of brochureware sites (30%) and a smaller still percentage of sites linking to online actions (17%).

Moving back to the twenty-cause field from these three illustrative examples, we find substantially higher rates of hosted online actions than linked online actions, contrary to expectations about how the relative ease of linked online tactics (versus hosted online tactics) would encourage diffusion of that tactical type. In all causes but two (education and environment) the percentage of sites hosting online tactics exceeded the percentage of sites linking to online tactics, and three causes had sites that hosted online tactics but no sites that linked to online tactics. In each of the two exception causes, the percentage of sites hosting online tactics was equal to that of sites with linked online tactics; there were no causes in which the number of sites linking to online tactics exceeded the number hosting online tactics.

Given this high level of variation in adoption rates, it is important to explore whether key structural characteristics of websites in each cause area can account for the different adoption rates. For instance, prior research has found that websites offering online tactics were less likely to be run by SMOs than by other types of actors (Earl 2006b). If this finding held across these twenty causes and some causes had markedly different rates of organizational affiliation, this

---

[2] Note that the percentages depicted in Figures 7.1 and 7.2 for each cause are not comparable; unlike Figure 7.2, Figure 7.1 lumps together all sites with any online activism.

would provide important initial inroads into understanding which diffusion processes may (or may not) be at work.

Starting with the least technically complex and most easily adopted form of Internet activism, we tested the influence of several characteristics of websites on the log-odds that a site would contain brochureware (Table 7.1, column 2). Only one variable showed a significant, positive association with brochureware: If a site was only a blog, its log-odds of being a brochureware site were higher. Two other significant variables were negatively associated with brochureware: The coefficient for organization-sponsored sites was significant at the 0.05 level, and the coefficient for sites with a broader range of news claims was significant at the 0.01 level. Although broader causes appeared to also be negative and significant, in unreported models testing for model sensitivity, this result did not hold so we do not discuss it further.[3] This suggests that organizational sponsorship and a broad focus on a variety of news and educational topics reduced the log-odds that a site would limit its vision of activism to brochureware. It is important to note – and we return to a discussion of this issue shortly – that organizational affiliation in the models does not mean SMO affiliation. Coders recorded any organizational owner or operator of a website, so organizations affiliated with websites run the gamut in our data from professional societies to think tanks to actual SMOs. The news breadth finding is contrary to our initial expectations that broader sets of causes, news topics, or both would signal less commitment to a particular cause and thus a higher rate of brochureware. It may be that sites that discuss a range of issues are also more complex sites generally, and that greater complexity is less compatible with relatively unsophisticated brochureware designs.

When dummy variables for the twenty causes were included to determine whether websites from causes were still significantly different from one another in adoption rates after accounting for the structural characteristics of sites, sites from several causes were significantly different from sites from the homelessness cause (the reference category) at the 0.05 level or below. This finding points to the possibility that in some cases the discourse of particular causes may likewise influence the types of Internet activism in which cause-oriented sites engage. However, with only a few structural characteristics of websites included, we were able to remove much of the cause-specific variation.[4] The other results remain largely unchanged in this model (again, while cause breadth appears significant, it does not stand up to sensitivity testing).

Turning to the opposite pole of Internet activism, we also tested the influence of the same variables on the log-odds that a site would contain hosted online

---

[3] Because several of the sites appeared in more than one cause sample, we also ran unreported models in which we dropped the second to the *n*th case of any site that appeared in more than one cause. The results were the same, although there was evidence to suggest that cause breadth was only significant when cross-cause redundancies were included and so we do not discuss it in the main text further.

[4] However, the pseudo-R^2 value suggests a large amount of overall unexplained variation.

TABLE 7.1. *Logistic Regression Predicting Types of Internet Activism on Websites*

	Brochureware Sites		Hosted Online Tactics	
	Model 1	Model 2	Model 1	Model 2
Multiple authors	0.0408	−0.0057	−0.5492[+]	−0.6445[+]
	(0.2534)	(0.2665)	(0.3320)	(0.3514)
Organization-sponsored	−0.8087*	−0.9804*	1.5076**	1.5643**
	(0.3596)	(0.3858)	(0.4846)	(0.5236)
Blog	1.2053**	1.0415**	−1.3786**	−1.3312**
	(0.2763)	(0.3008)	(0.3991)	(0.4245)
Directory	−0.4261	−0.4647	−	−
	(0.4754)	(0.5094)		
Movement affiliation	0.0548	0.0050	−0.2278	−0.1201
	(0.3523)	(0.3767)	(0.4973)	(0.5313)
Cause breadth	−0.0903**	−0.0969**	0.1581**	0.1642**
	(0.0340)	(0.0360)	(0.0388)	(0.0415)
News breadth	−0.1959**	−0.2578**	0.1570*	0.1772*
	(0.0704)	(0.0793)	(0.0768)	(0.0858)
Abortion		−1.1118		0.4451
		(0.6857)		(0.9081)
Civil liberties		−0.8104		1.5639
		(0.7855)		(0.9804)
Civil rights		−1.2782[+]		0.8210
		(0.7656)		(1.0084)
Education		−0.8580		1.2603
		(0.8305)		(1.0497)
Environment		−1.7222*		1.0342
		(0.8231)		(0.9972)
Globalization		−0.5454		1.2292
		(0.7466)		(0.9293)
Health		−1.5091*		1.9408*
		(0.7400)		(0.9354)
Human rights		−0.5975		1.4579
		(0.8041)		(0.9854)
Immigration		−1.2852[+]		1.7383[+]
		(0.7411)		(0.9411)
Intellectual property		−0.2101		0.9705
		(0.8965)		(1.1271)
Labor		−1.8162*		1.2823
		(0.7581)		(0.9352)
LGBTQ		−1.1696		1.8232[+]
		(0.7940)		(1.0003)
Nuclear power		−1.1447		1.0938
		(0.7373)		(0.9755)
Open source		−0.8392		0.8636
		(0.7343)		(0.9481)

(continued)

TABLE 7.1 *(continued)*

	Brochureware Sites		Hosted Online Tactics	
	Model 1	Model 2	Model 1	Model 2
Peace		−2.6147**		2.0999*
		(0.7568)		(0.9358)
Poverty		−1.6785*		1.0755
		(0.7586)		(0.9741)
Privacy		−1.4294*		2.2654*
		(0.7231)		(0.9379)
Right wing		−0.9941		1.3896
		(0.7219)		(0.9486)
Women's		−2.1559**		1.6704+
		(0.7967)		(0.9625)
Constant	0.4620*	1.9482**	−1.7062**	−3.1930**
	(0.2168)	(0.6690)	(0.2667)	(0.8828)
Observations	571	571	518	518

Standard errors in parentheses; + significant at 0.10; * significant at 0.05; ** significant at 0.01

tactics, the most technically complex type of Internet activism (Table 7.1, column 4).[5] As we might expect following the brochureware regression, the blog coefficient is significant at the 0.01 level, but is negative, suggesting that blogs are less likely to host online tactics. The breadth of the news material and the cause coverage on the site, in contrast, are significantly associated with higher levels of hosted online activity. As was the case with brochureware, the findings on these variables are opposite of our expectations. As we speculated earlier, perhaps sites with broad issue connections also tend to be more complex, and that technical sophistication seems a fertile environment for hosted online tactics. Most notably in this model, the sponsorship of an organization, which was significant at the 0.01 level, is associated with an increase in the log-odds that a site will contain hosted online tactics.

In the second model of hosted online actions in Table 7.1 (column 5), which includes dummy variables for each cause field to test for residual influences of causes on website adoption, we see limited specific effects of individual cause discourses after structural characteristics of the websites were accounted for. Other results are unchanged from the previous model.

DISCUSSION

Thus far our findings have (1) clarified the variability in the spread of different models of Internet activism across twenty cause areas and (2) shed light on the

---

[5] Readers should note that directory sites predicted perfectly the lack of hosted tactics, so the variable was dropped from these analyses. Also, as in the previous case, we ran unreported analyses in which we dropped the 2nd to the *n*th case of any site that appeared in more than one cause sample. Our results were unchanged except that the significance of news breadth was more questionable in those models.

microdynamics of diffusion by modeling the impact of structural characteristics of websites on the log-odds that, through their practices, websites embrace different visions of Internet activism. In this section, we also argue that those findings, when read in juxtaposition to prior research on online protest, can begin to open the black box of diffusion processes involved in the spread of different activist practices online.

Specifically, we find the results on organizational affiliation to be quite surprising given prior research. Although not analyzing an entirely comparable sample of websites, Earl (2006b) found that sites offering online tactics were less likely be operated by social movement actors than by other types of actors using data from a generalizable sample of websites in 2004 that hosted or linked to online petitions, online boycotts, or online letter-writing or e-mailing campaigns. Our data, drawn in 2006, suggest a different relationship between organizations (although we cannot speak to SMOs in particular, as Earl had studied) and online organization, online participation, or both.

To the extent that these two studies are in loose, nonprecise conversation, it would appear as though the role of organizations in promoting online protest has shifted over the past few years. By 2006, it seems that organizations might have been playing a role in promoting hosted online protest forms, which in turn suggests diffusion processes that feature organizations as primary actors.

We outline several scenarios that we regard as theoretical possibilities for future research. First, it is possible that organizations are the actors driving a fundamentally mimetic diffusion process (Strang and Soule 1998). In this scenario, organizations – professional societies, think tanks, SMOs, and the like – look around at other organizations' websites as models for their own websites. As organizations see other organizational sites hosting online tactics, they begin to incorporate these tactics into their own sites as well. This is the least interesting of the possibilities we imagine, but it could be tested with longitudinal data on the topic that includes the prior year's organizational adoption rate for hosted tactics. As that rate builds, one would expect mimetic pressure to build as well.

We regard two other possibilities as more likely, but still in need of research using longitudinal data. Hosted protest actions may not be present on sites for the direct utility they provide websites but rather as evidence of the site's legitimacy in the broader protest field. Drawing on new institutionalist understandings of isomorphism (DiMaggio and Powell 1983), it may be that offering online protest actions has come, over the past few years, to be seen as what legitimate advocacy organizations with online presences do. In this scenario, the spread of hosted online actions is not so much about their role in democratic participation as about their role in marking which actors are "in touch" and legitimate in the field, much as quality circles and other management fads were adopted for their representational value, not their efficiency.

There is some suggestive evidence to support this. In addition to the data used in this chapter, we have also collected data on what exemplary SMOs in each cause field did on their websites in 2006, which allows us to compare the practices of exemplary SMOs to practices in each cause field generally.

Unreported analyses of those data suggest that exemplary SMO websites are even more likely to host online tactics, with about 90 percent of those exemplary websites falling into this category.

But this begs the question of how exemplary websites might have come to be so involved in offering online protest tactics, which a third possibility addresses. Programming anything but the most basic website has become more complicated over time, as scripting techniques such as Ajax, web development applications such as Ruby on Rails, and server-side applications and languages such as PHP have become de rigueur. This has resulted in a booming web development sector that sells its expert design and programming services to organizations of all shapes and sizes.

For instance, Capital Advantage, which operates CapWiz, designs and hosts websites for organizations interested in issue advocacy. The company boasted more than 1,500 organizational clients in 2007 and claims to have handled 18 million messages from constituents to elected officials on behalf of these organizations in 2007 (Capital Advantage 2008). Convio, which acquired its competitor GetActive in 2007, offers similar services. Although it does not publish client numbers, it does list some well-known clients on its website, which include organizations like the League of Conservation Voters and the Dean for America Campaign (Convio 2008). Just as professionals have played a role in diffusing practices in other sectors (e.g., DiMaggio and Powell 1983; Edelmen and Suchman 1997), it is quite likely that these companies have helped to spur diffusion of hosted online tactics in the protest sector.

Although we do not have access to the longitudinal data that would be needed to test these possibilities, we do argue that even being able to suggest alternatives for likely diffusion dynamics at work is a large advance given the paucity of research on the diffusion of different practices associated with Internet activism.

CONCLUSION

There has been extensive research on the diffusion of protest *offline*, but relatively little work on diffusion processes at work *online*, with existing work focusing on information diffusion (Ayres 1999; Tarrow 1998b; Bennett 2005) or the diffusion of Internet access (DiMaggio et al. 2001), despite growing scholarly interest in the field of Internet activism. In this chapter, we have sought to redress this lack by offering an initial description of the distribution of several types of Internet activism across twenty causes. Our cross-sectional data mark the extent to which these practices of Internet activism have diffused since the inception of the World Wide Web, and their breadth offers a uniquely rich portrait of online activist undertakings across a diverse range of causes.

In our mapping of the spread of different types of Internet activism, we found a large presence of brochureware, as might be expected given the ease with which it is produced, and, also of note, a substantial presence of hosted online actions, a far less easily implemented form of Internet activism. Because our dataset includes data across twenty different causes, we were also able to show that the distribution of brochureware and hosted online actions varies noticeably by cause.

These findings enter the rather contentious debate over the political impacts of online organizing and participation. Where some have argued that online spaces will exacerbate offline inequalities, for example, due to the digital divide (Tilly 2004), others have cast these types of Internet activism as opportunities for new actors to engage in protest (Earl and Kimport 2008, 2009). Regardless of whether one considers online organizing and participation beneficial or dangerous, articulating the diffusion processes of types of Internet activism speaks to both sides of this debate, characterizing what types of activism occur online and how far they have spread.

Using logistic regression, we sought to explain variation in the adoption rates of different types of Internet activism using structural characteristics of the websites in our samples. Most interestingly, in contrast to prior research, organization-sponsored sites were significantly more likely to host online actions and significantly less likely to be brochureware sites. We offer three possibilities for this finding: (1) mimetic diffusion processes (Strang and Soule 1998); (2) isomorphism driven by legitimacy imperatives (DiMaggio and Powell 1983); and (3) the role of companies that develop and market systems to host online actions. There is some initial evidence for the second and third scenarios, and we leave it to future longitudinal research to further test these explanations. Our principal contributions have been to lay the empirical and theoretical foundation for more work in this area, as this aspect of diffusion has been so understudied.

8

Transnational Networks, Diffusion Dynamics, and Electoral Change in the Postcommunist World

Valerie Bunce and Sharon Wolchik

ELECTORAL CHANGE AND DIFFUSION DYNAMICS[1]

From 1996 to 2005, eight countries in postcommunist Europe and Eurasia held elections that replaced illiberal leaders or their anointed successors with leaders of the democratic opposition.[2] The impact of these elections varied. Some of the effects were important, but not earth-shaking – for instance, consolidating new and relatively fragile democratic orders (Bulgaria and Romania) or contributing to a more competitive politics in the context of mixed regimes that, although featuring some "democratic decorations," had tilted in an increasingly dictatorial direction over time (Georgia and Kyrgyzstan). However, some of these elections had dramatic consequences – for example, ending a dangerous interlude of de-democratization (Slovakia), contributing to significant democratic progress following a period of increasingly authoritarian politics (Ukraine), or producing a veritable leap from dictatorship to democracy (Serbia and Croatia).

Despite these differences, however, all eight elections were pivotal political events because of one overarching commonality: By removing authoritarian leaders from office and replacing them with leaders of the democratic

[1] We are thankful to the International Center for Non-Violent Conflict, the Smith Richardson Foundation, the Einaudi Center for International Studies, and the Institute for the Social Sciences at Cornell University for their support of this project. In addition, we thank Aida Baidalova, Keti Nozadze, Vlad Micic, Sara Rzyeva, Nancy Meyers, and Melissa Aten for their research assistance and Sidney Tarrow for his helpful comments on an earlier draft. The arguments presented in this chapter are based on more than two hundred interviews conducted from 2005 to 2007 with American and European democracy promoters and ambassadors, along with leaders of opposition parties, democratic activists, and civil society organizations. These interviews took place in Washington, D.C.; Philadelphia; Ithaca, New York; and Armenia, Azerbaijan, Croatia, Georgia, Serbia, Slovakia, and Ukraine.
[2] See, for example, McFaul 2005; Beissinger 2007, 2006; Tucker 2007; Demes and Forbrig 2007; Kuzio 2005; Way 2005a, 2005b; Bunce and Wolchik forthcoming, 2009, 2006a, 2006b.

opposition, these elections had the common characteristic of investing in subsequent democratic development. Although such changes in leaders and political coalitions cannot by any means guarantee subsequent democratic progress, they are in fact a necessary condition for such progress to take place. This is in part because dictators rarely become democrats, although they can pretend otherwise for a time when it serves their domestic and international interests. Another reason is that elections are vitally important to the democratic project. Just as improvements in democratic performance are associated with elections,[3] for example, so in the postcommunist region in particular, the victory of the liberal opposition has emerged as the best predictor of improved democratic performance since transitions from communism began nearly two decades ago.[4]

What explains this remarkable wave of electoral change? The easy answer – and one suggested by the very use of the term *wave* – is that cross-national diffusion dynamics were in play. This interpretation flows directly from four sets of arguments. First, it would be very hard to explain these elections in terms of purely domestic processes; that is, as eight separate instances of similar responses to similar domestic situations. One problem here, for example, is that these elections took place in quite different contexts, ranging from Bulgaria, which was rated "fully free" by Freedom House on the eve of the 1997 election, to Serbia and Kyrgyzstan, which were both ranked "not free" when their breakthrough elections took place. Second, the pattern of electoral shifts is consistent with a diffusion model, given the clustered character of these events with respect to both time and space and the common focus on elections as *the* site for democratic change.

Third, this region has a rich history of political change moving like wildfire across state boundaries. Here we refer, most obviously, to the wave of mass protests from 1988 to 1992 that had the remarkable and related effects of bringing down communism and communist states in the Soviet Union and Eastern Europe and, as a result, the Cold War international order. However, though unprecedented in their reach, these protests built in fact on earlier protests in the region that had also crossed state boundaries – for example, the protests in East Germany, Czechoslovakia, Poland, and Hungary that took place following the death of Stalin in 1953 and, earlier, the revolutions of 1848.[5] Finally, and also in support of an interpretation of diffusion, is the mounting evidence that democratic transitions tend to cluster within regions, and that the global reach of democratization during the Third Wave, along with cross-national patterns of democratic change in earlier periods, followed a dynamic quite consistent with a significant role for cross-national diffusion.[6]

---

[3] See Teorell and Hadenius 2009 and Lindberg 2006 and 2009.
[4] Bunce 1994, 1999a, 2003; Fish 1998 and 2005.
[5] See Bunce 1999b; Bunce and Wolchik 2006a and forthcoming.
[6] Starr and Lindborg 2003; Brinks and Coppedge 2006; and, for longer-term perspectives on the same question, Gleditsch and Ward 2006; Wejnert 2005; and Markoff 1996.

DEBATING DIFFUSION

These are suggestive, but not fully convincing, arguments. In particular, there are three problems, all of which, as highlighted in the concluding chapter by Sidney Tarrow in this volume, are quite common in studies of diffusion. One is that diffusion addresses the spatial movement of innovations, yet it is unclear what is innovative about these elections, aside from their outcomes. Even though the impact of diffusion is certainly an important question, as the introductory chapter in this volume emphasizes, it can hardly be assessed in the absence of identifying the innovation itself; that is, the causes of these electoral shifts. Indeed, there is little reason to assume a priori that new ways of "doing elections" were responsible for these outcomes, that there was a formula common to these eight electoral efforts that produced turnover in governing officials and parties, and that this formula in turn was transmitted among these eight electoral sites.

Another problem is that these arguments do not explain *how* these electoral challenges to authoritarian rule moved – or were moved – from one country to others. Diffusion processes, to draw on the introductory chapter, are always multidimensional, but that characterization hardly leaves analysts off the hook, particularly given competing perspectives in the literature on diffusion about the role of agency and structure (with the latter rarely standing alone, however, as the essays in this volume suggest) and the role as well of relational, nonrelational, and mediated diffusion.[7] Finally, these arguments seem to downplay the considerable obstacles to the diffusion of electoral challenges to dictatorial rule – obstacles that explain, for example, why the norm is for dictators to win, not lose, elections, even when they tolerate competition for political office. Here, we must remember that these elections were profoundly subversive political – and, indeed, economic – acts, with the two tied together because of the close relationship during communism between political power and economic resources and its easy translation after communism, especially in regimes governed by authoritarians, into patronage networks that leaders used to distribute money and jobs.[8] Thus, it is one thing to argue that innovations that change the reach and organization of the welfare system or that take a specific approach to public sector downsizing are able to move from one established capitalist order to another[9] and quite another to argue that electoral confrontations with incumbent dictators move from one country to others. If nothing else, dictators tend to be vigilant; they have considerable resources at their disposal to protect themselves and their allies; and they have a great deal to lose if they are removed from office.[10] Finally, just as dictators can be in fact quite popular, so oppositions, especially in mixed polities that

---

[7] See Tarrow 2005, especially the chapters by Tarrow and Sageman.
[8] See Bunce 1994; Fish 1998 and 2005.
[9] See Lee and Strang 2006 and Weyland 2005.
[10] See, especially, Kapuscinski 2006; and Silitski 2010, 2005a, and 2005b.

bridge dictatorship and democracy, tend to be both fragmented and unpopular. Their fragmentation reflects personal disputes, ideological differences in some cases, their inexperience with competitive elections, and continuing disagreements about the advisability of such strategies as running for office, boycotting elections, and collaborating with the regime; however, when coupled with their sorry electoral track record, divisions within and among opposition parties also contribute to public dissatisfaction with the opposition and the unwillingness of the public, even when the regime is unpopular, to transfer its allegiance to opposition parties. Particularly alienating from the perspective of the public is the tendency of opposition parties to "whine" about their location on the outskirts of power without seeming to take much responsibility for trying to exert more influence.[11]

ASSESSING DIFFUSION

In this chapter, we argue that the cross-national spread of electoral breaks with authoritarian rule from 1996 to 2005 in postcommunist Europe and Eurasia in fact reflected diffusion dynamics in play. We base this conclusion on both analyses of these elections (and a series of other elections that failed to bring oppositions to power) and more than two hundred interviews conducted from 2005 to 2007 with participants in these events in a variety of places in the United States, western Europe, and Armenia, Azerbaijan, Croatia, Georgia, Serbia, Slovakia, and Ukraine.

We build the case for diffusion in two stages. First, we review the wave itself, arguing that the pattern is consistent with diffusion, given not just the clustering of similar electoral outcomes over time and space, but also, more important, the presence in each case of a similar and distinctive approach to defeating dictators. It is precisely this approach – what we term the *electoral model* – that constitutes the innovation that moved from state to state in the postcommunist region. We then turn our attention to the "why" and "how" questions, concentrating on three factors in particular that supported the cross-national movement of the electoral model. Thus, we argue that this ensemble of strategies to win elections was unusually well configured for implementation in multiple sites – an argument about the modularity of the innovation that also figures prominently in the chapter in this volume by Sean Chabot. Despite the diverse regime settings, moreover, there were nonetheless sufficient similarities among regime contexts to support multiple applications of the electoral model. Finally, we focus on the critical role of transnational democracy promotion networks composed of local oppositions, activists from other countries in the region, and American democracy promoters. This network was responsible for developing the model; carrying it from place to place; amending the model in keeping with local conditions; and, finally, carrying out electoral challenges to authoritarian rule.

---

[11] See Bunce and Wolchik forthcoming.

Thus, rather than choosing among competing explanations for diffusion and between, at the extremes, a structural or an agency-based explanation, we embrace in effect all of the above by emphasizing the importance of the model itself, similar conditions, and transnational networks.[12] Our decision to embrace a three-part model that bridges explanatory families, however, was not a function of a resistance on our parts to "taking a stance." Rather, in our view, all three factors were necessary for the simple reason that the spread of subversive innovations of the kind of interest in this chapter has unusually stiff requirements. These exacting conditions, moreover, are also a major reason that the wave of electoral change missed some countries and why the wave appears to have come to an end – a set of issues we address in more detail in other work.[13]

DEFINING DIFFUSION AND ITS MECHANISMS

Following the lead of Givan, Roberts, and Soule in Chapter 1, we define diffusion as the "spread of some innovation through direct or indirect channels across members of a social system."[14] Diffusion, therefore, implies, on one hand, a significant change in ideas, institutions, policies, models or repertoires of behavior and, on the other hand, the subsequent movement of this change within a limited time span to new settings that in most cases are relatively close to the epicenter of change.[15] When applied to the case of interest here, diffusion refers to a new approach to defeating dictators through elections that was applied in one country and that then reappeared in a series of other countries in the postcommunist region – and elsewhere, as recent electoral confrontations between incumbents and oppositions in Mexico, Kenya, Togo, Ghana, and the Ivory Coast remind us.

How do we know when diffusion has taken place? We argue that a two-stage explanation is required. First, central to claiming diffusion is the ability to demonstrate that similar innovations appear in staggered fashion in multiple locales. Such a pattern, however, is suggestive of diffusion only in the absence of evidence demonstrating both how and why international transmission occurred.[16] Thus, unlike some students of diffusion, who argue in strong support of its role but who put off the question of what is driving the process

---

[12] For competing perspectives on diffusion, see Jacoby 2004 and 2006; Strang and Soule 1998; Lee and Strang 2006; Tarrow 2005; Bockman and Eyal 2002; Glenn 2000; McAdam et al. 2009; Elkins and Simmons 2005; Simmons and Elkins 2004; Beissinger 2002, 2006, and 2007; Osa 2001; Muiznieks 1995; and Diani 2003.

[13] See Bunce and Wolchik forthcoming, chapters 7, 8, and 10.

[14] Also see Rogers 1995.

[15] Ackerman and Duvall 2000; Aksartova 2005; Lee and Strang 2006; Beissinger 2002; Brinks and Coppedge 2006; Markoff 1996; Tarrow 2005 and Tarrow and della Porta 2005.

[16] For purposes of simplifying our discussion, we refer to the cross-national spread of innovation, rather than the more accurate characterization of the process as one that simply involves multiple sites – which can, of course, occur within, as well as across, states.

for later study, we see this issue as inseparable from the assertion of diffusion itself.[17] This is because, in the absence of insights into what propels innovations to travel, we cannot be secure in the claim that "clustered adoptions" reflect cross-national transmission of the innovation.

COMPETING EXPLANATIONS

In fact, there are several alternative explanations for cross-national similarities in adoption patterns. One is that domestic actors can simply be responding to similar conditions in similar ways, albeit at different times, given variations in domestic conditions. At the same time, diffusion can also be an illusion[18] when similar cross-national developments reflects the work of powerful inter-national actors orchestrating the introduction of innovations in a number of dependent countries. To provide two examples: Can diffusion explain the rise of communism throughout Eastern Europe (minus Greece) along with China following the end of the Second World War? It is true that the victory of com-munism was "innovative," and that the march to communism was a process that was both lagged in time, yet clustered in terms of geography. However, transnational transmission – the foundation of diffusion – is largely absent from this dynamic, because the victory of communist parties reflected, first, Soviet imposition of communism in many of the countries in Eastern Europe, and second, looking to both Yugoslavia and China, where communism was "home-grown," a common response to very similar local conditions.[19]

If common responses to common conditions or international orchestration of cross-national change are inconsistent with diffusion, then what kinds of dynamics can be hypothesized to drive the cross-national transmission of inno-vation? The literature presents two extremes, with a number of explanations falling between these poles. One extreme emphasizes the power of structural similarities among units – or what sociologists have termed structural isomor-phism. It is fair to say that this process is usually understood as an accidental by-product of similarities, with agents of change playing a limited role. The other extreme is actor-rich – for example, conscious decisions by local actors, given the appeal of positive precedents elsewhere, to import the innovation through the adoption of similar goals and strategies. Here, the emphasis is on purposive actions. In between are a variety of other arguments that contain elements of both structure and agency, planned as well as accidental cross-national adoptions of specific innovations – for instance, demonstration effects that change the calculus of outside observers by lowering the costs of emu-lation, while increasing the incentives to follow suit; the rise of transnational networks that support the spread of an innovation in both a purposive way and

---

[17] See, for instance, Brinks and Coppedge 2006.
[18] To borrow from Brinks and Coppedge 2006.
[19] And see Bockman and Eyal 2002, on misrepresenting the spread of neoliberal orthodoxy in Eastern Europe.

as a by-product of their geographical spread; and the characteristics of specific innovations with respect to their ease of transfer among sites.[20]

In our view, this thicket of competing explanations can be boiled down to three lines of argument that bridge structure and agency, purposive actions, and accidental transmission. The first is that diffusion occurs because the model itself is amenable to cross-national applications. This can be because the model is a tidy package of transportable tasks, because conditions in a number of locales provide opportunities for application, and because the model resonates with important local constituencies by tapping into their values and interests and by capitalizing on earlier efforts at change. The second is the presence of similar local conditions in both the "sending" and the "receiving" sites. These conditions, however, are not just objective, as in structural accounts, but also subjective. Thus, potential local adopters must perceive similarities in contexts before they translate appealing precedents in the neighborhood into relevant and "doable" actions. Finally, diffusion can occur because of the existence of transnational networks supporting the spread of the model. These networks typically bring together both domestic and international actors who share the same goals and who have converged on similar approaches to achieving these goals.[21] If all three of these explanations speak to the "why" question, the third also speaks to the "how" issues; that is, how innovations are transported from one context to another.

With these arguments in mind, let us return to the puzzle at hand: why and how electoral challenges to authoritarian rule moved across the postcommunist region. We begin by providing an overview of the eight electoral challenges to dictatorial rule. The purpose of this discussion is to flesh out the pattern of electoral change and provide evidence that a specific and similar innovation appeared in each electoral contest.

THE ELECTORAL WAVE

The story of the electoral defeat of dictators begins with four inter-connected political struggles that took place in Serbia, Bulgaria, Romania, and Slovakia from 1996 to 1998.[22] The first was the massive three-month-long protests in Serbia from 1996 to 1997 – protests that were motivated by Slobodan Milosevic's attempt to deny the opposition its significant victories in many of the local elections that took place in 1996.[23] These protests (as in the cases that followed) built on previous rounds of anti-regime mobilizations – in the Serbian case going back to the early 1980s and in Romania, Bulgaria, and Slovakia to

---

[20] See, for instance, Tarrow 2005; Beissinger 2006 and 2007; Glenn 2000; Bockman and Eyal 2002; Strang and Soule 1998; Simmons and Elkins 2004; and Elkins and Simmons 2005.

[21] See Tarrow 2005 and Keck and Sikkink 1998.

[22] For a more detailed discussion of the wave, see Bunce and Wolchik forthcoming, chapters 3 through 6.

[23] Lazic 1999 and Pavlovic 2005.

1989 (and even during the communist period, as in Slovakia from 1967 to 1968 and the miners' strikes in Romania during the 1980s). Although the Serbian protests failed in the short term (although victorious mayors, for example, were finally allowed to take office, their powers were significantly curtailed, especially in Belgrade, the capital), they contributed in important ways to a subsequent round of election-based protests in the fall of 2000 that succeeded in bringing Milosevic down.[24] Also helpful in producing a new generation of protesters and expanding the geography of anti-Milosevic sentiment were Milosevic's decisions following these protests to crack down on the autonomy of universities, local governments, and the media.[25]

The second set of struggles took place in Romania, where the liberal opposition finally came together and ran a sophisticated political campaign that succeeded in replacing the former communist incumbent president with a candidate with far stronger liberal credentials and commitments.[26] The third set of struggles took place in Bulgaria at roughly the same time. The Serbian protests next door had been very influential in motivating the unions, eventually joined by intellectuals and leaders of the opposition, to carry out large-scale protests that brought down the communist-led government and that led to a new election, in which a united liberal opposition emerged victorious.[27] The process then moved to Slovakia. In a pivotal meeting taking place in the Vienna airport at the end of 1997, leaders of the Slovak opposition, the American ambassadors to Slovakia and the Czech Republic, political activists from Romania and Bulgaria, and representatives of the International Republican Institute, the National Democratic Institute, Freedom House, and the National Endowment for Democracy came together to devise a strategy for unseating Vladimir Meciar, the illiberal Slovak prime minister, in the upcoming parliamentary elections. This meeting led to the OK98 campaign, in which all the components of the electoral model (as described later) came together – for example, the formation of a cohesive opposition (bringing together no fewer than eighteen parties); ambitious campaigns to register voters, advertise the costs of the Meciar regime, and get out the vote; and the deployment of both domestic and international election monitoring, as well as exit polls. As a result of their efforts and especially the turnout of first-time voters, Meciar lost the election.

The next application of the electoral model was in Croatia in 2000, where the death of the long-serving dictator, Franjo Tudjman, in 1999 had weakened the governing party and provided an opportunity for the opposition to finally win power. The Croatian opposition then applied the "Slovak model" to its own situation, with Slovak activists and European and especially American democracy promoters providing money, strategic advice, and even election playbooks.

[24] See St. Protich 2005; Bieber 2003; Jennings 2009; and Pribicevic 2004.
[25] Pavlovic 2005; Goati, 2000; Spasic and Subotic 2000.
[26] See, for example, Bunce and Wolchik forthcoming, chapter 3.
[27] See, especially, Petrova 2010 and Ganev 2007.

Later in 2000, Serbia finally experienced its own electoral breakthrough.[28] Here, there were several key differences – as is typical of foreign innovations when they are domesticated. One was that the struggle against Milosevic was severely constrained by the heavy authoritarian hand of the regime. Thus, for example, there were no external election monitors in Serbia in the fall 2000 elections; the media were closely controlled by Milosevic; the opposition faced continual threats; and the assistance provided by the international community was important, but located necessarily outside the borders of the state, given the political impossibility of a domestic presence as a result of the NATO-led bombing of Serbia in 1999 (although the Canadian Embassy substituted in effective fashion for the closed American embassy). Moreover, a student group, Otpor (Resistance), played the central role in the struggle against Milosevic, and it was the size, dedication, and geographical spread of this movement, along with the innovative electoral activities of the Center for Free Elections and Democracy (CeSID), which proved to be decisive in defeating Milosevic. Finally, the victory of the opposition (which was composed of eighteen parties that came together around the candidacy of a moderate nationalist, Vojislav Kostunica – thanks in part to the willingness of the far more charismatic Zoran Djindjic to play a secondary role) was delayed by Milosevic's refusal to cede power. In contrast to the previous cases discussed, in which authoritarian leaders immediately left office, Milosevic stepped down only after the opposition helped mount massive Serbia-wide protests.[29]

The Georgian opposition then followed suit in the 2003 parliamentary elections – although this produced a coup d'état by the opposition, as the long-serving president, Eduard Shevardnadze, resigned but in fact was not up for reelection.[30] In Georgia, the political context was less constraining than in Serbia, especially given the lackluster campaign run by Shevardnadze's allies, the defection of so many key players (such as Mikheil Saakashvili, the current president) from the ruling group to the opposition, and the relative openness of the Georgian media. However, the playbook was nonetheless remarkably similar – for example, the formation of both a united opposition and a youth group in support of political change (Kmara); the generation of opposition to regime vote totals that exposed regime fraud; close collaboration between the opposition and the third sector; and, finally, an extraordinarily ambitious campaign by Mikheil Saakashvili that brought him to virtually every village in Georgia.

The next successful use of elections to oust an authoritarian leader occurred in Ukraine a year later.[31] As in the Georgian case, a single charismatic politician – in this case, Viktor Yushchenko – played a critical role. As in both the

---

[28] See Bunce and Wolchik 2006a and 2009.
[29] St. Protich 2005 and Pavlovic 2005.
[30] Papava 2005 and Wheatley 2005.
[31] See, in particular, Kuzio 2005; Kubicek 2005; Way 2005a and 2005b; McFaul 2007; and Bunce and Wolchik forthcoming, chapter 5.

Georgian and Serbian cases, the successful political breakthrough exploited a record of a leadership that had grown increasingly corrupt, careless, and violent; benefited from defections from the ruling circles; built on earlier rounds of protests and recent successes in local elections; and reached out to diverse groups, with young people playing nearly as important a role as the one seen in Serbia with Otpor. Moreover, as in Serbia and Georgia, political protests after the election (which were as large as those in Serbia and lasted longer) were again necessary to force the authoritarian challenger to admit defeat.

The electoral model then moved to Kyrgyzstan, where it succeeded, as in Georgia, in deposing the long-serving president, despite the fact that these elections were also parliamentary, not presidential.[32] It is here where we see less evidence than in the previous seven cases of a well-orchestrated electoral challenge being mounted – although the United States instituted a major effort to improve the quality of the elections in Kyrgyzstan.[33] Instead, dissatisfaction with electoral outcomes in the south of the country produced protests that then spread to the north, where the capital, Bishkek, is located. The result in very short order was that the president of Kyrgyzstan, Askar Akayev, abdicated and fled to Moscow.[34] However, even here we find a variant on contagion effects. President Akayev, who had been in power since the early 1990s and who had become increasingly authoritarian over time, was so taken by his own fears of a "colored revolution" (as they have been commonly called) taking place in his own country that he wrote a book a month before his forced abdication about why such electoral challenges would never succeed in his country. It appears that a major reason that he left office so quickly was his own doubt about the accuracy of the very prediction he had made only a few months before the crisis.

PATTERNS OF DIFFUSION

This brief narrative highlights all the familiar components of a diffusion dynamic. The breakthrough elections took place in lagged fashion across a large group of countries located within the postcommunist region. Moreover, the contexts within which these elections took place were roughly similar. Though varying in their extent of both levels of repression and democratic "decorations," all these regimes nonetheless fell into that large space between full-scale democracies and full-scale dictatorships. Thus, more specifically, as mixed regimes they combined democratic institutions, such as parliaments, courts, a sprinkling of civil liberties, and at the least semicompetitive elections with authoritarian incumbents and political practices. Perhaps the most

---

[32] See, especially, Radnitz 2010 and Bunce and Wolchik forthcoming, chapter 6.

[33] Borbieva 2007.

[34] On the Kyrgyz case, see, especially, Weyerman 2005; Radnitz 2006 and 2010; and Fuhrmann 2006.

important indicator of diffusion, however, is that these elections marked a sharp departure from the past in two ways. They all ended the rule of dictators, and oppositions used both new and yet similar strategies to win power – what we have termed in other work the electoral model.

Though familiar to most citizens, political activists, and political scientists in established democracies, the tasks associated with the electoral model were new to this region and very difficult – and often dangerous – to carry out. These tasks involved, for example, exerting considerable pressures on the regime (in alliance with their international allies) to reform electoral procedures; organizing large-scale voter registration and turnout drives; forming a united opposition; carrying out unusually ambitious political campaigns that forced opposition candidates for the first time to go outside the major cities; and conducting (where politically tolerated) sophisticated public opinion polls, parallel tabulation of votes, and exit polls.[35] All these features were critical because they made it harder for authoritarians to win elections and to stay in power. Moreover, they often made all the difference. Electoral turnout had declined over time in most of these countries, because citizens had become divided and demobilized, as well as skeptical about the ability of the opposition to win and even about the advisability of such a victory.[36] Winning citizens over, in short, was difficult, because it involved a three-part proposition: registering them to vote, getting them to vote, and finding ways to encourage them to support the opposition. It is telling, for example, that electoral turnout was unusually high in many of these elections (especially in Slovakia, Croatia, Serbia, and Ukraine) and that most of these elections were in fact very close (especially in Bulgaria, Slovakia, Serbia, and Ukraine). Also revealing is what happened in the 2000 Serbian election. With two hours left before the polls closed, CeSID, a nongovernmental organization involved in voter turnout, registration, and parallel vote tabulation, realized that turnout in key areas was too low to guarantee a victory for the opposition. As a result, they mobilized an ambitious and targeted get-out-the-vote campaign at the last minute that delivered a narrow victory to Vojislav Kostunica, the opposition presidential candidate.

In addition to the core features of the electoral model outlined previously, there were other similarities across these electoral episodes in strategies deployed and the distinctiveness of those strategies in comparison with previous elections. For example, in many of these elections, extensive use was made of rock concerts, street theater, marches, and unusually widespread distribution of posters, stickers, and T-shirts to expand interest in the election and voter registration. In addition, a large number of new organizations were formed to monitor elections, get out the vote, tabulate the vote, and engage young people; close ties were forged for the first time between civil society groups and the opposition; and in more repressive polities, protests were organized to force

---

[35] See, especially, Gel'man 2005; van de Walle 2005 and 2006; Howard and Roessler 2006; and Garber and Cowan 1993.
[36] See, for instance, Djordjevic 2005 on Serbia.

recalcitrant dictators to admit defeat and leave office. Central to the success of these protests, moreover, were conversations during the campaign between opposition leaders and members of the security apparatus.

Once we step back from this wave of electoral change, we see some other patterns that are typical of diffusion dynamics. One is that, though maintaining a core set of tasks, the model was nonetheless amended as it made its cross-national journey – for instance, the use of parliamentary elections to oust presidents, the elaborate coordination of food and shelter for protesters in Kyiv and other major cities in Ukraine, and the addition of massive public protests in more authoritarian political contexts. At the same time, we see a familiar cycle, wherein the "early risers"[37] tended to combine unusually supportive contexts for change, more planning, and a more faithful application of the model than "late risers," in which domestic conditions were less supportive and where the role and appeal of attractive precedents outrun careful local preparations.

Also important in this regard was the learning that took place not just among groups sharing the goal of subverting the status quo, but also on the part of the defenders of politics "as usual." This is why, for example, even in other cases in the region where oppositions broke with past practices and managed to unite when running for office, as in Armenia, Azerbaijan, and Belarus from 2003 to 2008, they failed nonetheless in their quest to win power.[38] Just as they did not deploy other strategies included in the electoral toolkit, so they were blocked in many cases from doing so because of the preemptive actions of their authoritarian opponents – a dynamic that reminds us of the important roles in diffusion processes of both learning and repeated interactions between regimes and antiregime social movements.[39] At the same time, the electoral showdowns in these three states demonstrate, as in Ronald Herring's chapter, the central importance for the evolution and form of contentious politics of the competition over framing. Thus, unlike their counterparts in Serbia, Ukraine and the like, authoritarian leaders in these contexts succeeded in painting oppositions as inexperienced leaders and electoral turnover as destabilizing events, and they buttressed their cases by pointing, for example, to the political and economic disarray (albeit quite exaggerated) in Georgia, Ukraine, and Serbia after their electoral breakthroughs. For all these reasons, not surprisingly, the wave of electoral change in the postcommunist region finally came to an end.

THE BENEFITS OF THE ELECTORAL MODEL

Elections are, in many respects, ideal sites for contesting the power of authoritarian leaders. Authoritarians feel compelled to hold regular – and at least

---

[37] As Mark Beissinger 2002 has termed them.
[38] See Bunce and Wolchik forthcoming, chapter 8.
[39] See Chapters 1 and 11, this volume, and McAdam 1983.

semicompetitive – elections because of international pressures to do so and because of calculations on the part of authoritarian incumbents that they can control the results while using the elections to "smoke out" the opposition, recalibrate patronage networks, and legitimate their rule to both citizens and the international community.[40] Moreover, democracy has become a global norm; elections are central to public understandings of democracy and voting is associated in the public mind with evaluating the regime and making choices (choice, for instance, is the root word for election in many Slavic languages).[41] Elections are also ideal activities for challenging authoritarian rule, because they occur at regular intervals, thereby facilitating planning while asking citizens to become reengaged in politics, but only for a circumscribed period of time. Because of their ties to political participation and regime assessment, moreover, elections are also associated with popular protest cycles.[42]

Beyond these general points about elections are some specific characteristics of the electoral model that make it a good candidate for cross-national application. One is the core argument underlying the model. Thus, its very purpose is to exploit electoral opportunities for turnover in regimes and governing officials by limiting the ability of the regime to control elections while selling the opposition to the citizenry and thereby enhancing their capacity to win power. Therefore, it is a model that is designed to solve three related constraints on democratic change in mixed regimes: the collective action problems that limit the ability and the willingness of citizens to reject authoritarian politics; the collective action problems that limit as well the ability of oppositions to mount effective challenges to the power of authoritarian leaders; and, finally and rarely recognized, the collective action problems built into a sprawling and poorly coordinated international democracy promotion community.[43] In addition, the electoral model has a record of success that dates back to the 1986 election in the Philippines that led to the ouster of Ferdinand Marcos and the Chilean referendum in 1988 that had the surprising outcome of rejecting the "shoo-in" proposal put forward by the Pinochet dictatorship. Such successes are widely recognized for the simple reason that elections make the news, especially if they feature surprising outcomes – largely because they are discrete events that are widely covered by the media and that are easily used by the media to summarize a country's politics and even its likely future directions. Thus, electoral challenges to authoritarian rule have received much international attention, and they have influenced politics in some surprising places. For example, just as protesters in Lebanon in 2005 made repeated references to the Orange Revolution in Ukraine in 2004 and the opposition in Kenya in 2007

---

[40] Schedler 2006 and Lust-Okar 2004 and 2005.
[41] See, especially, Bratton et al. 2004 and Dalton et al. 2007.
[42] Trejo 2004 and McAdam and Tarrow 2009.
[43] Tucker 2007 and Bunce and Wolchik forthcoming, chapters 2 and 9.

named itself after that very revolution, student leaders of a movement opposing the constitutional amendments proposed by Hugo Chávez in Venezuela in
2007 indicated that they had been influenced by the accomplishments of the
student movement in Serbia in 2000.[44]

A final asset of the electoral model, as Mark Beissinger[45] has observed, is
that it is an unusually modular innovation.[46] Most innovations associated with
struggles for political power are unwieldy bundles of activities. By contrast,
the electoral model combines clear premises, clear goals, and a tidy bundle
of tasks and strategies. Indeed, during its travels through the Balkans, the
electoral approach produced a playbook of activities that was easy to share
across national boundaries – though not always easy, we must remember,
to implement, especially in more authoritarian settings where democratizing
elections were attempted later in the wave.

SIMILAR CONDITIONS

Despite its regionwide reach, the fall of communism and communist states from
1987 to 1992 produced a far less "regional" region – that is, a far more diverse
and less connected set of regimes than had been the case during the communist
era. Although correct, this observation ignores several critical points. One is
the rise in this region of an extremely attractive model of simultaneous and
rapid transitions to democracy and capitalism provided by the experiences of
Poland, Hungary, the Czech Republic, and Slovenia in particular.[47] This model,
we must remember, featured rates of economic growth considerably above the
regional norm, stable polities, and membership in the EU and NATO. Just as
important is the one commonality among these trend-setting states: their sharp
break with authoritarian rule through the defeat of the communists and the
introduction of significant economic reforms.[48] In addition, to downplay the
potential of the postcommunist region for diffusion is to ignore the fact that by
far the most common successor to communism in the region was mixed regimes
that straddled democracy and dictatorship.[49] These regimes shared a number
of other characteristics as well. These commonalities included not just a communist past, but also (1) recent statehood or recently regained sovereignty;
(2) earlier rounds of political protests; (3) culturally heterogeneous populations, which illiberal leaders often used to divide and demobilize the liberal
opposition; and (4) generally poor economic performance, rapidly growing
socioeconomic inequalities that contrasted sharply with communist-era patterns, or both. With some variation, this profile describes every country in the

---

[44] Choucair 2005; Rodenbeck 2005; MacFarquhar 2005; Romero 2007; and McKinley 2006.
[45] Beissinger 2007.
[46] And see Tarrow 1998a and 2005 on this argument.
[47] Bunce 2006.
[48] Bunce 2003.
[49] Also see Levitsky and Way 2002 and forthcoming, and Diamond 2002.

region where successful electoral breakthroughs took place, along with some other countries where significant attempts at challenging authoritarian rule also occurred – for example, Armenia, Azerbaijan, and Belarus.

SUBJECTIVE SIMILARITIES

These similarities, however, are objective in nature. Although they enhance the willingness and the ability of citizens and oppositions to model themselves after neighboring countries that had experienced electoral breakthroughs, they hardly guarantee that this will happen, especially given the considerable threats to the status quo posed by electoral turnover in regimes governed by authoritarian leaders. Here, what seems to be critical is an assumption of fundamental similarities on the part of both those who carried out such challenges and those who wanted to follow in their footsteps. In our interviews, we found considerable support for this assumption – which is surprising, given the tendency in this region of the world, as in others, for many citizens to make a sharp distinction between the distinctive politics, history, and culture of their own countries and those of other countries. Moreover, there is a very strong subregional mindset in this part of the world that draws a thick boundary between Eastern and Central Europe on one hand and the Soviet successor states on the other. It is critical to recognize in this regard that the electoral model did not just move across countries, but also "jumped" three key divides within this region – between the Balkans and states located in the northern tier of Eastern and Central Europe (Bulgaria, Romania, and Croatia versus Slovakia) and then between these countries and three Soviet successor states (Georgia, Ukraine, and Kyrgyzstan). This surprising pattern, in combination with the movement of the model from relatively democratic to relatively authoritarian contexts, suggests a more complex story of the assumptions underlying cross-national transmission than one based on a list of objective similarities.

What we discovered in our interviews is that in the minds of many opposition leaders, political activists, and intellectuals, just as communism produced similar contexts, so leaving communism successfully had a common set of preconditions. Although recognizing that certain legacies and situations made the break with communism easier or more difficult, this "to do" list was understood nonetheless to be applicable across the region. Thus, for example, it was widely assumed that a successful break with communism required broad antiregime movements that brought together disparate oppositions and citizens; exploitation of opportunities for change as a result of both divisions among the elites and changes in the international system that weakened authoritarians; progress in reaching out to authoritarian reformers and political "fence-sitters"; and mass mobilization against the regime. It was also assumed that failed challenges preceded successful ones – that is, that valuable lessons could be culled from earlier confrontations with the regime. This understanding of how authoritarianism could be challenged was not just well known to political activists throughout the region and had the additional selling point of having succeeded in bringing down communism; it was also amenable to recycling, with some tinkering, to the new conditions posed by mixed regimes that featured authoritarian leaders but, to varying degrees, competitive elections.

As a result, just as both older activists and newer ones learned from one another, so the dissident past – which, we must remember, was a dissident, but not a distant, past – carried another powerful lesson: the value of sharing strategies across national boundaries when the common motivation was one of defeating dictators in the streets, at the bargaining table, or at the polls.[50] Further facilitating this perception of similarities across both time and space was continuity in dissident communities. For example, some of the very people who had been in Charter 77 in Czechoslovakia during the communist period later participated in the struggle against Meciar in Slovakia and, indeed, against dictators in Croatia and Serbia. Similarly, many of the most important dissidents in Serbia, dating from the 1970s and 1980s and the antiwar movement of the 1990s, played key roles in the defeat of Milosevic.

SELF-INTEREST

We would be remiss in our discussion of perceived similarities if we did not recognize the power of self-interest in nudging oppositions to construct an interpretation of their political situation that was remarkably similar to situations in the neighborhood where dictators were defeated. After all, for the opposition the electoral model held the promise of winning power, rather than continuing to sit on the sidelines alienating publics and bickering with one another about whether to cooperate with the regime, win some seats in parliament and support modest reforms, or boycott elections entirely. Put in stark terms, what opposition would not like to win power; what opposition would not like a playbook that shows how to accomplish that; and, therefore, what opposition would not appreciate precedents showing that these feats could be accomplished? In this sense, self-interest constructed a self-serving perception of common contexts and transferable strategies – even if these perceptions amounted in some cases to wish fulfillment. For example, it can be argued that there is a significant difference between the situations in Slovakia in 1998 and in Kyrgyzstan in 2005, let alone in Armenia and Azerbaijan in the same year.

At the same time, it is important to recognize that self-interest also motivated exporters. They were eager to guarantee the success of their electoral breakthroughs by encouraging similar developments in neighboring countries. This was a particularly powerful argument in the cases of Bulgaria, Romania, Croatia, and Serbia, where shared borders placed a premium on a collective democratic effort. However, these assumptions were sometimes misplaced. Dissident cultures, as in Russia, were not always receptive to the ideas and strategies put forward by successful practitioners of electoral change.[51]

---

[50] Also see Kenney 2002 on solidarity and regional outreach during the 1980s.
[51] See, especially, Mendelson and Gerber 2005.

Regional outreach, moreover, was facilitated by the changing nature of democracy assistance in the region. Membership in the EU in 2004 carried with it a transition for Slovaks, Czechs, Poles, and Hungarians in particular from being the recipients of democracy aid to becoming donors – and donors with not just money and projects, but also considerable expertise in struggling against authoritarianism in the communist, as well as postcommunist, world. The recent decision by the European Union to focus assistance on the countries that neighbor the expanded EU – the European Neighborhood Policy – facilitated this process.[52] As a result, over the past few years casual ties have become more institutionalized, although with the proviso that external assistance was for building democratic capacity, not challenging dictatorial rule.

Thus, postcommunist structural similarities, the self-interest of both senders and receivers, common political goals, similar political opportunities as a result of the tensions between authoritarian politics, yet regular and semicompetitive elections and political habits and networks that dated back in many cases to the communist era all worked together to facilitate the geographical spread of electoral challenges to authoritarian rule. Although these factors hardly guaranteed that the model would remain the same or necessarily produce the same results, they nonetheless rendered this region, as during the communist era, a supportive site for the diffusion of political change. Like the electoral model itself, so similarities among these countries – in structure and in the perceptions of similar conditions among political actors – created opportunities, incentives, and capacity for the successful cross-national diffusion of the electoral model. In this sense, the phrase "similar conditions" oversimplifies what is really a more complex story of an environment unusually conducive to the diffusion of both the electoral model and electoral change. It is not surprising, therefore, that this region stands out, in comparison with others, with respect to both more attempts to defeat dictators at the polls and more success in accomplishing this objective.[53]

AMERICAN ORCHESTRATION?

The previous discussion hinted at the importance of not just local actors in democratizing elections, but also transnational collaborative networks that were involved in all the phases of the innovation process – that is, developing, implementing, and transferring the electoral model. It is precisely this question – the "who" and the "how" of transmission, rather than conditions facilitating transmission – that forces us to confront an earlier argument that casts a shadow on the interpretation of diffusion – that is, the role of powerful international actors orchestrating changes across a group of weaker countries. Vladimir Putin, Hugo Chávez, and the Chinese leadership have argued

---

52 See Fischer 2005.
53 See Bunce and Wolchik 2006b.

in concert that these electoral "revolutions" (as they prefer to characterize them) are the work of the United States, which, in their view, is bent on both exporting its political model to other countries and, as a result, drawing those countries into its political, economic, and security orbit.[54] Thus, even though the electoral model is portable and cross-national conditions similar enough to support transfer, the transmission process can nonetheless be reduced to the United States – in collaboration with, say, the EU and American-based foundations such as the Open Society – orchestrating the defeat of dictators throughout the postcommunist region. From this perspective, for example, even though common strategies for defeating dictators speak to the power of a single player, the lags in adoption merely reflect variations in the electoral calendar.

There is little doubt that the United States has been very supportive of democratization through free and fair elections, has favored the postcommunist region over other parts of the world in its efforts to support democratic development in general, and was a strong and consistent supporter of democratic change in all the countries that experienced electoral breakthroughs.[55] Moreover, a recent statistical study of USAID democracy and governance outlays from 1990 through 2003 has suggested that, of all the forms that American democracy assistance takes, investments in elections have the strongest relationship to improvements in democratic performance.[56] At the very least, therefore, it is fair to conclude that the United States played a role in the electoral breakthroughs that took place in the postcommunist region from 1996 to 2005.

However, it would be mistaken to conclude, at the same time, that these electoral episodes can be reduced to the machinations of the American government and democracy promotion community. The first problem with this interpretation is that the electoral model itself was not invented by the United States. Rather, it developed through trial and error in the Philippines, with the eventual success in defeating Marcos in turn providing important lessons to the Chilean opposition. What is striking about this story is that both these events played a pivotal role in weakening American commitment to support of dictators during the Reagan and then the Bush I administrations. Moreover, the United States has actively promoted free and fair elections throughout the postcommunist region. However, elections are still regularly stolen – as we saw most recently in the 2008 Armenian elections (which did not stop the United States from continuing development assistance through the Millennium Challenge Account, despite the tie of that assistance to democratic performance).

---

[54] See, for example, Herd 2005; Nygren 2005; Silitski 2005b; and, see, especially, the interpretations of the 2005 election in Kyrgyzstan in Kniazev 2005 and the interview with Vladimir Meciar in Fukic and Capin 1999.

[55] See Bunce and Wolchik forthcoming, chapters 2 and 7.

[56] Finkel et al. 2006.

Third, the relationship between American pressures for genuinely competitive elections, on one hand, and electoral breakthroughs, on the other, is uneven. Just as the United States (along with its European allies) has pressed hard for free and fair elections in Belarus, but to no avail, as the 2001 and 2006 presidential elections in that country demonstrate, so it provided limited electoral assistance in the case of Kyrgyzstan in 2005. Moreover, there is little evidence that the United States supported either the coups d'état, albeit with some basis in elections, in both Georgia in 2003 and Kyrgyzstan in 2005.[57] Indeed, in the Georgian case, pressures on Shevardnadze in the summer of 2003 to clean up the Georgian elections that were to take place later in that year were not followed up in any consistent way. Thus, although the United States was very supportive of the defeat of Meciar in 1998, the victory of the opposition in Croatia in 2000, and the defeat of Milosevic in 2000 – and all three cases slide easily from campaigns for free and fair elections to campaigns mounted by the United States, in collaboration with other actors, in support of regime change – American involvement in the other countries where electoral breakthroughs took place was either limited or inconsistent, although the United States was quick to side with those challenging the official results of the Ukrainian election in late 2004.

However, a more general point here requires emphasis. Although democracy promotion has risen on the American foreign policy agenda, especially since the Carter administration (and, thus, before the end of the Cold War), American commitment to the defeat of dictators, to put it mildly, has never been a consistent goal of American foreign policy. This is especially the case when this priority collides with concerns about political stability, oil, and national security, not to mention the practical politics of base placement,[58] and when the United States learned – for instance, from what happened in Palestine – that electoral competition can produce the "wrong" winners.[59] Thus, although the United States may have targeted the defeat of dictators in three of our cases, in the remainder and in most countries it has been far less willing to do so. Instead, the focus has been on supporting civil society and free and fair elections.

TRANSNATIONAL NETWORKS

Another and more fundamental problem with reducing these electoral breakthroughs to the machinations of the United States is that this assertion misrepresents both how American democracy promotion and efforts to challenge dictatorial rule actually work on the ground. For example, American democracy assistance has focused much less on opposition development than on the growth of civil society organizations (although the United States did play a role in helping fragmented oppositions become more cohesive in Slovakia, Croatia,

---

[57] See, especially, Mitchell 2009 and Radnitz 2010.
[58] See, for example, Cooley 2008.
[59] See Cooley 2008; Bunce and Wolchik forthcoming, chapter 7; and Kaush and Youngs 2009.

Serbia, Bulgaria, and Romania). Second, outside groups also played a role, as in the substantial support Russia provided to Viktor Yanukovych in the Ukrainian elections in 2004 – support that by Russian accounts (though hardly endorsed by the Kremlin) far outstripped direct campaign contributions by the United States. Third, American support lacks the consistency and the coordination that is in keeping with the idea of an American "plot" – although this was less true, it is fair to say, for the cases of both Meciar and Milosevic. Finally, both the participants in these elections and members of the American democracy promotion community who were on the ground during these elections all agree that although American support was helpful, it was beneficial only at the margins.[60] Moreover – and again, by all accounts – it was most helpful with respect to identifying strategies for campaigning and getting out the vote; long-term support for civil society; withdrawal of support for illiberal incumbents (though this was relatively slow in coming in Georgia, Ukraine, and Kyrgyzstan); and rapid, as well as quite vocal, critiques of unfair elections (as in Ukraine and Serbia, in particular).[61]

Perhaps the most important qualification is that all the successful electoral breakthroughs were a product of complex transnational collaborations that brought together not just American democracy promoters – and even, in some cases, U.S. ambassadors – but also two other key groups: regional democracy promoters who had carried out their own electoral breakthroughs, and experienced, dedicated local activists willing to work hard, think in new ways, and take personal risks. With the exception of Kyrgyzstan, moreover, these collaborations involved significant planning. Such planning is necessary, given, for example, the details and the difficulties involved in forming effective oppositions that participate in elections, rather than boycott them, and that succeed in mounting effective campaigns; convincing voters to register, vote, support the opposition, and demand that their votes count; winning the election, while gathering the data necessary to demonstrate that victory, and convincing citizens that the opposition tally is more accurate than the "official" version; and, finally, preparing themselves and citizens for the possibility that victory will not lead to taking office. As argued earlier, moreover, there were a number of factors in place that laid the groundwork for such planning – for example, the many similarities, perceived and objective, between the countries where electoral breakthroughs took place and other mixed regimes in the region.

Also important was the existence of practice runs with earlier elections, particularly at the local level (which was critical in Croatia, Serbia, Georgia, and Ukraine); prior rounds of political protest; invigoration of divided and dispirited dissident networks; and even earlier experiences with public opinion polling, election monitoring, and exit polls (all of which, for example, were already in place in Bulgaria, Romania, Slovakia, and Georgia). But when all is said and done, there were international coalitions that were particularly

---

[60] See, especially, Carothers 1999, 2004, 2007a, 2007b; Demes and Forbrig 2007.
[61] See Bunce and Wolchik forthcoming, chapters 3–7.

vibrant, flexible, persistent, and geographically expansive, if not restless, in the postcommunist region. If electoral challenges to authoritarian rule were a moving target, given the timing of elections and changing political opportunities, so were the people who promoted the electoral model as a regionwide political weapon.

Thus, Bulgarian and Romanian activists, emerging from their successful defeat of dictators, then shared their strategies for success with Slovak activists, who then involved themselves, along with the Bulgarians and the Romanians, in both the Croatian and the Serbian elections. Serbian activists, in turn, building on a longer-term relationship between the older Serbian opposition and the Georgian opposition, shared the "secrets of their success" with their Georgian counterparts before the breakthrough election in 2003. The story continues with Ukraine in 2004, and to a lesser extent in Kyrgyzstan in 2005.

The importance of these ties was emphasized repeatedly in the interviews we conducted with American and European democracy promoters and with members of the opposition, political parties, youth organizations, and nongovernmental organization (NGO) leaders in Croatia, Georgia, Serbia, Slovakia, Ukraine, and Washington, D.C.[62] Perhaps the most common theme, however, was the deeply held belief among local activists throughout the region that the struggles for democracy in countries that fell short of democratic standards in the postcommunist region were in large measure the *same* struggle. Illiberal leaders and their allies, it is widely assumed, use similar strategies, in part because of their experiences under communism (where, we must remember, there were also regular elections) and in part because they committed similar transgressions and provided, as a result, similar opportunities for political change.

Thus, for "graduates" of successful electoral revolutions, the assumption is that their experiences are relevant to oppositions in neighboring countries where such revolutions are needed, but have not yet occurred. Just as interesting is a strong belief that they have a responsibility to share their insights about effective strategies for political change through elections and later through other mechanisms, such as assistance in the development of more robust local governments and civil society. The activities of the Pontis Foundation in Bratislava in training democratic activists in Belarus, Ukraine, and even Uzbekistan are cases in point. In part, these activities stem from the belief that their democracy is not safe until it is embedded in a larger democratic community; in part, it reflects a local version of the EU model of spreading democracy (helped by the European Neighborhood Policy); and in part, it is simply a tradition carried on from the communist era, wherein dissidents felt compelled, because they were struggling against the same enemy, to share their ideas and strategies with others in Central and Eastern Europe and the Soviet Union.[63]

---

[62] Also see Meladze 2005; Kandelaki 2005; and Devdariani 2003.
[63] Kenney 2002.

Importers of these strategies, moreover, also assumed that they could and should model themselves after the successful local cases – albeit recognizing the importance of modifications based on local conditions. Again, in the interviews we conducted, it was frequently observed that although local conditions and local struggles were important, knowing that electoral challenges to authoritarian rule had been done elsewhere successfully and learning from participants in these cases about how it was done – in short, both precedent and emulation – were critical to both the decision to try to defeat dictators and in the quality of the implementation of the electoral model. From the vantage point of local activists, therefore, electoral breakthroughs elsewhere contributed to optimism and energy, and, because of shared information, to strategies as well.

CONCLUSIONS

This chapter has argued that diffusion dynamics were in play in the cross-national spread of electoral challenges to authoritarian rule in the postcommunist region from 1996 to 2005. As evidence, we pointed first to the clustering over time and space of these electoral episodes, as well as striking similarities in the innovative strategies oppositions and their domestic and international allies used to defeat dictators. Second, we identified three factors that enabled the cross-national transmission of the model. Just as the model itself was a tidy to-do list that tapped into self-interest and was easy to share among opposition communities (though hard to implement, especially in more authoritarian political settings), so similarities – objective and widely perceived – among "sending" and "receiving" countries facilitated the adoption of the model in a variety of countries. However, central to transmission was the hard work of a transnational network, co-organized by the United States, private foundations based in the West, the European Union (albeit to a lesser extent), regional democracy promoters, and local oppositions and NGOs. It was this community that fashioned, applied, and exported the model.

This case study of one wave of innovation has some implications for our general understanding of diffusion. One is that the claim of diffusion rests not just on new ways of doing things and patterns of adoption, but also on evidence regarding how and why innovations move from one setting to others. This two-stage explanation is important because it allows for the elimination of alternative explanations for clustered commonalities – for example, similar conditions giving rise to similar innovations and powerful external actors forcing similar innovations on less powerful actors. Second, it can be argued that, for subversive innovations, the commitment to choosing among different diffusion models may be misplaced. It may be the case that there are stiff requirements for an innovation that challenges the status quo in a fundamental way to embark on a successful cross-national journey. Thus, where conditions are not so similar or not perceived as being similar by key actors, where the model in question lacks easy transportability, where goals converge, but interests are untapped, and/or where local actors lack both a game plan and international and regional allies, subversive innovations may be easily blocked from leaving their home site. Indeed, this is one explanation of why some attempts to defeat dictators failed in this region and why the electoral wave came to an end, as well as why the revolutions of 1989 that brought down communism were limited in their regional reach.

9

Diffusing the Rumor Bomb

"John Kerry Is French" (i.e., Haughty, Foppish, Elitist, Socialist, Cowardly, and Gay)

Jayson Harsin

Scholars of contentious politics and social movements in sociology and political science (Tarrow 1998a) have used the concept of diffusion to help theorize the spread of a social movement and its claims for change. However, with few exceptions, they have not had much dialogue with communication studies of similar scholarly objects. Recently, scholars such as Ayres (1999) have developed the concept of social movement diffusion with regard to the Internet, although the set of references is limited almost entirely to sociology and political science. Ongoing interdisciplinary work is needed to understand the dynamics of diffusion in a highly complex, ever-changing culture of media convergence. Groundbreaking studies that focused on social movements and "mass media" in the past (Singer 1970) are outdated models for understanding a context in which journalism practices, news business values and markets, and media consumption have seen dramatic changes in the past twenty years, thanks to the arrival of cable, satellite, Internet, cell phones, infotainment, globalization of media businesses, narrowcasting, and downsizing resources in the news business (Harsin 2006). An interdisciplinary conversation may stand to enrich the conceptual development of diffusion.

This chapter builds on the interdisciplinary concept of framing in diffusion processes by bringing recent scholarship and concepts in media studies and political communication into conversation with work on social movements and contentious politics. More specifically, this article will use Henry Jenkins' (2006) concept of "convergence culture" to launch a discussion about the ways that ideas, issues, and beliefs are diffused or circulated in contemporary, highly electronically mediated, cultures.

Another new concept for discussing that circulation will be the "rumor bomb." A case study on the claim that John Kerry "looked French" in the 2004 American presidential campaign will illuminate the importance of these concepts at the intersection of interdisciplinary considerations. In short, this chapter has two main aims: (1) to develop the concept of diffusion in relation to the recent media studies and political communication concepts of "convergence culture" and the"rumor bomb"; and (2) to conduct a case study that determines the diffusion range of the "rumor bomb" that John Kerry was French across multiple media forms, while documenting the types of frames in which the rumor bomb appeared and then theorizing why the rumor was successfully diffused.

LITERATURE REVIEW

Diffusion and Convergence Culture

According to Michaelson (quoted in Ayres 1999), diffusion is "the process by which an innovation (any new idea, activity, or technology) spreads through the population." Diffusion in highly electronically mediated societies such as the United States has been completely transformed with the arrival of what Henry Jenkins has described as "convergence culture."

In *Convergence Culture* (2006), Jenkins describes a "collision" of old and new media forms that, in his considerations of fans, demonstrate an increased agency of cultural consumers vis-à-vis producers. In fact, the new "participatory" aspect of the Internet (evidenced by fan films, for example) has, in his view, produced a culture in which the fan is receiver and producer of media (including old media, through the influence of their own new media productions). Although Jenkins is surely right in his documentation of new media's participatory productive aspects, he fails to consider the ways in which convergence is carefully studied and exploited by shrewd political public relations practitioners, in ways that attempt to both control and produce participation in new media and everyday life. The *type* of participation thus has huge importance for conceptions of participatory democracy (Barber 1984).

Convergence of media business, technological, cultural, and political phenomena has produced an American political culture and citizenship that has transformed older practices of journalism, political discourse, and citizens' interventions (Harsin 2006; Gans 2003; Jamieson 1988). This convergence of factors includes the news media's growing valorization of tabloidization and infotainment and audiences' consumption of it, and the importance and effects of speed on news practices, because of market competition; influence of the Internet (especially blogs); the breakdown of traditional news gatekeeping; the fragmentation of mediated political discourse into sound bites on the news, and the tailoring of political messages to these constraints of the news format; and the twentieth-century drive for technocratization of mass democracies, accompanied by the infiltration of political communication by public relations, itself modeled on the strategies and successes of wartime propaganda. These convergences are predominant in the United States but are spreading elsewhere in conjunction with the commercialization and concentration of a global media system (Ewen 1998; Thussu 1998; Swanson 2004; McNair 2006).

Thus, at least three kinds of convergence culture are under consideration here. First, in terms of cultures of media consumption and production, convergence culture refers to the way consumers of media are also producers of media, and there exists a two-way or mutual influence in terms of content and production. This is closest to the original formulation by Jenkins, although he considered its impact on fans, consumers, and traditional producers of media content, not politics and diffusion of ideas and movements. A second kind of convergence culture involves the complex overlapping or convergence of multiple phenomena mentioned previously: speed and transitoriness in news, consumer goods, attention, movement of people and ideas; market values determining "old media" (e.g., TV and newspapers), including news or infotainment; Internet content and agendas affecting the content and agendas of old news and media products; and the professionalization or technocratization of mainstream politics. A close relative of these overlaps is the increasing connection between politics and entertainment, in which competition and voting seem to mirror entertainment practices such as reality television (Corner 2003). Similarly, significant numbers of young Americans report that they receive most of their news from late-night comedy shows, such as Jay Leno, *The Daily Show*, or *The Colbert Report*. There is also evidence that news consumption for many Americans is not limited to one media form, but moves across the different forms of convergence culture, from cable news to comedy shows, blogs, and newspapers (Pew Center 2008).

The Rumor Bomb

Within this news and political culture of speed, word compression, and infotainment, and the manipulation of their convergence by astute public relations gurus and political actors, a crisis of verification has ensued. The relationship between tenuous claims and their diffusion points to a common strategy in contemporary – especially American – political practice: the rumor bomb.

As I use the term,[1] rumor bombs include the following characteristics:

1) *A crisis of verification.*

A crisis of verification is perhaps the most salient and politically dangerous aspect of rumor. Berenson (1952) defines rumor as a kind of persuasive message involving a proposition that lacks "secure standards of evidence" (in Pendleton 1998). Something major may not be the case. An official source or a leak asserts something is the case, but the reporter is unable to verify the claim through direct observation or through other reliable sources, in accordance with professional rules of reporting and codes of ethics (Mencher 2000: 42–5, 755–57), but for market value reasons, the statement or story is published anyway. Another aspect to the crisis of verification comes through claims that are deliberately

---

[1] The concept's definition is up for grabs. The scholarship on rumor across sociology, psychology, and communication studies agrees on very little (Berenson 1952; Pendleton 1998; Bordia and Difonzo 2004).

ambiguous; they could be verified in a way that depends on one's interpretation of the claim. Take, for instance, the widely circulated claim
by President George W. Bush that "[t]here's no question that Saddam
Hussein had al Qaeda ties" (Bush 2003). What does "ties" mean here?
Clearly some took it to mean that Hussein had a close working relationship with al Qaeda and, thanks to other such statements, even had a
hand in 9/11. This is impossible to verify until the terms are defined. So
the rumor is diffused by mainstream news and the Internet alike, with
serious repercussions in public life and foreign policy.

2) *A context of public uncertainty or anxiety about a political group, figure, or cause, which the rumor bomb overcomes or transfers onto an
opponent.*
The United States is shocked and anxious after the 9/11 attacks. Why
did they happen? Is the U.S. government in any way to blame? Is there
a historical context of the problem? The rumor bomb that there was an
Iraq–al Qaeda "link" worked to dispel anxiety about government leadership, responsibility, and a plan for reestablishing security via preemptive
war against a clearly identifiable (attackable) enemy.

3) *A clearly partisan source, even if an anonymous source (in, for example,
the Blair, Clinton, Bush, and Sarkozy governments), which seeks to profit
politically from the rumor bomb's diffusion.*
The Swift Boat Veterans for Truth claimed that John Kerry lied about his
war record. They claimed they were a nonpartisan group. However, a
major Republican donor was funding them, a major Republican lawyer
was defending them, and a major Republican communications consul-
tant designed their ads (Media Matters for America 2004). Witness also
how Scott McClellan, former press secretary to President Bush, has publicly stated that Bush misled the American people (and the world) about
the threat of Iraq (Gonyea 2008).

4) *A rapid diffusion of a statement (even an image) via highly developed
electronically mediated societies where news travels quickly.*
As will be discussed shortly in the case study, a report in the *New York
Times* that a Bush adviser said Kerry was French set the agenda for
other major newspapers, TV news programs, and websites, in some cases
within a few hours of the report.

The rumor bomb, then, is a particular form of diffusion, "the process
by which an innovation (any new idea, activity, or technology) spreads
through the population" (Michaelson in Ayres 1999). Rumor bombs
have been documented as a staple of contemporary global media systems,
and are thus not limited to American media and politics (Harsin 2008).

Although rumor bombs are a global phenomenon, the post-9/11 American
mediated political culture has been particularly marked by a series of rumor
bombs, including Iraq–al Qaeda ties, weapons of mass destruction in Iraq, and
covert transportations of those weapons to Syria. The campaign leading to

the 2004 presidential election was also rife with rumor bombs. Looking back on the campaign on election day, *Washington Post* columnist Howard Kurtz noted: "Some of these episodes were harmless distractions (unless, like former AP reporter Polier, you were hounded by journalists over a false Internet rumor that made its way into the newspapers). But in other cases, the campaign was hijacked by sidebar stories that the media pumped up or twisted out of shape" (Kurtz 2004). In a scandalous CBS report that turned out to be based on forged documents, the Bush family was said to have influenced a makeover of the President's Air National Guard service, including an instance in which he allegedly failed to show up for a physical exam.

But Kerry was largely on the receiving end of the rumor bombs. The Swift Boat Veterans for Truth disputed the truthfulness of the event for which Kerry received military decorations in Vietnam, drawing widespread news attention until, after three weeks of ads and several months of e-rumors in circulation, it was reported that one of the Swift Boat accusers, Al French, had lied about being an eyewitness, and another accuser's own navy record disputed his own recollection of the events (www.factcheck.org/article231.html; www.truthorfiction.com/rumors/k/kerry-swiftboats.htm). In addition, in February 2004 the online Drudge Report claimed that Kerry had had an affair with an intern, which the intern and Kerry then denied. But it was back in the spring of 2003 that one of the most durably vexing rumors of the campaign was launched against Kerry: He was said to be French-looking. Unlike some of the other rumors, this one was difficult to ignore, deny, or refute. And unlike some of the other rumors, such as the Swift Boat Veterans claims or the Kerry-intern-affair rumor, the "Kerry is French" rumor was not limited to a short time frame but appeared off and on from April 2003 through the election. At first glance the claim may seem preposterous, but it is also not clear what exactly the statement means. That was part of its circulatory success.

It is this rumor episode, "John Kerry is French," that I wish to analyze in this chapter. To understand why it would be politically effective to call John Kerry "French," I will need to revisit the turbulent Franco-American relations around the invasion of Iraq in the winter of 2003, which becomes a context for some important coverage of the 2004 American presidential election. Thus, the following study documents the rhetorical construction of national identities via important news frames and circulation (Americanness and Frenchness), which then becomes the cultural context for employing a rumor bomb as a political weapon: the rumor that John Kerry is French. This cultural–historical (and political–economic) contextualization of the frames that composed the rumor bomb that Kerry is French is also an answer to calls for frame analysis to be more nuanced by exploring the cultural contexts and power relationships that surround instances of framing (Carragee and Roefs 2004). I view the Kerry rumor as evidence of ongoing trends in anti-deliberative American spectacular democracy (Harsin 2006), avoiding policy debate while endeavoring to construct public opinion (as it commonly appears as a statistic in news) and manage political perception. In addition, the study shows how rumors facilitate political branding as products of astute, if ruthless, readings and manipulations of the intermedia agenda-setting opportunities and changing old news media values toward tabloidization. Finally, the thick description of this rumor's circulation on major cable and mainstream news channels, newspapers, and Internet sites shows how a rumor bomb may create an intermedia discourse about a topic such as the war in Iraq or the suitability of a candidate for president. Thus, I argue that episodes such as the one analyzed here point toward the need for interdisciplinary political communication studies to politicize speed, as Paul Virilio counsels, but also to repoliticize authorship, intention, content, and style in a world in which techniques of branding sell not just clothing, but also news, presidents, values, and wars.

"F" the French[2]: On the Construction of *l'Americainicité*

To understand the French Kerry rumor as a political strategy, one must go back to the 2003 deliberations over the American proposal to invade Iraq. In the second week of March 2003, more than two months after Germany and France announced they would oppose a U.S.-led invasion of Iraq in the UN, after images of Americans with "Invade France" posters at pro-war rallies and others pouring French wine into gutters, two congressional representatives, apparently outraged at France's opposition to a U.S. invasion of Iraq, moved to change the name of French fries to "freedom fries" in the House cafeteria. On a similar note, Florida congresswoman Ginny Brown-Waite sponsored House Resolution 1265: the American Hero Act of 2003. The resolution called for the removal of all American servicemen's remains from cemeteries in France and their relocation to the United States. Explaining her reasoning for the bill, Brown-Waite said, "France has consistently turned its back on the United States. . . . They forget, if it weren't for us they would be speaking German today" (Reid 2003). The bill never went anywhere, but the symbolic gesture was noticed by journalists around the world.[3] Brown-Waite was reelected with 64 percent of the vote in 2004. However, it is not clear to what degree these media representations and public speech reflect widespread feeling or construct it.

An interview with French President Jacques Chirac sheds more light on the role the media played in constructing a Franco-American rivalry, fueling American anti-French public opinion, and destroying a more careful consideration of the arguments for and against going to war in Iraq. In this arguably

---

2 "F" refers to the expletive "fuck," if you'll pardon my French; this was made the title of a website and a T-shirt slogan.

3 A LexisNexis search of major U.S. newspapers turns up sixty articles about her bill from mid-March to May 1, 2003. In Europe, the story attracted attention in France, Spain, Germany, and Portugal. The wire services, such as Agence France Presse, United Press International, and the Associated Press, extended its reach across every continent (LexisNexis search, December 12, 2005).

Francophobic media culture, Chirac went on the popular CBS TV news-magazine *60 Minutes* on March 16, 2003, supposedly to explain his case to the American people. Journalist Christiane Amanpour, instead of asking Chirac careful questions about his argument against an invasion, tried to appeal to his shame for not boarding the war bandwagon. "Mr. President," said Amanpour, "you know that since you have taken the position you have there has been *a massive backlash* in the United States at *almost every level of society*" (my emphasis). Amanpour failed to explain what the "position" was to which she was referring, as if it were known to viewers beyond the simple knowledge that Chirac opposed an invasion of Iraq. By the end of the interview, she had associated Chirac with Hussein on the basis of rumor.

The news frenzy about France's opposition to the United States and about Americans' disgust with France also fit into a long-standing historical discourse of Francophobia. When France is used as a binary opposition for U.S. identity, it has been historically documented as looking like this, with a few more recent oppositions[4]:

France/French	United States/Americans
Strict, even policed, cultural practices	Open cultural practices define the melting pot
Colonizers	Rebelled against colonialism
Lascivious, hypersexual, Pepe le Pew	Well-behaved, respectful, privately sexual
Extravagant, corrupted, foppish	Sparing or modest
Formal, unrelaxed	Relaxed
Cowardly	Brave
Effete/homosexual	Masculine
Delusions of grandeur, but Old World passé	Actually potent, New World Order
Lecherous	Gentlemanly
Antiglobalization, backward	Proglobalization, forward-looking
Communists/socialists	Capitalist democrats
Freedom-hating, indicated by excess of government and social rules, customs, and laws	Open and free
Foul-smelling	Clean
Arrogant, rude	Modest, friendly
Anti-Semitic	Multicultural and accepting
Anti-American	American
Speak French	Speak Spanish
Kerry: Arrogant, foppish, effete, elitist	**Bush:** Cowboy/regular guy, democratic, strong

---

[4] These categories are based on Vaissy (2003) and my own survey of content stereotypes across hundreds of mainstream American newspapers, TV shows, and websites in 2003.

These oppositions are portrayed to frightening perfection in the following *Saturday Night Live* parody of a French tourism ad, which aired less than a year before the Bush–Chirac fallout.

France: rolling country sides, sprawling vineyards, quaint cafes. France: home to the world's greatest painters, chefs, and anti-Semites. The French: cowardly, yet opinionated; arrogant, yet foul-smelling; anti-Israel, anti-American, and, of course, as always, Jew-hating. Paris: the city of whores, dog feces on every corner, and effete men yelling anti-Semitic remarks at children. The real crème de la crème of world culture. With all that's going on in the world, isn't it about time we got back to hating the French?
(http://snltranscripts.jt.org/01/01rfrance.phtml)[5]

All these characteristics form the durable clichés of the American discourse of Francophobia. Furthermore, this attempted parody of a French tourism ad is a window into supposed values that were circulating in contemporary American culture. These opinions that contribute to the binary oppositions integral to American national identity have been well documented (Vaissy 2003). It was not uncommon for these oppositions to appear almost systematically in American popular news media in 2003 and 2004. To understand how Kerry was branded French and how affective transfers were executed and attachments invited, it is important to understand the cultural context that I have begun to describe through the example of the *Saturday Night Live* video, late night comedy, Internet sites, and TV and print news. It is also helpful to consider the Bush administration's international diplomatic situation at the time.

That situation was marked by the Bush administration's diplomatic failures in the UN and with Turkey, among others.[6] The Bush administration presented these events in a paranoid frame, which the media willingly took up as a good drama. France became the scapegoat for this damaged American mind. Strategically, France became a useful tool to discredit the war opposition (some half of the U.S. population) by branding it French and un-American (Vaissy 2003). Similarly, John Kerry's loose "connections" to France became a perfect receptacle for Bush administration foreign and domestic policy failures. Many (more than 50 percent in February 2004 [Morin and Milbank 2004]) believed Bush lied about weapons of mass destruction and al Qaeda–Iraq links. But no matter, because this conspiratorial reaction could be reversed or redirected at the persecutor, the Frenchman John Kerry. Just as France stood in for Germany and Russia and others in the world, Kerry could stand in for all the supposedly anti-American Americans who protested the war. The play of images and attachments was ripe: after all, although Kerry was a decorated veteran, he was also an outspoken protestor of the Vietnam War. But now, to protest the war was French – that is, treason. Thus, the "Kerry is French" rumor bomb can be seen to serve several aims: (1) it would avoid rational critical debate

---

[5] Retrieved September 21, 2006.
[6] On the diplomatic failures with Turkey, for example, see www.usatoday.com/news/world/iraq/2003–03–16–military-usat_x.htm.

about Iraq, reasons for going to war, and errors in planning and executing the campaign in Iraq by redirecting emotional attention to the discourse of French cowardice and betrayal at the outset of the war, which reframed support of the war as a matter of patriotism; (2) by linking Kerry to France and the discourse of French military ineptitude and cowardice, it sought to harm John Kerry's ostensible advantage over George Bush in terms of Kerry's military heroism; (3) related to the attempt to undermine Kerry's heroic military ethos, it sought to undermine simultaneously Kerry's ability to be a commander in chief who could make decisions in the national interest, which it was said would take a backseat to what was good for Europe and France, which circled back to French military and economic ineptitude; and finally, (4) it sought to undermine Kerry's masculinity proffered by war heroism by drawing on the stereotype that French men were effete, which was to say, more or less homosexual. The news media (old and new) happily enabled the diffusion of these rhetorical ploys.

ORIGINS AND CIRCULATION OF THE FRENCH KERRY RUMOR BOMB

It was in this hyperreal Francophobic cultural climate that the Bush administration decided to launch the rumor/slur that John Kerry was French. It appears to have begun in the same way that other forms of increasingly strategic rumors begin: in the form of a leak from an anonymous source. In the midst of this anti-French frenzy, shrewd Bush strategists looked toward the fast approaching reelection campaign and saw an opportunity to discredit the most likely opponent.[7] The fact that a Bush administration official is attributed with the characterization helps distinguish the rumor bomb concept from simple rumors. A rumor bomb is first of all a political strategy to discredit, distract, or both by making claims that are difficult to immediately verify or refute, which themselves are designed to play into new tabloidization values of news organizations and consumers. There is no question that the Bush administration official had a particular interest in the Democratic primary when he or she was asked to comment on the candidates. Thus began the rumor bomb of the French John Kerry.

On April 22, 2003, the *New York Times* reported that an anonymous source in the Bush administration had observed that Democratic presidential candidate John Kerry had a distinctive look; in fact, he said, "he looks French." Other major newspapers followed. According to LexisNexis, thirteen national newspapers (including the *New York Times, Washington Post, Boston Globe,* and *USA Today*) had put the rumor bomb on their agendas. Soon the Internet was abuzz with talk about "the French-looking" John Kerry. An Internet search of "April 23, 2003" (and the following few days), "Kerry," and "French," gives an illustration of its diffusion, from abcnews.com to "Betsy's Blog."

[7] In April 2003, John Kerry had a narrow lead over Howard Dean in New Hampshire (www.prospect.org/webfeatures/2003/05/franke-ruta-g-05-08.html).

Other conservatives complicated the strategically ambiguous claim, giving it a number of twists. One that stuck most was perhaps that of *Wall Street Journal* columnist James Taranto who, just two days after the leak, described Kerry as the "haughty, French-looking, Massachusetts Democrat." He repeated this mantra regularly on the *Wall Street Journal*'s online opinion page. As recently as November 2007, if one searched the online *WSJ* Opinion Journal archives, one found more than two hundred editorials in which the phrase was repeated. What is fascinating, perhaps, from the perspective of diffusion and agenda-setting is that strategic phrases that mean nothing precisely but have great affective power begin with conservative sources in the Bush administration, in this case the *Wall Street Journal* and the *Washington Times*, but then they are taken up by more legitimate news organizations and offered to the rumor mill. Two months after the rumor's launch, and writing about what was to come in the following months in the campaign, *Newsweek* magazine's editor, Eleanor Clift, demonstrated uncanny prescience. "Remember the anonymous Bush strategist quoted some months ago suggesting Sen. John Kerry looks French," Clift recalled. "There will be two GOP campaigns: the flag-waving one on the surface that Bush is involved with, and then the sub-rosa campaign waged by surrogates that will be less gentlemanly" (June 20, 2003). Indeed, the repetition of the rumor bomb by columnists, congressional allies, and pundits in new and old media forms allowed it broad diffusion.

METHOD

The second half of this chapter is a study addressing the following research questions:

1) How wide was the diffusion area of the content "John Kerry is French" across multiple news media forms?
2) What frames were used to circulate the claim that Kerry was French?
3) In what ways did the French frame(s) interweave with other circulating frames in the broader media culture's campaign discourse?

The study begins with a content analysis of mainstream American news media, print and TV, with the coding "John Kerry" and "French." The first content analysis is complemented by a content analysis of the same terms on the Internet, using Google to provide a map of the rumor bomb's diffusion. Next, a frame analysis was conducted to understand in what way "French" was framed, and thus what it meant to be Kerry and French in these articles and newscasts.

Framing as a concept has been notoriously loose across the social sciences, but as I use it here it reflects definitions by Gitlin (1980) and Entman (1993). Gitlin and Entman both emphasize the subjective way events and people are contextualized with "persistent patterns of cognition, interpretation, and presentation, of selection, emphasis, and exclusion" (Gitlin 1980: 6–7). Journalists and editors thus organize verbal and visual discourse, and thus present information in a way that invites the receiver to process it on the producer's terms of "selection, emphasis, and presentation." But such presentation includes "tacit theories about what exists, what happens, and what matters." Political-communication scholars such as Robert Entman (1993) and cognitive linguists such as George Lakoff (2004; Lakoff and Johnson 1980) have also stressed the importance of frames for fixing the terms for debating problems and solutions to, as well as moral judgments of, important public issues. In the case of campaign discourse, framing can also set terms for evaluating candidates, and such selection and presentation of candidates can take precious attention away from their policy proposals. Thus, framing is studied in this chapter for its power to emphasize John Kerry's competence for the presidency as a matter of his alleged Frenchness, thus inviting viewers and readers to see him that way instead of as someone, for example, whose identity could be based on his health care, environmental, and foreign policy proposals. Relatedly, it may suggest that such proposals be viewed through his alleged Frenchness, even if it does not mention such proposals.

The study uses an intensive keyword "content" search of hundreds of American daily newspapers, magazines, TV news scripts, wire releases, late night comedy routines, and Internet sites and discussion, on LexisNexis and Google to analyze the pervasive intermedia discourse "John Kerry is French" between April 1, 2003 (the first documented occurrence of the rumor bomb was April 22, 2003) and November 4, 2004, the end of the election campaign. On Lexis-Nexis only the headlines and first paragraphs for keywords "French" and "Kerry" were searched, as a compromise to the unmanageable findings of more than three thousand stories retrieved in a "full text" search. Focusing on the headlines and first paragraphs allows a close reading of all the stories, instead of a study based on sampling methods that force the researcher to skip some stories in the set or population. As a sample of the thousands of "full text" articles, however, it allows one to see the frames for stories that foregrounded the French rumor bomb, instead of mentioning it in passing.

FINDINGS ON THE FRENCH KERRY RUMOR

First, there were eighty major newspaper stories in 2003 that dealt with the rumor bomb that John Kerry was French. It appears that much of the talk about Kerry's alleged Frenchness began on the Internet and was later taken up by the mainstream traditional news organizations. Coverage was also helped by major reiterations from the Bush administration, their surrogates in Congress, and on the radio. Although the anti-French rhetoric did not die down much before 2004, characterizations of Kerry as French did seem to subside a bit until January, and then picked back up as the election approached in 2004. I have classified the TV and print news, wire, magazine, Internet, and late night comedy data into five classes or frames of "French connections," which served as dubious forms of evidence (indexical signifiers) to brand Kerry negatively:

(1) speaks French; (2) relatives or French family; (3) French public opinion – "France loves Kerry!"; (4) looks French, or is "French-looking," often qualified by "haughty" or "socialist"; and (5) a miscellaneous class of assertions, such as "seems French," "has French ideas" (occasionally supported through an analogy of France's tax system to that which Kerry allegedly proposed), "seems too French," "acts French," "would say '*bonjour*.'" Some texts contained all five classes of "connections."

Speaks French

Roughly 15 percent of the texts I examined discussed Kerry's Frenchness in terms of his ability to speak fluent French, or by stressing that he and his wife spoke French. When, in March 2004, Fox News show host John Gibson asked his guest if Republicans would be able to effectively make John Kerry French, his guest responded, "They can if they want." Why? Gibson asked. "Because Kerry speaks French."

Other times, the strategy seemed to be to follow tabloid genres that follow celebrities into their romantic lives. It was reported that Kerry whispered French into the ear of his wife, Teresa Heinz Kerry, on their first date. Other times, it was enough to simply roll a tape of Kerry speaking French – the French kiss of death.

Interestingly, it did not seem to matter that George W. Bush spoke Spanish to Cuban- and Mexican-American audiences. Or, rather, it mattered in the way it could slide into an already existing American binary identity construction against France. Haughty France and its language was transferred to Kerry, and democratic populist (i.e., American) Spanish was transferred to Bush. The contradiction that many Republicans have at times supported English-only legislation and defined themselves against an influx of their southern neighbors didn't seem to matter. French was an elitist, effete, East-Coast second language. Mexican Spanish was the language of the new American proletariat. It magically trumped Bush's own elitist background and fit nicely with his appeals to ordinariness, to being a common man, indexed by his grammatical ineptitude and malapropisms (nucular, misunderestimating, strategery). To attend to grammar was elitist, liberal, effete, French. As with the entire French connection rumor, a claim to masculinity underpinned it. Real men are men of action, not words. The president is a man of his word, not words.

Family Connections

Another popular device in the Frenchification of John Kerry was the rumor bomb that he was French by blood or nationality. These suggestions were often absurd, as they were ambiguous about Kerry's birthplace, even though by U.S. law, one cannot run for president of the United States unless one is born there. Nevertheless, American networks would send correspondents on expensive trips to Bretagne to report from St. Brieuc, where Kerry's father once owned a home and where Kerry was reputed to have spent summers in his youth. The usual coverage would move from acknowledging the rumor of Kerry's French connection against the onsite backdrop in Bretagne, then appear to provide evidence for the rumor, noting that Kerry spoke fluent French and lived there at times, and would end with interviews with French citizens who expressed their unbridled enthusiasm for his presidential bid. In one "Fox Special Report with Brit Hume" (February 24, 2004), correspondent Greg Palkot reported from Saint Brieuc, France: "John Kerry country. Huh? That's right. Kerry spent summers here as a boy, staying in the house of his grandfather." Palkot explained that one of the grandfather's daughters married a Frenchman, producing Kerry's first cousin Brice LaLonde. Palkot ended by connecting St. Brieuc to World War II and American sacrifices for France: "Nazi troops occupied the town. American troops liberated the town. Three U.S. soldiers killed here are remembered," Palkot eulogized. Not only is it never explained what this could possibly have to do with debates over policy or presidential leadership, but it also repeats the most common emotional appeal to support Bush's indignation toward Chirac: the shame of betrayal after the debt of World War II. The frame for this story becomes one of melodramatic betrayal, in the context of the Iraq War.

Family connections stories accounted for a little more than 10 percent of the total French connections, but I just demonstrated that this category also often overlapped with the others.

French Public Opinion

The third major category of Kerry's French connection consisted of how popular Kerry was in France. Given the American cultural climate, the audience could make the inference without much help: Popular in France means anti-American. Electing Kerry would be like committing treason. This sort of story is closely related to the French relatives–bloodline connection. Who would want to be popular with the French, who are being characterized as traitorous and cowardly? For example, Fox News host John Gibson, of *The Big Story with John Gibson*, said of a *Le Figaro* poll, taken October 15, 2004, "If the French could vote, 72 percent would vote for John Kerry. Why is it the French are so angry with the United States?" (Gibson 2004). Here, Kerry is linked with the oft-repeated rumor that France opposes the United States because it hates or is angry with the United States for inscrutable reasons. In fact, Chirac told Amanpour in March 2003 that he opposed the war out of concern for a good friend. A local TV station's news script for March 17, 2004 read: "Drudge Report [a much frequented political news blog] cites French going wild for Kerry.... Stay tuned to see one possible explanation for why President Bush is so misunderstood by the French. [commercial break] John Kerry is as popular in France as cheese." These stories accounted for roughly 15 percent of the texts I examined.

Looks French – Haughty or Socialist

Another 16 percent of the stories analyzed simply treated Kerry as visual–biological evidence for Frenchness, or, alternately, they suggested he was French through the alleged French ideas he was said to have. This is a convenient, effective form of ambiguous rumor. When people say "Kerry looks French," what do they mean? Do they mean there is a kind of phenotype, suggesting one is in the presence of a racial theory? Do they mean he looks French figuratively? Do they mean he has a *cultural* disposition they perceive as essentially French? In this way the cultural – and the racial – essentially seemed to mutually reinforce one another in their ambiguity. The binary oppositions we have already visited suggest a mythical French identity, behavior, and thoughts by default, as if it is in the blood. But if one is not by blood French, perhaps one has been corrupted by French culture? This was the original White House leak in the spring of 2003. Kerry, someone said, "looked French." This was soon qualified, as mentioned earlier, by pundits such as James Tarantano, to John Kerry, the "haughty, French-looking Massachusetts senator," or by Rep. Tom DeLay, who referred to Kerry as "the socialist French-looking senator from Massachusetts." Republican Senator Gordon Smith (OR) told the *Los Angeles Times* (Wallsten and Barabak 2004), "It's not John Kerry's fault that he looks French. But it is his fault that he wants us to pursue policies that have us act like the French. He advocates all kinds of additional socialism at home, appeasement abroad, and what that means is weakness in the future." This one at least provided support for the claim, though the grounds beg further elaboration. What policies exactly are "socialist?" Clearly, this repeats the old binary clichés of the cowardly/appeasing French, the radical socialist/communist French, and possibly even effete French. These accounted for 16 percent of the texts I analyzed.

Miscellaneous: Foreign Policy Puppet of France and Gay

This sprawling category accounted for 24 percent of the texts analyzed. Their strongest repetition was of military ineptitude or homosexuality as indexically French. Campaigning in Pennsylvania on October 2, 2004, Bush told reporters that if elected, "Kerry would subject American troops to 'a veto from countries like France.'" In the context of the last two years of heavy French bashing, the inference for many was likely that Kerry would weaken the country by making it militarily inept and deferential to France or Europe; he would be soft on terrorism, supposedly like France. At the Republican national convention, Democratic party turncoat Zell Miller proclaimed, "Kerry would let Paris decide when America needs defending." Sometimes, the connection between Kerry, the French, and French opposition to the U.S. invasion of Iraq was made explicit. On May 19, 2004, CNN anchor Wolf Blitzer appeared on Judy Woodruff's *Inside Politics* to pronounce, "One word that usually gets Republican tongues wagging about John Kerry is the word French. The French, of course, among other things helped to strain the alliance between the United States and its European allies over the war in Iraq. John Kerry's French connections have made him the target of some ribbings."

Another story that was part of a larger assault on Kerry's masculinity was the insistence that Kerry's Frenchness betrayed some kind of effeteness, or even homosexuality. "Whit Ayres, a Republican strategist," told a reporter that "Kerry's Francophilia 'plays into this stereotype of the effete, French-speaking, northeastern Massachusetts liberal elitist. The fact that his position on Iraq seems reasonably close to that of [French president] Jacques Chirac is just icing on the cake'" (Milligan 2004). Some analyses claimed that an important aspect of the campaign was a war to claim hegemonic masculinity and thereby brand the opponent as deficient in masculinity. The *New York Times* featured a story on May 23, 2004 titled "Kerry's Gender Gap: Yes, Democrats Can Win (Some) White Male Voters." That story claimed that Kerry had a problem getting white males to identify with him. He was seen as elite and effete. "Up to now, Mr. Kerry has relied on cosmetic changes," the article said. "When Republicans accused him of being aloof, liberal and, worst of all, looking French, he conspicuously peppered his speeches with terms like 'fight' and 'strength' and, of course, 'bring it on.'" Kerry further tried to perform his masculinity by riding a motorcycle to his appearance on the *Tonight Show*, having himself filmed while hunting, and emphasizing his war record in his ads. But the effete French brand pursued him into the election's settled dust. One of the most memorable rumor bombs dropped on Kerry's masculinity came from Fox News. Fox News correspondent Carl Cameron (anonymously) posted a story titled "The Metrosexual and the Cowboy" to the Fox News website. Cameron invented quotes of Kerry asking his supporters at a Tampa Bay gathering, "Didn't my nails and cuticles look great? What a good debate" ("Fox Posts Reporter's Kerry Spoof on Website" 2004). A Fox spokesman apologized for the incident, saying it was written "in jest," although it had no ironic signal that it was "fake news."

The mainstream news media steered clear of explicit statements of the homosexuality rumor, but the Internet was full of it (see, for example, the viral Internet video "Kerry Loves Edwards," "Kerry and Edwards in Love," or "Kerry and Edwards are gay," which was especially prominent on kerrysucks.com, a site that is no longer active in 2009 at the time of this writing). Indeed, this theme was consistent with portrayals of Kerry at the Republican National Convention, where a video mockingly represented Kerry as a French poodle named Fifi Kerry who debated the president's dog Barney. The appeal to homophobia was so obvious to some in the media that the *New York Times'* Frank Rich responded with a column (September 5, 2004) titled "How Kerry Became a Girlie Man." The French slur was, he said, "code for faggy." As mentioned above, the clear anchoring of Frenchness in military ineptitude, cowardice, and even homosexuality had the potential to undermine Kerry's seeming masculine credibility, and military leadership and heroism. If George W. Bush was dogged by rumors of dodging military duty in the Air National Guard, at least he wasn't gay (which, of course, Kerry sought to counter in his outing of Vice President Cheney's daughter as a lesbian).

Internet and Rumor Convergence

As mentioned earlier with regard to the "Kerry is effete or gay" rumor, the Internet works as both old media agenda setter and old media rediffuser at different times in a complicated dynamic. To further investigate the new-old media convergence around the rumor bombs, I complemented my LexisNexis searches by Google searches[8] for Kerry's French connection. In general, those searches revealed that the French connection rumor circulated widely on the Internet in all the forms I found in the mainstream news media. A search of "'John Kerry' and French" produced 1,790,000 hits. The set of terms "Kerry 'French-looking' (anonymous White House figure) April 2003" produced 24,200 hits. "Kerry and 'French-looking Massachusetts Democrat'" produced only 605 hits, but 186 hits alone registered on the influential *Wall Street Journal*'s Opinion website. The terms "Kerry and 'French Connection'" produced 15,900 hits. But when one searched "'John Kerry' and Haughty" the result leapt up to 40,600. The phrase "Kerry is gay" produced 216 hits. But "'John Kerry' and effete" produced 28,200. "Kerry and Edwards in love" produced 522. Perhaps an indicator of how Internet speech can connect to and generate speech in other forms and places, the terms "'John Kerry' and French and T-shirt and stickers" produced a significant 171,000 hits.

Unfortunately, the form of Internet speech known as the viral chain message was unable to be included in this study. But a mainstream news story on the eve of the election provides some insight into how such forms contributed to the rumor bomb's diffusion within a culture of media convergence. On November 2, 2004, United Press International's Jean Kropowski wrote of a last-day effort by the Republican National Committee to win votes through an e-mail message that quoted the French daily *Le Monde* as endorsing John Kerry for president. The message encouraged the reader to "send this to a friend" (clearly a very different kind of participatory culture of convergence than the one described by Jenkins).

Overall, these Internet texts range from the do-it-yourself (such as the selection of allegedly homoerotic photographs of Kerry and Edwards in a viral video slide show put to Marvin Gaye's "Sexual Healing," which appeared on YouTube and other video-hosting sites and was embedded in hundreds, perhaps thousands, of blogs) to the very center of resource-rich, institutional electoral politics (the Republican National Committee's election day mass e-mail). Speaking of the "Kerry and Edwards are gay" rumor bomb, Salon.com's Eric Boehlert (2004) nicely summed up the volatile dynamic between old and new media, professional and everyday political actors, tabloidization and diffusion: "It's a creepy GOP talking point first floated by Matt Drudge [online]

---

8 Search results retrieved September 15, 2006.

and then hammered with typical subtlety by the *Washington Times*' right-wing editor-in-chief, Wesley Pruden. For some reason, the AP took the bait and decided the angle was newsworthy." Obviously, many of the sites listed in these "hits" do not have the number of readers or viewers that some of the newspapers and TV news broadcasts had. But they do generally mirror the frames of old news media, and in some cases, there is evidence that new media have provided the frame itself (as in "Kerry and Edwards are gay").

CONCLUSION: DIFFUSING RUMOR BOMBS, (UN)ACCOUNTABILITY, AND SPECTACULAR DEMOCRACY

The "Kerry is French" case study demonstrates an episode in which Americans are both frequent spectators at and active participants in a public state of affairs in which rumor bombs are deliberately launched into an intermedia diffusion process as strategies of tabloidesque distractions that are nevertheless used to justify what appear to be logical non sequitur political claims and policies (such as the unsuitability of a candidate for president). One need not be nostalgic for an ideal speech situation and public sphere that never existed to note changes in the character of mediated political discourse that exclude voices and ideas and offer a spectacle of democracy, complete with staged news conferences, fake news, and pseudoevents.[9]

The convergence of new news values, speed pressures for scoops and less time for verification, and wartime propaganda strategies domesticated into political public relations have all transformed the production, circulation, and reception of American politics, and there is evidence that other countries are following suit (Harsin 2006, 2008; Swanson 2004; Esser and Pfetsch 2004; McNair 2007). Competitive news market pressures to secure audiences and raise profits have resulted in news values that have increasingly embraced tabloid-lifestyle stories, scandals, and rumors that were more recently the primary material of tabloid papers and celebrity magazines, such as the *National Enquirer, Tiger Beat*, and *People* magazine (historically, yellow journalism and the penny presses were rife with this type of story before the professionalization of journalism in the late 1920s). With the success of reality television and cults of celebrity (from Monica Lewinsky and Princess Diana to David Beckham and Paris Hilton), we have witnessed strategies in mainstream journalism to blend genres to attract entertainment audiences. Astute political public relations consultants have read these cultural changes and sought to make politics and the news genres that blur with reality TV and entertainment overall.

Why are rumors such as "John Kerry is French" appealing for some audiences, and what are the ramifications for theories of democratic politics? As John Corner has recently noted (2003), in 2002 8.7 million votes were cast in the biggest phone-in ever for the *Pop Idol* election campaign in the UK. The

---

[9] The classic work that documents historical changes in the character/style of American political discourse is Jamieson's *Eloquence in the Electronic Age* (1988).

show began in 2001 with 5.6 million viewers, and concluded with an audience of 15 million. Corner asks us to compare those numbers with the 4.5 million who watched the 10 o'clock news during the "real" election campaign, or the 2.5 million viewers of the Paxman–Blair interview on *Newsnight* that asked crucial policy issues regarding Blair's reelection (Corner 2003: 1). These kind of comparisons suggest some reasonable speculations. There is all sorts of evidence that citizens in various democracies are disillusioned with the process of politics and ideas of representation. They have become cynical and dropped out of the spectacle of democracy (Delli Carpini 2004). Why so many voters for *Pop Idol*? Such voting gives audiences the satisfaction that their votes really matter and they enjoy the process of participation. As many theorists have suggested, the development of Western consumer societies has involved a blurring of political will and citizenship with self-expression and voice through consumption (Cohen 2003; Corner and Pels 2003). The enormous success of entertainment culture and the channeling of identifications into celebrity have understandably encouraged political strategists and MBAs in newsrooms to mimic what sells.

Of course, Kerry lost the election, but what did the French rumor bomb have to do with it? It worked nicely as a strategy in synchronous discursive diffusion with other attacks and rumor bombs; and media convergence culture facilitated that diffusion, as agenda setting ping-ponged between old and new news media, and the participatory nature of the new media allowed bloggers to diffuse the rumor bomb in conjunction with the other attacks. Kerry was a semiotic vessel tossed about and sometimes effectively anchored in a sea of interweaving discourses and intertexts from 2003 to 2004. In the context of the Iraq War and the war on terrorism, Kerry's opponents sought to brand him within a discourse of American patriotism precisely by associating him with an important excluded element – the French. According to a widespread nationalist, pro-war, Francophobic discourse in the winter and spring of 2003, the French were cowards, fair-weather friends, disloyal, undependable, arrogant and haughty, militarily inept, communist/socialist, and effete. These brand connotations were used effectively by Kerry's opponents, whose rhetoric was taken up and presented on a news and entertainment (in the case of late night talk hosts such as Leno, Letterman, and Conan O'Brien) network to offset a counter-discourse offered by the Kerry public relations effort. According to them, Kerry was smart, dignified, masculine, and militarily heroic.

At the Democratic National Convention, Kerry's Vietnam experience was portrayed using verbal and visual symbols that deliberately recalled popular patriotic war products such as *Saving Private Ryan* and *Band of Brothers*. Thus, in his acceptance speech, Kerry narrated, "Our band of brothers doesn't march together because of who we are as veterans, but because of what we learned as soldiers. We fought for this nation because we loved it and we came back with the deep belief that every day is extra. We may be a little older, we may be a little grayer, but we still know how to fight for our country" (Kerry

2004). But Kerry was also in a rhetorical bind, in the sense that he wanted to capitalize on his war heroism to build his brand, yet that brand was vulnerable to challenge by images and words about his antiwar activism on his return home. The latter part of Kerry's identity, his history, did not easily fit into the simplistic branding narratives that contemporary political communications demand (Jamieson 1988). Kerry's image managers astutely played the tension between his heroism and antiwar qualities against the context of accusations that Bush lied about weapons of mass destruction. In his campaign film, Kerry is thus quoted as saying he "felt the government had not been truthful with the American public," so it was his civic duty to question that government's war policy (Corn 2004). Similarly, Kerry faced a problem with his initial support for the Iraq War, which he then came to oppose. He wished to challenge the "flip-flopper" opponent's negative brand by identifying with the American people: He had trusted the president not to go it alone and only as a last resort based on careful intelligence work (Healy 2004). Kerry's opponents played the French card to try to symbolically reverse the Kerry camp discourse. He was not a heroic military man, said the French connection discourse, because Kerry is French and the French are cowards and lying opportunists. The French coward frame circulated well in its intertextuality with the rumor bomb from the Swift Boat Veterans, who tried to claim that Kerry had lied about his bravery in Vietnam. The aim there appears to be to fight accusations that Bush lied by making Kerry defend himself against similar accusations. It was an "I'm rubber, you're glue" state of political discourse.

The findings of this study contribute to our knowledge about contemporary political communication, but in particular, it enriches our understanding of how and multiple reasons why "an innovation," a rumor about Kerry's alleged "Frenchness," was diffused in a complex media convergence culture. It documents the rumor bomb communication tactics used by the Bush administration in the last election to discredit John Kerry, as well as about the Kerry public relations team's responses and tactics of its own. Those tactics reveal a political culture in which branding has become the dominant form of primary political discourse (i.e., originating from political persuaders) in its attempt to circulate and set new and old media agendas. The norm is a war of distractions produced by political actors and media enablers who pay careful attention to their embeddedness in an entertainment context (as mentioned previously: *Band of Brothers*; *The Simpsons*; *Saturday Night Live*; *The O'Reilly Factor*; *Saving Private Ryan*). The articles that circulate the rumor that Kerry was French are small compared with the total number of articles on and references to (such as late night talk shows and comedy) John Kerry in the media. But when viewed in conjunction with other major tactics and events in the campaign, one begins to see some of the recurring strategies of the Bush agenda-setting and branding effort and how their frames interweave in diffusion. Other rumors in the context included Iraq–al Qaeda links, weapons of mass destruction, and Kerry's cowardice in Vietnam and thus allegedly illegitimate medals. Here an intertextual and discursive look at these phenomena reveals an *overall* negative branding strategy, of which the rumor bomb "John Kerry is French" played an integral part.

Here also is a concrete study that answers Gaonkar and Povinelli's (2003) calls for studies not just of meanings in texts but also of matrixes of circulation. The rumor that John Kerry is French (-looking) has a kind of circulatory capital based on its producer's sensibility to the rhetorical concept of "kairos" or timing (Jasinski 2001). The same team of communication experts who helped produce the diplomatic crisis with France then used that moment as an opportunity to launch the arguably absurd claim into a media agenda whose news values were ready to open it into a broad circulatory culture, moving between traditional broadcast and print news, talk and comedy shows, cable and mainstream, political speech, and websites and forums – convergence culture. The deliberately ambiguous form, the timing, the political economy of news, the repetition by political allies, and the power of new media address all coincided to produce a particularly wide-ranging circulatory culture.[10] Thus, the positioning of this set of frames about "Frenchness" in relation to other "frame games" answers recent calls to develop the complexity of frames by attending to their cultural context and relationship to different forms of power (Carragee and Roefs 2004). Here research projects of publics and agency that celebrate the democratic potential of the Internet must be complicated by taking into account agency as it is actually practiced via media institutions, their news values and newsgathering practices, the political economy of which they are a part, and the marketing and public relations firms to whom professional political speech is outsourced. Contentious knowledges circulate, but they are not always circulated from below, from subaltern publics and agents.

The news media did very little to interrupt antideliberative strategies of political persuasion such as those documented in this study. On the contrary, they repeated and diffused them, encouraging a tabloid frame for electoral decision making. Kerry's family ties or linguistic ability have no clear rational connection with his suitability for the presidency, yet the news media happily circulated these red herrings and ad hominems because they hold market value. Here political economy considerations of circulating political discourse are crucial (McChesney and Schiller 2002; Gans 2003). Instead of hearing mainly about the problem of health care or Iraq, and each candidate's positions on them, precious news time was squandered on tabloid-like associations – potentially explosive rumors about Frenchness in the context of the Franco–American fallout of one year before. As far as the French opposition to the U.S. invasion of Iraq at a crucial time of media publicity on the UN and American public deliberation to that policy choice, the old news media did little to provide the public with diverse ideas, opinions, and arguments on that issue (a problem of political economy and its impact on information and framing). Thus, one may politicize the style of mediated political discourse and the market values that

---

[10] Its circulatory range is undeniable. However, its uptake by citizen-spectators cannot be known. Audience studies or polls three years after the fact are of questionable value.

contribute to its systematic distortion. But there are also actual people, not just systems, who intend to limit political communication to this form, this way of being political. What can the lesson be here for diffusion and contentious politics scholars? If it is so hard for citizens, politicians, and international leaders to set the American media and public agendas in terms of rational policy claims (and reasons for and against, for example, a war that has now cost hundreds and thousands of lives, resources, and dollars), it may not augur well for activist publics that wish to diffuse their claims and ideas broadly to set policy agendas. If they are to do it, they must astutely read media business needs, and learn the viral and other communication techniques of diffusion so dominant in a new convergence culture of news/entertainment/consumption, in which new media are just as likely to set the agenda of old media as vice versa. As John Kerry would say: *fin.*

PART III

DIFFUSION, SCALE SHIFT, AND ORGANIZATIONAL CHANGE

10

From Protest to Organization

The Impact of the 1960 Sit-Ins on Movement Organizations in the American South

Michael Biggs and Kenneth T. Andrews

For the past three decades, scholars of social movements have debated whether collective protest is the product of prior organization, as predicted by resource mobilization and political process theories. In this chapter, we consider the other side of this relationship: whether the diffusion of protest leads to the growth of movement organizations. This tackles the third question posed by Givan, Roberts, and Soule in the introduction to this volume: What is the impact of diffusion? This question is rarely asked, as studies of diffusion devote much greater attention to the onset and spread of innovations than to their long-term consequences (Soule 2004; Strang and Soule 1998). Although the consequences of the diffusion of protest for movement organization have attracted remarkably little attention, various theories converge on the prediction that the effect will be positive. People drawn into protest are available to be recruited as new members, and activists have reason to consolidate the enthusiasm of defiance by expanding existing organizations or founding new ones.

This chapter considers a historically and theoretically influential case: the 1960 sit-ins by black college students in the American South. The sit-ins have been credited with revitalizing a civil rights struggle that had been floundering in the late 1950s. Local campaigns were set in motion, new leaders emerged, established organizations increased their efforts, and a new organization was created – the Student Nonviolent Coordinating Committee (SNCC). Using data on 334 cities in the American South, we investigate whether cities where sit-ins occurred were more likely to experience organizational expansion, measured by membership growth or the establishment of local affiliates or representatives. Various organizations are considered: the venerable National Association for the Advancement of Colored People (NAACP), including its youth councils and college chapters, and three organizations that took the form of activist

The authors would like to thank Susan Olzak for incisive comments, and Megan Rolfe for research assistance.

networks – the Congress of Racial Equality (CORE), the Southern Christian Leadership Conference (SCLC), and SNCC. Our analysis controls for each city's organizational ecology on the eve of the sit-ins as well as its sociopolitical characteristics, thus enabling us to isolate the impact of protest on subsequent organization.

The chapter begins by reviewing the literature on the relationship between protest and organization. The second section sketches the historical context of the 1960 sit-ins. Qualitative evidence shows that CORE and SCLC, in particular, were keenly aware of the opportunities provided by the rapid diffusion of protest. The third section describes the data used in the quantitative analysis. Considering the South as a whole, it is surprising that aggregate figures reveal no substantial increase in membership and no great expansion of organizational presence for existing organizations. Results from our analysis of 334 cities are presented in the fourth section. Again, the results are surprising: Controlling for prior organizational ecology and sociopolitical characteristics, the occurrence of sit-ins had no discernible positive effect on subsequent organization growth or expansion. These unexpected results are scrutinized in the final section, in which we address the implications of our findings.

THEORETICAL EXPECTATIONS

Scholars of social movements seek to explain two distinct but related phenomena: collective protest or contention and formal organization. There are many empirical analyses of the diffusion of movement organization, generally the formation of local affiliates of existing organizations (e.g., Biggs 2003; Conell 1988; Conell and Voss 1990; Hedström 1994; Hedström et al. 2000; Voss 1988, 1993). Likewise, there are many analyses of the diffusion of protest (e.g., Andrews and Biggs 2006; Biggs 2005; Conell and Cohn 1995; Myers 1997, 2000; Soule 1997). Controlling for variation in sociopolitical characteristics, these studies consistently demonstrate "positive feedback": The occurrence of protest in one place (in geographical or social space) makes the occurrence of protest nearby more likely; the formation of an organization in one place makes the formation of another nearby more likely. The relationship between protest and organization, however, is rarely analyzed empirically. This omission may be due in part to differing time scales: waves of protest unfold over weeks or months, whereas organizations expand over years.

One side of the relationship between protest and organization has been the subject of theoretical controversy: the effect of movement organization on collective protest. Reacting against theories that viewed protest as a consequence of social disintegration, scholars in the political process and resource mobilization traditions (e.g., Shorter and Tilly 1974; McAdam 1982) originally argued that organization was a necessary condition for protest. Such arguments tended to conflate preexisting social networks with formal movement organizations. Against this view, Piven and Cloward (1977) contended that movement organizations – at least bureaucratic organizations that focused on recruiting a mass membership – stifled rather than stimulated collective protest. The controversy is illustrated by the debate over the role of movement organizations in the wave of sit-ins that occurred in 1960 (Killian 1984; Oberschall 1989; Morris 1981, 1984; Polletta 1998). Our event-history analysis of this episode found only modest positive effects of organization on protest (Andrews and Biggs 2006). In a similar analysis, unionization had no effect on strikes by French coal miners from 1890 to 1935 (Conell and Cohn 1995).

The other side of the relationship – the effect of collective protest on movement organization – has attracted far less attention. Scattered remarks suggest a theoretical consensus that protest helps to build organization, at least when protesters remain optimistic about the prospect of success and when repression is relatively modest. According to Piven and Cloward (1977: xx), "activists' conviction that formal organization is a vehicle of power" leads them to recruit protesters as members of movement organizations – although Piven and Cloward view that conviction as an illusion. To similar effect, McAdam (1982: 147) argues that "the ad hoc groups and informal committees that typically coordinate the movement at its outset are ill-equipped to direct an ongoing campaign of social protest." Therefore, we should expect "formal movement organizations . . . to replace indigenous institutions as the dominant organizational force within the movement."

Different theoretical perspectives converge on the hypothesis that collective protest has a positive effect on movement organizations. It is worth distinguishing three different sorts of positive effect.[1] One is the founding of new movement organizations. Another is the formation of additional local affiliates of existing organizations. This is important because an organization composed of multiple local units spread across the country is likely to behave very differently from an organization consisting of a single headquarters (Skocpol 2004). A third effect is growth in the membership of movement organizations. Are such positive effects of protest on organization confirmed by empirical analysis? A crucial methodological point is that such effects can be identified only by controlling for prior organization – because prior organization may also affect protest (even if the precise effect is a matter of dispute, as we have seen). In other words, we need to estimate the effect of protest at time t on organization at time $t + 1$, controlling for organization at time $t - 1$ as well as for sociopolitical variables at time $t - 1$.

One promising domain of investigation is the relationship between strikes and union membership, because lengthy time series are available. Qualitative explorations of the relationship suggest that strike waves often precede an influx of union members (Cronin 1989; Franzosi 1995). In a quantitative analysis of the United States and France from 1880 to 1914, Friedman (1998: 37–42) suggests a strong positive effect, but this finding seems to be a statistical

---

[1] This does not exhaust the possible positive effects; another would be an influx of financial resources (e.g., Jenkins and Eckert 1986).

artifact.[2] Curiously, the most convincing demonstration of a positive effect on unionization does not involve strikes: Isaac et al. (2006) show that "New Left" protest (encompassing the civil rights, feminist, and antiwar movements) increased the membership of public sector unions in the United States from 1950 to 1981. Turning from membership to organizational founding, Minkoff has collected data on movement organizations in the United States from 1955 and 1985. A series of analyses find that collective protest had a *negative* effect on organizational founding for the civil rights movement (Minkoff 1995; Meyer and Minkoff 2004) and had no statistically significant effect for the women's movement (Minkoff 1997).[3] These analyses control for prior organizational density.

Taken together, these empirical findings are curious. There is little evidence that collective protest has a positive effect on movement organization. Indeed, for organizational founding the opposite holds: More protest leads to fewer new organizations. Thus far the empirical data examined have been aggregated at the national level. Data disaggregated into spatial units such as cities provide greater analytical leverage, because we can investigate whether places where protest occurred were more likely to have membership growth or to form local affiliates than places without protest. The proliferation of local affiliates of a movement organization is also a substantively important process to investigate.

HISTORICAL CONTEXT

The sit-ins that spread across the South in the spring of 1960 constitute an especially relevant case for studying the relationship between protest and organization. By mobilizing thousands of activists across the South to engage in disruptive protest, the sit-ins struck participants and observers at the time as a watershed moment. This view has been endorsed by sociologists. Morris, for example, sums up this episode as the "origins of a decade of disruption" (1984: 195). McAdam and Sewell argue that the first sit-in in Greensboro,

---

[2] Friedman analyzes union growth as a function of the "quasi-striker ratio" (this year's strikers divided by last year's members), so the basic model is:

$$\frac{M_t}{M_{t-1}} = a + b \frac{S_t}{M_{t-1}} + e_t$$

where M stands for union members and S for workers involved in strikes. The dependent and independent variables share the same denominator, and so the model can be rewritten:

$$M_t = a M_{t-1} + b S_t + e_t M_{t-1}$$

The model's fit stems from the fact that last year's union membership is a good predictor of this year's, irrespective of the effect of strikes.

[3] Using Minkoff's data, Olzak and Ryo (2007) found that protest in the prior year has a positive and significant effect on the tactical and goal diversity of the population of civil rights organizations.

North Carolina was a "transformative event," exemplifying the way in which "very brief, spatially concentrated, and relatively chaotic sequences can have durable, spatially extended, and profoundly structural effects" (2001: 102). The sit-ins, they claim, "revitalized all of the major civil rights organizations" and "the impact [on the movement] was as dramatic as the event itself was unpredictable" (ibid.: 108).

A brief historical sketch sets the scene for our analysis. The sit-in tactic – physically occupying space reserved for whites only – had been pioneered by activists associated with CORE and NAACP youth councils in the 1940s and 1950s, primarily in border states and the upper South (Meier and Rudwick 1973; Morris 1981). However, these early efforts failed to inspire large-scale protest, because they received little media coverage and they were geographically distant from the concentrations of black college students in the South. On Monday, February 1, 1960, four freshmen at Greensboro's North Carolina Agricultural and Technical College occupied the lunch counter of Woolworth's (Chafe 1980; Wolff 1970). The initial event involved minimal planning and no involvement of movement organizations. The store manager decided to ignore the protesters, rather than having them removed or arrested. When the store closed, the students promised to return the following day, and when they arrived back on campus, they found "a beehive of activity" (Raines 1977: 79). Students turned to Dr. George Simkins, president of the Greensboro branch of the NAACP, who contacted the national office of CORE about providing assistance to the students. Simkins recalled that he "thought the organization [CORE] might be more experienced at the sort of operation under way," having recently read a CORE pamphlet about sit-ins in Baltimore (Powledge 1991: 201, Wolff 1970: 35–6). The size of the protest grew throughout the week culminating in a major protest the following Saturday with hundreds of students. That evening a mass meeting of sixteen hundred students decided to suspend protest for the purpose of "negotiation and study" (Chafe 1980: 88).

By then, the confrontation in Greensboro had drawn the attention of students elsewhere. Sit-ins spread quickly in the following week to other North Carolina cities and then onward to cities in Florida, South Carolina, and Virginia. By mid-April protest had occurred in more than sixty cities in every Southern state except Mississippi. In a previous article (Andrews and Biggs 2006), we investigated the diffusion of protest across 334 Southern cities in the ten weeks following February 1. Our analysis demonstrates that the key determinant of protest was the number of black college students. Movement organizations facilitated protest, primarily through cadres of activists in CORE and NAACP college chapters; the membership of NAACP and the presence of SCLC was not significant. News media played an important role in the diffusion of protest by circulating information about sit-ins in nearby cities.

Shortly after the first protest began in Greensboro, the sit-ins activated leaders and organizers connected to formal movement organizations. Both NAACP and CORE sent representatives to North Carolina to support student protesters. For example, CORE contacted its local chapters barely a week after the first sit-in, reporting on the efforts of two field secretaries to assist students in North Carolina and urging members to contact Woolworth's national office and to organize sympathy picket lines.[4] Two weeks after Greensboro, student leaders met in Durham with established civil rights leaders including Martin Luther King (Meier and Rudwick 1973). Thus, within two weeks of the initiating event, the major civil rights organizations had sent leaders to North Carolina to observe and support the emerging protest movement. CORE field-workers, in particular, spent the spring traveling to cities where protest had been initiated to organize training workshops in the techniques of nonviolence (ibid.). The national organizations also attempted to mobilize support among their members and local affiliates. NAACP and CORE sent letters to local affiliates encouraging them to support the sit-ins by organizing sympathy pickets, boycotting national chain stores that had segregated lunch counters in the South, and writing to chain stores to express opposition to segregation.

Civil rights organizations directed new resources toward sustaining the sit-in campaigns. For example, CORE hired Len Holt, an attorney from Norfolk, Virginia, as a new field secretary in mid-April; he worked with activists in cities such as Memphis and Tallahassee.[5] The field staff grew from two to five full-time field secretaries by April (Meier and Rudwick 1973). During the spring, CORE received inquiries about establishing local chapters in Durham and Atlanta,[6] but the staff was too focused on the protest already under way to shift attention toward building local affiliates. By summer, CORE's field director, Gordon Carey, appears to have been less distracted by the demands of sit-in campaigns. He traveled to multiple cities seeking to establish contacts and lay the foundation for local chapters.[7]

Like CORE, SCLC did not have a sustained program for building local affiliates. Wyatt T. Walker, SCLC's executive director, advocated strongly for a staff position and resources for this purpose, but he reported in 1961 that the "growth of the affiliate program was arrested due to a shortage of personnel and the two great crises of the past year, the jailing of Dr. King and the Freedom Ride. There has simply been no opportunity to do what needed to be done."[8] As with CORE, the desire to build local affiliates was circumscribed by the exigencies of sustaining a protest campaign.

---

[4] Memo to all CORE groups and members of the Advisory Committee from Marvin Rich, February 9, 1960, CORE Papers, Reel 26.

[5] Letter from Carey to Wyckoff, February 26, 1960, CORE Papers, Reel 40; Carey to Fullerton, March 18, 1960, CORE Papers, Reel 42.

[6] Letter from Carey to Martha and Peter Klopfer, February 26, 1960, CORE Papers, Reel 42; Letter from Robinson to Wyckoff, March 1, 1960, CORE Papers, Reel 40.

[7] Report on Florida Contacts and Field Work, Gordon R. Carey, July 28, 1960, CORE Papers, Reel 40.

[8] Report of the Director, October 1960–September 1961, delivered at the Annual Convention, September 20, 1961, SCLC Papers, Part 3, Reel 8; for a detailed description of SCLC's plans for a larger affiliate program, see Memo to Wyatt Tee Walker, Staff Expansion, October 23, 1961, SCLC Papers, Part 2, Reel 13.

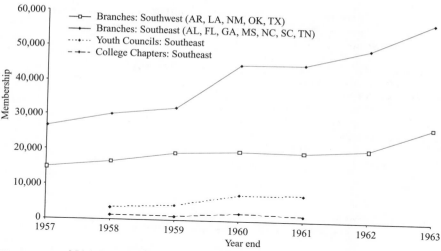

FIGURE 10.1. NAACP Membership in the South, 1957–1963

The most direct organizational legacy of the sit-ins was the establishment of SNCC, which emerged from a conference of student activists held at Shaw University in April 1960. The Shaw conference was organized by Ella Baker, SCLC's executive director at the time. Given SCLC's sponsorship of the conference and King's role as keynote speaker, SCLC was in a key position to shape the organizational direction of the sit-in movement. However, Baker herself urged the students toward establishing an independent organization – an outcome that was far from certain (Carson 1981). At the time, she famously wrote in the *Southern Patriot* about the "frustration and the disillusionment that comes when the prophetic leader turns out to have heavy feet of clay" – a thinly veiled critique of King and his leadership style (Ransby 2003: 245).

All the established civil rights organizations played active roles in supporting the 1960 sit-ins. Nevertheless, the impact of that experience on the growth and expansion of movement organization remains unclear. On one hand, staff and resources were mobilized, and staff inevitably came into contact with hundreds of newly committed young activists. On the other hand, the demands of responding to the emerging movement in 1960 and beyond may have undercut the opportunities to institutionalize protest by recruiting new members and establishing new local affiliates. To determine the impacts of the sit-ins, we turn to our empirical analysis.

DATA

NAACP was the largest and longest established civil rights organization. It recruited members into local branches, and also two separate types of local affiliates (with separate membership): youth councils and college chapters. Figure 10.1

TABLE 10.1. *Movement Organizations in 334 Southern Cities, 1959–1962*

Total Membership			
	End of 1959	End of 1960	End of 1961
NAACP Branches	70,265	82,682	79,597
Number of cities with:			
	End of 1959	+1960 charter	+1961 charter
NAACP youth council	117	131	140
NAACP college chapter	13	16	18
	Early Feb 1960		Dec 1961/Feb 1962
SCLC presence	22		30
	End of 1959	Nov 1960	June 1962
CORE chapter	12	16	22
		Oct 1960	
SNCC delegate		39	

depicts membership at year end.[9] At the end of 1959, on the eve of the sit-ins, branches in the South had 51,539 members. A year later, membership had increased by 26 percent, to 64,690. By comparison, there had been a 10 percent increase from 1958 to 1959. Youth councils and college chapters should be especially important because students were disproportionately involved in the sit-ins. Membership returns for these units are fragmentary, so it is possible to reconstruct time series only for the Southeast. In 1960, membership in youth councils increased by 70 percent, from 4,347 to 7,384, whereas college chapter membership doubled, from 1,040 to 2,161. In all three series, growth was not sustained in the following year, and indeed, college membership fell by almost a quarter from 1961 to 1962.

For quantitative analysis, we focus on 334 Southern cities with a population of at least ten thousand and a black population of at least one thousand.[10] Table 10.1 shows the extent of organization before the sit-ins occurred and at two later points. We consider two points in time to check whether organizational expansion in the aftermath of the protest wave was sustained over the longer term. NAACP branch membership approximates the trends shown in Figure 10.1.[11] For youth councils and college chapters, we measured whether they were present in each city at the end of 1959.[12] Because of the paucity of membership returns in the following years, we measure newly chartered councils or chapters during 1960 and 1961. These are used to estimate the number

---

[9] The NAACP's Southeast and Southwest regions are not coterminous with the Southern states in our analysis. This difference in geographical coverage explains why the membership figures in Table 10.1 are higher.

[10] We include states of the former Confederacy plus Maryland, Kentucky, and West Virginia.

[11] Some branches encompassed a county rather than a city. When the county contributed more than one city to our dataset, the membership is distributed evenly between those cities.

[12] There are no extant returns for youth councils or college chapters for 1959 from Kentucky, Maryland, and West Virginia; for these states we have used the returns for 1958.

of cities with at least one youth council or college chapter, respectively.[13] Youth councils and college chapters alike expanded modestly after the sit-ins.

Unlike NAACP, the other civil rights organizations did not focus on recruiting members. CORE, SCLC, and SNCC were essentially networks of activists. Again, we measure whether each organization was present in the city. For SCLC, this is defined as the existence of a local affiliate (usually a church) or the residence of someone on the executive board. Unfortunately, there are no reliably dated lists of affiliates from the eve of the sit-ins until the beginning of 1962.[14] Over that period, SCLC expanded by just over a third, from 22 to 30 cities. For CORE, presence is defined by the existence of an affiliated chapter (or one in the process of applying for affiliation). CORE expanded steadily from the eve of the sit-ins to late 1960, and then again to mid-1962, almost doubling the number of chapters from 12 to 22 over the entire period. SNCC was formally founded at a conference in Atlanta in October 1960. Delegates came from 39 cities, giving this fledgling organization a greater geographical extent than either SCLC or CORE.

Leaving aside SNCC, these aggregate figures do not suggest that the wave of sit-ins in 1960 had a dramatic impact on established organizations. To further assess the impact of the sit-ins, we analyze cross-sectional variation across cities. There are two types of dependent variables. One is the organization's membership in the city, which is applicable only to NAACP. The other is a dichotomous variable for the organization's presence in the city. Statistical models are estimated for the membership or presence of each organization at one or two points after the sit-ins of spring 1960.

The key independent variable is a dichotomous variable for the occurrence of a sit-in, defined as the physical occupation of space from which blacks were excluded (usually a dining facility), at any time between February 1 and April 14, 1960. These ten weeks encompass the rapid diffusion of sit-ins across the South; sit-ins occurred in 66 of the 334 cities. Only a few additional cities experienced sit-ins in succeeding weeks, and there was a general hiatus of protest over the summer vacation. Aggregate time series data on movement

---

[13] This is not the same as the total number of affiliates, because a few cities had more than one, as, for example, where there were multiple colleges.

[14] In a previous article (Andrews and Biggs 2006), we used a list of affiliates apparently dating from February 3, 1960 ("Affiliate List," Folder: Directory, 1960, SCLC Papers, Part 2, Reel 13). On further scrutiny, we consider the second part of this list to be an entirely separate document, from a later date (quite possibly after 1962). The variable we used therefore exaggerated the extent of SCLC (as present in 34 cities). Fortunately, the corrected variable (22 cities) makes very little difference to the results. SCLC presence now has no effect (whereas before the effect was substantial but not statistically significant). The same error also entered an article (Biggs 2006) on individual participation in the sit-ins. The corrected variable now has no effect on protest (whereas before the effect was strong and statistically significant), although it still has a positive effect on NAACP membership. This correction strengthens that article's main finding, that frequent church attendance made protest less likely. Corrected tables are available at http://users.ox.ac.uk/~sfos0060/1960.shtml and http://users.ox.ac.uk/~sfos0060/1960survey.shtml.

activity also indicate the abrupt decline of protest following the spring of 1960 (McAdam 1983: 739). Needless to say, this variable does not capture subsequent sit-ins, and this limitation should be emphasized especially for our analyses of organization at the end of 1961 or in 1962. The variable is strictly a measure of the *initial* wave of confrontational protest.

There are two further sets of independent variables. One set pertain to the city's organizational ecology on the eve of the sit-ins: NAACP branch membership (square root) and dichotomous variables for the presence of an NAACP youth council, an NAACP college chapter, SCLC, and CORE.[15] Another set of independent variables capture sociopolitical characteristics likely to affect both collective protest and movement organization.[16] The resources and autonomy of the black community are measured by the male unemployment rate and the percentage of the male labor force relegated to unskilled occupations. Political opportunities are measured by four variables: the presence of the Southern Regional Council (SRC), an organization promoting interracial cooperation; the percentage of blacks in the county, which is often used as a proxy for the degree of repression exercised by whites; the existence of a state poll tax, used to disenfranchise blacks; location in the Deep South, where repression was more severe. There are also two demographic variables: the number of black students enrolled in college (logged), and the black population (logged).

RESULTS

Table 10.2 summarizes the results of the statistical models, identifying those coefficients that are statistically significantly different from zero at the 0.05 level. (See Appendix Tables for detailed results.[17]) In Models 1A and 1B, the dependent variable is membership of the regular NAACP branch (as in Table 10.1), so negative binomial regression is used. The other models use logistic regression. In Models 2A and 2B, the dependent variable is whether an NAACP youth council was newly chartered in the city during 1960 (26 cities) and 1961 (34 cities), respectively.[18] The latter model drops thirteen observations, because the presence of a college chapter in 1959 perfectly predicts the absence of newly chartered youth councils in 1961. Model 3 is the same for NAACP college chapters; the years 1960 and 1961 are combined because of the small numbers (11 cities). In the remaining models, the dependent variable is simply organizational presence (as in Table 10.1).

---

[15] NAACP branch membership is transformed by taking the square root because we expect a diminishing marginal effect; a logarithmic transformation is not appropriate because many cities have zero members.

[16] For explication of these independent variables, see Andrews and Biggs 2006.

[17] In Appendix Tables 10B and 10C, each model's ability to discriminate between cities with and without organizational presence is measured by the area under the Receiver Operating Characteristic (ROC) curve, which can range from 0.5 (no discrimination) to 1 (perfect discrimination).

[18] Note that the returns did not distinguish the "rechartering" of lapsed units from the chartering of new ones, but the former were a small minority.

TABLE 10.2. *Determinants of Organizational Presence and Membership*

	NAACP Branch Members		Youth Council		College Chapter
	End of 1960 1A	End of 1961 1B	1960 Charter 2A	1961 Charter 2B	1960–61 Charter 3
NAACP branch members, end of 1959 (√)	+	+			+
NAACP youth council, end of 1959	+				
NAACP college chapter, end of 1959					
SCLC presence, early Feb 1960			+	N/A	
CORE, end of 1959					
Black population (logged)					
Black college students (logged)				+	
Black % of county					+
Poll tax in state				−	
Deep South					
Sit-in, spring 1960					

	SCLC Presence	CORE Chapter		SNCC Delegate
	Dec 1961/Feb 1962 4	Nov 1960 5A	June 1962 5B	Oct 1960 6
NAACP branch members, end of 1959 (√)	+	+		
NAACP youth council, end of 1959	−			
NAACP college chapter, end of 1959	+			+
SCLC presence, early Feb 1960				
CORE, end of 1959		+		
Black population (logged)				
Black college students (logged)			+	
Black % of county		−		+
Poll tax in state			−	−
Deep South			−	−
Sit-in, spring 1960				+

N = 334 (321 in Model 2B).

+ or − indicates effect that is statistically significant at the 0.05 level (two-tailed test).

Other independent variables include: black unskilled %, black unemployed %, SRC presence, black % of county (squared orthogonal).

The most striking result is the absence of any positive effect: When we take into account the city's prior organizational ecology and its sociopolitical characteristics, the occurrence of sit-ins in the spring of 1960 has *no* discernible effect on subsequent organizational expansion. In the negative binomial regressions, the coefficients are −0.20 and 0.25, close to zero. In the logistic regressions, the odds ratios range from 0.20 to 3.9, not significantly different from 1; even for the highest odds ratio, the *p*-value is only 0.12. If the sociopolitical variables are omitted from the models, then the occurrence of sit-ins does have a statistically significant and positive effect in three models: NAACP youth councils chartered during 1960 (Model 2A), college chapters chartered during 1960–61 (Model 3), and SNCC delegates (Model 6). This finding helps to interpret the negative results of the full models: The sociopolitical variables predict with considerable accuracy which cities were likely to experience sit-ins (as shown in Andrews and Biggs 2006); therefore, the sit-ins variable yields little additional information. The same factors were conducive to disruptive protest and also to subsequent organizational expansion.

The results for the sociopolitical variables are straightforward. Organization was more likely to expand in cities with wider political opportunities and more potential supporters.[19] When we consider organizational ecology, the analyses suggest that the newer organizations were more likely to expand where NAACP was strong.[20] Higher NAACP membership at the end of 1959 makes the subsequent presence of SCLC and CORE (as least in Model 5A) more likely. The presence of an NAACP youth council at the end of 1959 raises the probability of a delegate going to SNCC's founding conference. Nevertheless, prior organization has a negative impact in two instances. The presence of an NAACP college chapter makes the subsequent presence of SCLC less likely; the presence of CORE reduces the probability of a delegate to SNCC. This pattern suggests some degree of competition for activist students.

In sum, cities with sit-ins had neither more members nor a greater probability of organizational presence than cities without sit-ins – after we control for prior organizational ecology and sociopolitical variables. The effect of protest was minimal in explaining cross-sectional variation.

Hypothetically, this minimal effect could be attributed to a lack of opportunity for expansion in the 66 cities where sit-ins had occurred in the spring of 1960. Figure 10.2 shows the presence of various types of organizations. The great majority of the cities had an NAACP branch and a youth council. The other organizations, however, were remarkably sparse. Two-thirds of the cities lacked SCLC presence, whereas four-fifths had no CORE chapter. For NAACP college chapters and SNCC, the appropriate denominator is the 34 cities with a black college: Almost half of those cities had no college chapter, although only

---

[19] The only surprise is the negative effect of black population in Model 6.
[20] The very high odds ratios, for example, in Model 5A (Appendix Table 10C) for the effect of CORE in 1959 on CORE in 1960, reflect the fact that the former is a very powerful predictor of the latter.

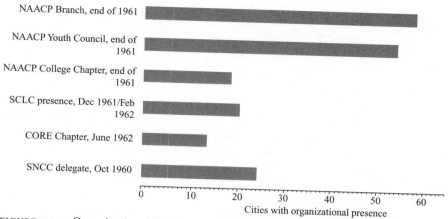

FIGURE 10.2. Organizational Presence in 66 Cities Where Sit-Ins Occurred in Spring 1960

a quarter failed to send a delegate to SNCC. Even when considered together, the organizations most closely associated with the sit-ins – NAACP college chapters, SCLC, CORE, and SNCC – failed to achieve comprehensive coverage. In 23 cities out of the 66, none of those organizations was present. In a significant number of cities, then, sit-in protest did not produce any new organizational affiliate of a civil rights organization.

CONCLUSION

The sit-ins led directly to the founding of a new organization, SNCC, and were followed by a modest expansion of existing organizations. Nevertheless, the diffusion of sit-in protest did not generate any equivalent diffusion of local movement organization. How can these findings be reconciled with the theoretical expectation that protest will lead to organizational expansion? We should begin by acknowledging possible limitations of our analysis. Our measure of protest is restricted to sit-ins that occurred by April 1960, so it omits later protest events. But the incorporation of later events in other cities would make the limited expansion of CORE, SLC, and SNCC still more pronounced and therefore more puzzling. College students constitute an unusually mobile population – going home during the summer, moving away after graduation – and this might confuse our cross-sectional analysis. But this would not affect the aggregate figures for membership and local affiliates throughout the South (Table 10.1).

Given that our findings are unlikely to be an artifact of data or method, how can they be explained? For NAACP, two factors can be considered. It already had a mass membership: about 1.5 percent of the total black population in these Southern cities. Although there was scope for growth, it is also true that few membership organizations of any sort – aside from trade unions – have recruited more than 1 percent of their target population (Skocpol 2004; Skocpol et al. 2000). In addition, although NAACP provided considerable support to the student protesters (and the college chapters were especially important), the leadership did not embrace disruptive protest. The organization as a whole remained associated with an older generation and with institutional tactics such as litigation.

CORE and SCLC, by contrast, were closely associated with the sit-ins. In both cases, the leadership did not see the formation of local affiliates as a top priority; they also did not depend on membership dues for income. CORE hired new staff in 1960 and attempted to form local affiliates in the South, but it soon shifted attention to the Freedom Rides in 1961 (Arsenault 2005). SCLC was a network of activist congregations, and although some had ties to black colleges, ministers may have found it difficult to organize the new generation of student activists that emerged in 1960. Contrary to accepted wisdom, a survey of black colleges shows that students who frequently attended church were less likely to take part in the sit-ins (Biggs 2006).

More generally, the ethos of the sit-ins was more conducive to protest than organization. Observers at the time viewed the student protest as a critique of established civil rights leaders and organizations (Lomax 1960; Polletta 1998). Activists established various committees and ad hoc organizations to manage the campaign in each city, and soon founded SNCC (Searles and Williams 1962; Wehr 1960). But this organization – modestly titled a Coordinating Committee – was very different from the bureaucratic model offered by NAACP or the SCLC's charismatic leadership. SNCC celebrated its informality as a "band of brothers" who put their "bodies on the line" (Carson 1981: 180; Polletta 2002: 55). More prosaically, the established strength of NAACP – with branches in most Southern cities – freed SNCC, SCLC, and CORE to devote their energies to sustaining and innovating protest.

We conclude that the sit-ins of 1960 did not provide a massive impetus for local organization building. This finding challenges a widely held view in the study of social movements and poses two important questions about the diffusion of collective protest and movement organizations. One question is theoretical: Why does a sudden eruption of protest coincide in some cases with the rapid growth of movement organizations but not in others? The other question is historical: If the diffusion of sit-ins in the spring of 1960 did not transform the organizational ecology of the movement in the South, exactly how did these events have an enduring impact on the struggle for civil rights?

TABLE 10A. *Determinants of Organizational Membership*

Negative Binomial Regression	NAACP Branch Members					
	1A: End of 1960			1B: End of 1961		
	coeff.	s.e.	p	coeff.	s.e.	p
Black unskilled %	−.012	.015	.44	−.003	.016	.87
Black unemployed %	−.027	.037	.46	−.048	.034	.15
Black college students (logged)	.002	.107	.99	.006	.110	.95
SRC presence	.226	.329	.49	.217	.334	.52
Black % of county	−.019	.014	.16	−.005	.013	.72
Black % of county (squared orthogonal)	.000	.001	.74	−.001	.001	.53
Poll tax in state	−.276	.265	.30	−.352	.270	.19
Deep South	−.538	.289	.06	−.596	.308	.05
Black population (logged)	.347	.216	.11	.399	.222	.07
NAACP branch members, end of 1959 ($\sqrt{}$)	.129	.024	.00***	.100	.023	.00***
NAACP youth council, end of 1959	.767	.316	.02*	.620	.329	.06
NAACP college chapter, end of 1959	−.549	.695	.43	−.569	.701	.42
SCLC presence, early Feb 1960	.082	.547	.88	.337	.562	.55
CORE, end of 1959	−.089	.698	.90	.049	.706	.94
Sit-in, spring 1960	.247	.418	.56	−.195	.414	.64
Alpha (overdispersion)	4.410	.402	.00***	4.608	.409	.00***
Spearman's rho	.857			.821		

N = 334.

coeff: coefficient s.e.: standard error p: p-value (two-tailed) *** p < 0.001, ** p < 0.01, * p < 0.05

TABLE 10B. *Determinants of Organizational Presence (i)*

Logistic Regression	NAACP Youth Council 2A: 1960 Charter odds	s.e.	p	NAACP Youth Council 2B: 1961 Charter odds	s.e.	p	NAACP College Chapter 3: 1960–61 Charter odds	s.e.	p
Black unskilled %	.97	.04	.34	.96	.03	.09	.93	.15	.66
Black unemployed %	.94	.08	.45	.98	.05	.71	.72	.25	.34
Black college students (logged)	1.03	.20	.88	.82	.14	.25	12.26	12.15	.01*
SRC presence	1.04	.65	.95	1.32	.69	.60	55.60	140.32	.11
Black % of county	1.02	.03	.39	.96	.02	.07	1.57	.47	.13
Black % of county (squared orthogonal)	1.00	.00	.65	1.00	.00	.81	.94	.04	.09
Poll tax in state	.48	.27	.20	.15	.08	.00***	.01	.02	.07
Deep South	2.01	1.22	.25	.63	.32	.36	4.93	9.83	.42
Black population (logged)	1.13	.45	.75	3.08	1.31	.01**	.07	.10	.08
NAACP branch members, end of 1959 (√)	.94	.03	.00**	.97	.03	.27	.90	.09	.31
NAACP youth council, end of 1959	7.43	5.20	.00**	2.77	1.37	.04*	1,130	3,991	.05*
NAACP college chapter, end of 1959	1.40	1.23	.70	N/A (perfectly predicts no charter)			.01	.02	.07
SCLC presence, early Feb 1960	3.32	2.40	.10	.25	.25	.17	11.60	21.80	.19
CORE, end of 1959	1.51	1.27	.63	.79	.76	.81	.01	.02	.08
Sit-in, spring 1960	2.57	1.70	.15	.57	.34	.35	.24	.43	.43
ROC area	.854			.799			.993		

N = 334 (321 in model 2B).
odds: odds ratio s.e.: standard error p: p-value (two-tailed) *** p < 0.001, ** p < 0.01, * p < 0.05

TABLE 10C. *Determinants of Organizational Presence (ii)*

Logistic Regression	SCLC Presence 4: Dec 1961/Feb 1962			CORE Chapter 5A: Nov 1960			CORE Chapter 5B: June 1962			SNCC Delegate 6: Oct 1962		
	odds	s.e.	p	odds	s.e.	p	odds	s.e.	p	odds	s.e.	p
Black unskilled %	1.05	.05	.39	.91	.12	.45	1.00	.05	.95	1.02	.05	.66
Black unemployed %	1.00	.12	.97	1.22	.29	.41	.97	.10	.77	1.05	.08	.57
Black college students (logged)	.71	.20	.23	.98	.53	.97	1.50	.42	.15	3.48	.87	.00***
SRC presence	.83	.70	.83	12.43	36.44	.39	.92	.75	.92	2.57	1.62	.13
Black % of county	1.03	.05	.57	1.44	.30	.08	.89	.04	.00**	1.00	.03	.89
Black % of county (squared orthogonal)	1.00	.00	.30	1.00	.01	.51	1.00	.00	.60	1.00	.00	.22
Poll tax in state	2.96	2.22	.15	.00	.01	.04*	.13	.11	.01*	.70	.39	.53
Deep South	.89	.86	.91	11.78	20.54	.16	2.57	2.03	.23	5.31	3.77	.02*
Black population (logged)	1.23	.65	.69	.01	.02	.07	2.41	1.16	.07	.30	.13	.01**
NAACP branch members, end of 1959 (√)	1.08	.04	.05*	1.53	.33	.05*	.99	.03	.62	1.03	.03	.18
NAACP youth council, end of 1959	3.59	3.43	.18	6.95	16.59	.42	1.28	1.05	.76	13.29	9.58	.00***
NAACP college chapter, end of 1959	.03	.05	.04*	.00	.01	.07	.14	.18	.12	1.90	1.78	.49
SCLC presence, early Feb 1960	467.14	654.22	.00***	.76	1.56	.89	3.63	3.32	.16	1.83	1.40	.43
CORE, end of 1959	1.61	2.13	.72	121,464	577,047	.01*	23.96	24.02	.00**	.12	.13	.05*
Sit-in, spring 1960	3.95	3.48	.12	2.08	3.54	.67	1.48	1.27	.65	1.04	.74	.96
ROC area	.952			.997			.921			.941		

$N = 334$.

odds: odds ratio s.e.: standard error p: p-value (two-tailed) *** $p < 0.001$, ** $p < 0.01$, * $p < 0.05$

Dynamics of Diffusion

Mechanisms, Institutions, and Scale Shift

Sidney Tarrow

What are the pathways through which a new form of collective action, a new collective action frame, or a new social movement spreads? Do such collective phenomena diffuse autonomously, or in response to the institutional practices to which they are directed? Under what conditions does the horizontal diffusion of contention give way to broader configurations of conflict – what Doug McAdam and this author have called "upward scale shift" (Tarrow and McAdam 2005; Tarrow 2005)? These are the questions I will take up in this chapter.

Research in the past has focused centrally on the "fact" of diffusion (e.g., does an act of contention diffuse or doesn't it?); it has often traced the pathways of diffusion across geographic and social space; and it has tried to show how, and under what circumstances, diffusion produces new organizations and transmits new collective action frames. These are all important contributions to our understanding of contentious politics. But in each respect, existing research leaves lacunae in our understanding of the dynamics of contention:

- First, the "fact" of diffusion can be easily confused with the simultaneous or near-simultaneous emergence of contention in structurally similar situations.
- Second, although diffusion always involves emulation, contention can diffuse across geographic or social space through a combination of mechanisms with different outcomes and valences.
- Third, as Andrews and Biggs show in their contribution to this volume, when preexisting organizational ecology is taken into account, the diffusion of a new form of contention may have no discernable effect on subsequent organizational expansion (Chapter 10).

This chapter will focus on three aspects of the dynamics of diffusion that may help us to unravel these puzzles: the key mechanisms that drive diffusion; its

I am grateful to Jan Kubik, Doug McAdam, and the editors of this volume for advice on producing this attempted synthesis.

interaction with institutions and institutional change; and the significance of upward and downward scale shift as part of the diffusion process.

How do we proceed? For reasons of parsimony, this chapter will give less attention to both collective active frames and the spread of new social movements than to the diffusion of new and innovative forms of collective action. I will argue, first, that although analysts have frequently noted the fact of diffusion – and even charted its geographic spread (McAdam and Rucht 1993; Soule and Zylan 1997) – we have little evidence about the concrete mechanisms that drive it. I will identify three main mechanisms of diffusion, which have demonstrably different effects on its reach and outcomes. Second, I will argue that diffusion is seldom self-generating out of the claims and inventions of activists; it results from their interaction with, and often mirrors, the institutions they attack and their practices. Third, I will argue that we need to distinguish between horizontal diffusion and the shift in the scale of contention. Although the former can spread contention broadly across geographic and social divides, it is only the latter that can turn simple incidents into waves of contention, broad social movements, and revolutions.

Here is an example of diffusion that illustrates how mechanisms, institutions, and scale shift came together in a major cycle of contention.

SOLIDARITY FROM THE LENIN SHIPYARD TO POST-LENINIST STATE

On June 30, 1980, Polish communist authorities announced an increase in meat prices, triggering a vast wave of contention that would ultimately undermine the country's communist system and pave the way for the collapse of the socialist bloc. As Jan Kubik begins the story:

The next day workers in several factories... went on strike. During July the strike wave engulfed several regions. On August 14, 1980, several dozen workers began an occupational strike in the Gdańsk Lenin Shipyard. As the strike in the Shipyard grew and the workers from other plants joined in, the authorities agreed to grant wage increases and met some other demands, but only for the Lenin employees. (Kubik 2009: 3072)

There was always a chance that the Gdansk workers would accept the wage increases and go back to work, but under pressure from the base, their representatives ultimately refused, and the strike spread. As Kubik continues:

During the night of August 16 the Inter-factory Strike Committee (*MKS*) was formed and immediately formulated a list of twenty-one demands, including a demand to create a trade union independent from the Communist Party. By the end of the month over 700 thousand people were on strike in about 700 enterprises in all 49 regions of Poland (ibid.).

The strike soon broadened well beyond the confines of an industrial dispute, as intellectuals and artists, peasants and students, and even state workers lent their support, and Catholic clerics offered certification by the country's deep religious beliefs (Kubik 1994). By September, more than thirty Interfactory

Founding Committees had emerged, forming the Independent Self-governing Trade Union "Solidarity," with a National Coordinating Committee (KKP) as its governing body. Already the new union had about 3 million members.

Of course, an independent trade union and a state socialist regime could not coexist for long. With each move forward by the union, the state intervened with delays, challenges, and occasional repression. As Kubik recalls:

The party-state would provoke a crisis either by dragging its feet when it came to implementing the negotiated decisions or attacking the Union activists (including physical assaults); the Union would respond with strike alerts or strikes. An agreement would ultimately be reached and produce a moment of calm until another provocation would restart the whole cycle (2009: 3074).

Ultimately, on December 13, 1981, martial law was declared, Solidarity's leaders were rounded up, and the regime survived for another eight years. But while the struggle changed its form, it was far from over. As Kubik writes: "A multi-faceted 'underground society' emerged, whose activities ranged from clandestine publishing and private theater performances to spectacular rallies and marches often dispersed by the special riot police units" (ibid.).

Slowly, but with increasing determination, the movement openly reconstituted itself, emerging from clandestinity and forming a National Council in 1987 (ibid.). After a new strike wave in 1988, a series of roundtable discussions was held in January 1989, national elections were held in June, and Solidarity candidates won 161 seats in the Sejm and 99 in the Senate. What had begun as an isolated strike of shipyard workers on the Baltic coast produced the first noncommunist government in a state socialist regime.

This story has been told and retold in many versions[1] but it still holds fascination. Why is this? Apart from its inherent interest to students of world politics, it offers three main lessons for students of diffusion:

- First, Solidarity did not spread through "contagion" – a patternless spread of contention across an entire society resembling the spread of a disease. It diffused through a combination of old and new networks: old ones, such as the KOR (Komitet Obrony Robotników, Workers' Defense Committee), factory councils, and even party cells; and new ones, like the interfactory councils. Not only that, but after the movement was forced underground, Catholic practices were socially appropriated and Catholic social doctrine served as a spiritual glue holding the movement together (Kubik 1994).[2]
- Second, Solidarity did not simply "emerge" as a self-starting social movement. It took its initial form within the logic of industrial relations and shifted to its later forms through a series of interactions with the state and the state's moves. Even the ultimate form of its rise to power – the "round

[1] In addition to Kubik (1994 and 2009), the basic story, with some differences of interpretation, is told by Ash 1983, Bernhard 1993, Laba 1991, and Staniszkis 1984.
[2] I am grateful to Jan Kubik for summarizing these mechanisms of diffusion in private correspondence with the author.

table" format, which spread to other parts of East-Central Europe – was the result of interaction with a regime which did not want to recognize the legitimacy of the union by sitting across a rectangular table from its representatives.

- Third, although Solidarity spread across Poland through a process of horizontal diffusion, what ultimately explained its success was *upward scale shift* – that is, a transition from lower to higher levels of the political system.

In the remainder of this chapter, I will follow up on these observations by first specifying the varieties of mechanisms of diffusion we can see in the contributions to this book; second, exploring the ways in which new forms of contention emerge from the interaction between institutional actors and new movements; and third, investigating the conditions that shift contention downward and upward in scale, sometimes – but by no means always – producing broader patterns of contention, regime change, and even revolutions.

I begin with the mechanisms of diffusion of collective action.

MECHANISMS OF DIFFUSION: A TILLIAN PERSPECTIVE

In his studies of what has come to be called "the repertoire of contention," the late Charles Tilly wrote that the existing repertoire grows out of three kinds of factors: a population's daily routines and internal organization; the prevailing standards of rights and justice; and the population's accumulated experience with collective action (Tilly 1986: 10). Tilly also emphasized social learning: what people *know* about how to contend in various places and at different periods of history constrains changes in the repertoire and provides the raw materials for innovation. If this is true, then there are both inducements for and constraints on the spread of new forms of contention in both structural conditions and cultural understandings.

In his work on Britain, Tilly showed how both inducements and constraints worked historically, as state building and capitalism triggered the invention of new forms of contention (Tilly 1995a, 2008). As the early modern state consolidated, people resisted its domination with tax revolts, conscription riots, and petitions; as market capitalism took hold, grain seizures, strikes, and turnouts were used to resist its pressures; and as electronic communication partly displaced print and face-to-face contacts, the possibility for rapid spatial diffusion expanded (Tilly 2004).

Take the strike: Its emergence and development were dependent on changes in capitalism. If there had been no capitalists assembling workers in factories and exploiting their labor power, there would have been no strikes. Or consider the demonstration: Had there been no centers of power such as tax collection offices, prefectures, or city halls, demonstrators might have milled around in the streets but would never have developed the orderly progression to places of power. Capitalism and state building were the major macroprocesses triggering the development of the modern repertoire of contention (Tilly 1995a).

But once invented, in response to the broad structural changes Tilly out-
lines, new forms of contention did not "sit still." Although some – like the
strike – were most at home where there were dense concentrations of workers,
others were "modular" – for example, they could be adapted to other venues,
different social groups, and diverse configurations of conflict (Tarrow 1998;
Tilly 1995a). Even the strike was imitated and modified far beyond its industrial origins and outside the structural relations that had produced it. Once its
efficacy was demonstrated, it spread from industry to services and from there
to educational institutions.

The same was true of other contentious performances. Petitions, which
had proven useful when seeking redress from individual state officials, were
employed as a political tactic against slavery; turnouts against local capitalists
transformed into demonstrations against all manner of antagonists; protesters
refusing to leave a particular official's office transmuted into the sit-in. Countering the specificity and locality of the repertoire of contention was its modularity
and transferability across space and into different sectors of movement activity.
With globalization and internationalization, both the speed and the modularity
of diffusion increased.

In his early work, Tilly imputed fundamental changes in the British repertoire from the eighteenth to the nineteenth century, but without specifying the
mechanisms of diffusion that brought it about. In his last book, *Contentious
Performances* (2008), he summed up these mechanisms as what he called
"parliamentarization." He showed how, between the late eighteenth and the
early nineteenth century, British claims-makers shifted their targets to Parliament just as they were discarding the parochial, bifurcated, and particular
repertoire of the past.

But the connection Tilly drew between the change in the British repertoire
and the rise in Parliament's power was approximate and imputed, rather than
specific and demonstrable. Even though diffusion has been a well-recognized
part of the study of contentious politics for decades, we still know little about
the mechanisms of which it is composed. The idea of patternless "contagion"
was long ago dismissed, but much of the research on diffusion (including many
of the contributions to this volume) focus more on the *fact* of diffusion than
on the mechanisms that drive it. The distinction is important, because of the
possibility that similar forms of contention may develop almost simultaneously
in different settings either randomly or because actors face similar constraints
and inducements.

Think of the wave of protests against International Monetary Fund (IMF)
conditionality that began in the late 1970s and endured through the 1980s
(Walton and Seddon 1994). These protests were triggered by near-identical
pressures from an external institution, sometimes abetted by, but often opposed
by domestic authorities. They *may* have involved mechanisms of diffusion, but
in the absence of evidence about *how* protests diffused from one site to another,
they were probably similar but independent reactions to the same stimulus.

How does a new form of contention spread, and what lessons does this have for contention in general? We can identify three main pathways of diffusion: relational, nonrelational, and mediated.[3]

- By *relational diffusion* I mean the emulation of new forms of contention on the part of actors with preexisting relationships of trust, intimacy, or regular communication to those who have initiated those forms.
- By *nonrelational diffusion* I mean the emulation of new forms of contention on the part of actors who learn, through impersonal means such as the media, of the actions of those who have initiated those forms.
- By *mediated diffusion* I mean the emulation of new forms of contention on the part of actors with no preexisting ties to those who have initiated those forms through the intervention of third parties who maintain relationships of trust with both initiators and adopters.

The general tendency of students of social movements has been to focus on the first process – relational diffusion – because innovations travel most easily along established lines of interaction.[4] Like the spread of hybrid corn or the adoption of new medical practices, the adoption of new forms of collective action often follows the links of interpersonal interaction among people who know one another or are parts of networks of trust. But in this age of almost instant communication, new forms of protest often spread among people who have never met. And in an age of massive immigration and cheap and easy transportation, information about collective action can also spread through third parties – brokers – who connect people who would otherwise have no contact with one another.

From his study of the spread of the Salafist jihad, Marc Sageman allows us to identify all three main pathways of diffusion: relational, nonrelational, and mediated. According to Sageman, social bonds and personal networks were important in the spread of the Islamist network (Sageman 2004: chapter 5). In his view, not only did Islam and Arabic provide a universal faith and a common language to jihadis, but interpersonal trust, family ties, and common local origins also helped to create "small world networks" among people who identified with one another and were prepared to emulate one another's actions (ibid.: 139). This is what I call *relational diffusion*. It transferred information along established lines of interaction through the attribution of similarity and the networks of trust that it produces (Lee and Strang 2006).

Sageman also observed *nonrelational diffusion* among people who had few or no social ties. By historical accident, the Islamist movement's growth

[3] These ideas grew out of joint work with Doug McAdam and Charles Tilly (McAdam et al. 2001), and then with McAdam alone (Tarrow and McAdam 2005), and are elaborated in my *New Transnational Activism*, 2005.
[4] See the discussions in Jackson et al. 1960; McAdam 1999; McAdam and Rucht 1993; Pinard 1971; Rogers 1983; Strang and Meyer 1993; and Soule 1997.

coincided with the coming of the Internet, "making possible a new type of relationship between an individual and a virtual community" (Sageman 2004: 160–3). This not only sped the diffusion of the movement but favored its "theorization": a kind of "folk theory" that defines some thing or activity in abstract terms and locates it within a cause–effect or functional scheme (Strang and Meyer 1993). The media, and especially the Internet, encouraged the diffusion of an extremely one-sided reading of Islam, reducing the level of discourse to the lowest common denominator and identifying the suicide bombing as a tool that would bring glory to the martyr and success to the cause (ibid.: 162).

Sageman also observed *mediated diffusion.* In the jihadi networks he studied, he identified a number of movement "nodes" that connected individuals within a geographic cluster and were linked across these clusters by a small number of weak ties (ibid.: 169 ff.). What kept these weak links alive was the mechanisms of brokerage – the connection of two unconnected sites by a third, which works through movement "halfway houses," immigrants, or institutions. Brokers may never participate in contentious politics, but their key position between otherwise unconnected sites can influence the content of the information that is communicated.

Each of these pathways can be observed in the contributions to this volume:

- *Relational diffusion:* In her chapter on the diffusion of the "sexual harassment" frame from the United States to Western Europe, Conny Roggeband pinpoints the role of Dutch feminists who had been living in the United States for several years, who used a *Redbook* survey to highlight sexual harassment in the Netherlands (this volume, Chapter 2). Even in France, seldom willing to follow American examples, feminists of the AVFT (the European Association against Violence Towards Women and Work) were informed by American and French Canadian examples. In Germany, she concludes, "the first awareness programs against sexual harassment in the workplace ... were inspired not only by U.S. feminism, but also by other European examples." "These European initiatives," she concludes, "were clearly informed by the U.S. example through direct links like international feminist networks, personal contacts and visits" (ibid.).
- *Nonrelational diffusion:* Roggeband also points to the role of the media and available feminist literature in the diffusion of the American approach to sexual harassment in Europe (ibid.). This process was at the heart of the diffusion of the "John Kerry is French" rumor during the 2004 U.S. presidential campaign. As Jayson Harsin writes, "the repetition of the rumor bomb by columnists, congressional allies, and pundits and new and old media forms allowed it broad diffusion" (Chapter 9). What was key to the "success" of the "Kerry is French" message was that – although its origin lay in the Bush–Cheney electoral machine – it was diffused by media sources whose interest was less in undercutting Kerry's reputation than in "making news."

- *Mediated diffusion:* Sean Chabot's chapter on the diffusion of the Gandhian repertoire is a good example of mediated diffusion (Chapter 6). Valerie Bunce and Sharon Wolchik's chapter on the diffusion of the "electoral model" of democratic revolutions is another. In the first case, Chabot shows, diffusion worked through the intermediation of American civil rights advocates who traveled to India to meet Gandhi; in the second, the American democracy promotion community, both public and private, played a central role in bringing groups together, transferring campaign and electoral strategies, and providing resources for campaign literature, public opinion surveys, civic groups, and independent media (Chapter 8).

WHY MECHANISMS MATTER

Why is it important to specify these different trajectories of diffusion? Why not simply register the "fact" of diffusion or trace its geographic or social scope? It is important because the outcomes of diffusion vary according to the mechanisms that drive it. For example, in relational diffusion, trust enables communication between originators and adopters and thus the emulation of practices by the originators. But depending on trust also limits the range of diffusion to networks built on personal ties. In such cases, diffusion may be strong but narrow. The history of the limited spread of peasant rebellions illustrates this factor: Only when peasants were somehow "connected" to other peasants did trust networks allow rebellion to be diffused; in highly localized peasant societies in which trust seldom spread beyond a single village or clan, diffusion was limited.

In nonrelational diffusion, "theorization" makes it possible to rapidly transport a message to a new venue. But the need to reduce the message to "folk wisdom" reduces its complexity and can produce a simplistic version of the performances that receivers can interpret as they like, often in sites to which they are ill adapted. The Internet, which has created much excitement about the possibility of online mobilization, can diffuse contention far and wide; but it is possible that Internet-based mobilization may not create the trust networks that are needed for sustained diffusion.

Finally, in mediated diffusion, brokerage by third parties speeds the transfer of information but gives these intermediary actors leverage in reshaping the message. This seems to have been the case for the diffusion of the Gandhian version of nonviolence as it was adopted and adapted to the United States by the civil rights movement. Here, the pervasive institutionalized forms of politics of the United States reshaped the doctrine, giving it a Christian cast. This worked well for churchgoing middle sectors of the black population in the South, but not in the northern ghettoes, where nonviolence gave way to violent riots that alienated many African Americans, as well as the movement's liberal white supporters. Had the Gandhian model of diffusion awaited direct relational diffusion, it would have had to wait a long time; and without its translation by movement brokers, it might not have been adapted to American conditions.[5]

Institutions and Interactive Diffusion

This takes us to my second argument about the dynamics of diffusion. In our studies of the diffusion of social movements, we have often followed the lead of students of technical innovations. But technical innovation is essentially institution-free. What I mean by this is that the progress of an innovation is largely dependent on its resistance or acceptance by a receiving population (Rogers 1995). To the extent that institutions matter, they either guide the paths of diffusion or provide diffusers with resources – for example, with research grants. The innovation itself is free-floating: Its acceptance or diffusion depends ultimately on the networks through which it travels and on its adaptation to the task it was designed to solve.

The diffusion of collective action is different: It interacts in complex ways with both political institutions and can bring about institutional change. Consider the influence of American and European institutions on the diffusion of the American frame of sexual harassment from Roggeband's chapter. Whereas American feminists were helped by the Equal Pay Act of 1963 and by the Civil Rights Act of 1964, their European counterparts had no such structuring legislation on which to build. Dutch activists strategically reframed the issue, dropping the American emphasis on "hostile environments," and sought state funding to create a "complaints office," but ultimately, facing limited support at the national level, they cooperated with other feminist groups to place sexual harassment on the agenda of the European Commission. To adapt to European institutions, European feminists adopted a professional scientific language that became the currency in transnational communication between feminists, policy makers, and politicians (Roggeband, Chapter 2; Marks and McAdam 1996).

Institutional encounters often change how movements frame their messages. In their chapter on the creationist–intelligent design controversy in the United States, James Stobaugh and David Snow show how "frames . . . are probably rarely diffused in whole cloth but are more often reconstituted in a fashion in which core ideas or values are laminated with ideas and constraints that are consistent with the temper of the times *and the institutional structures in which the collectivity or movement is embedded* (Chapter 3, this volume, emphasis added). Focusing on the single legal institution of the Supreme Court, Stobaugh and Snow show how, following the setback of the *Epperson v. Arkansas* case, creationists "had to find another means of countering the teaching of evolution" (ibid.; Binder 2002). The result was the amalgam called "creation science," and the argument that it should be taught alongside evolution to allow student

---

[5] For an extended examination of how such "translation" can work in the case of human rights norms, see Merry 2003.

choice. Not only did the Supreme Court reshape how antievolutionists shaped their message, but different levels of the federal court system also appeared to function as a significant constraint on frame construction and deployment for both sets of contestants. Stobaugh and Snow conclude that "different institutional contexts may impose different sets of constraints on framing processes that in turn affect the character of what is diffused" (Chapter 3, this volume).

So far, institutional effects on diffusion have been portrayed as static: for instance, a given movement adapts to a given institutional context. But institutions are not static; they evolve in a process of interaction with contentious politics. The challenge for diffusion researchers is to try to understand how institutional change and changes in collective action affect one another.

This is not a new idea. More than two decades ago, Doug McAdam showed how the diffusion of the tactics of the civil rights movements interacted iteratively with state responses (McAdam 1983). Each time the movement found itself stymied by state responses, it would innovate in the forms of collective action it employed. State responses were similarly dependent on what the movement did: When repression turned out to fill the jails to overflowing, the police would truck protesters to temporary sites and in some cases adopt the more permissive techniques that later came to be called "protest management" (McCarthy and McPhail 1998).

National traditions of protest condition how a state makes policy to anticipate new contention. Consider the limited U.S. resources that were initially mobilized in both the Afghanistan invasion and the Iraq War. Many critics have noted the relatively small number of troops employed, the use of mercenary forces filling the gaps that would otherwise have had to be filled by conscription, and the low level of sacrifice demanded of the American public. Why did the Bush administration try to fight a war on two fronts with inadequate forces? The reason seems to me to lie in the history of contentious politics triggered by our last major foreign misadventure – in Vietnam – where both mass mobilization at home and troop demoralization in the field combined to shake the foundations of American power. It was fear of a repetition of the recent history of contentious politics at war that led the Bush administration to attempt to fight two wars with inadequate troops and soldiers of fortune.

Interactive diffusion also links non-state institutional and contentious actors. In his chapter, Ronald Herring describes a doubly articulated dialectic: for instance, the ways in which "oppositional politics confronts organized promotion and official sanction" (Chapter 5). Herring develops the concept in the context of the "framing contest" between pro-GMO and anti-GMO forces in the arena of food production over the past decade. "Much of the dialectic," he writes, "is precisely mirrored: The pro-biotech narrative perfectly inverts, for example, the opposition's framing of authoritative knowledge from "GMOs: Unsafe and Untested" to "GMOs: Tested and Safe.""

Interactive diffusion also links the moderate and extreme wings of social movements with state strategy in cycles of radicalization and moderation (Tilly and Tarrow 2006: chapter 5). Donatella della Porta and Tarrow traced the pathways of diffusion in the Italian cycle of protest in the late 1960s and early 1970s through two contradictory yet mutually dependent processes – escalation and institutionalization (della Porta and Tarrow 1986). Combining data on ordinary protest events with data on organized violence, they developed the following explanation.

- *Escalation:* When different movement sectors compete for support, some leaders respond by escalation: the substitution of more extreme goals and more robust tactics for more moderate ones in order to maintain the interest of their supporters and attract new ones.
- At the same time, others respond by *institutionalization:* the substitution of the routines of organized politics for the disorder of life in the streets, buttressed by mass organization and purposive incentives.
- Faced by these competing forms of collective action, states can respond with *facilitation* of those who are willing to work within institutional practices and with *repression* of those who do not. Facilitation produces co-opting of moderates and isolates those whose involvement is most intense into a clandestine world in which their only means of expression is violence.

The result is *polarization:* increasing ideological distance between the wings of a once unified movement sector, divisions between its leaders, and – in some cases – terrorism. Della Porta and Tarrow found that the Italian protest cycle ended in a paroxysm of organized violence but also in the routinization of contention. Escalation and institutionalization – fed by repression – produced a split in what had once been seen as a single movement. But in the meantime the scale of conflict gravitated upward into the political system, culminating in the kidnapping and murder of Aldo Moro, a leading figure in the Christian Democratic party. This takes us to scale shift.

Scale Shift

Scale shift is a complex process that not only diffuses contention across space or social sectors, but also creates instances for new coordination at a higher or a lower level than its initiation. Scale shift makes a big difference to contention because it leads to new coordination at a different level and thus involves new actors and institutions. Contentious actors often deliberately "venue shop" – often to higher or lower levels of the polity – in order to seek coordination at a level more favorable to them. This was the strategy of the National Association for the Advancement of Colored People (NAACP) in taking school discrimination to the Supreme Court in the 1950s. It was also the strategy of the Women's Christian Temperance Union, which shifted its targets from the national to the state and local levels trying to find a venue in which its message against the evils of alcoholism would be best received (Szymanski 2003).

Scale shift can operate either downward or upward:

- *Downward scale shift* is the coordination of collective action at a more local level than its initiation. A good example is civil rights groups' responding to the Supreme Court's striking down of racial discrimination at the national level by registering African American voters in Mississippi (McAdam 1988).
- In contrast, *upward scale shift* involves coordination of collective action at a higher level (whether regional, national, or even international) than its initiation.

Although downward scale shift can often bury contention in the recesses of individual or group life, upward scale shift is one of the most significant processes in contentious politics. It moves contention beyond its local origins, touches on the interests and values of new actors, involves a shift of venue to sites where contention may be more or less successful, and can threaten other actors or entire regimes.

Figure 11.1 describes two main routes through which upward scale shift can operate: a *direct diffusion* route that passes through individuals and groups whose previous contacts or similarities become the basis of their mobilization; and a *mediated route* through brokers who connect people who would otherwise have no previous contacts. We saw an example of the first route when so many factories adopted the tactic of the Lenin shipyard that Polish authorities were forced to recognize Solidarity's legitimacy. We saw the second route when the parish priests adopted the strikers' cause, if not their tactics, and Catholic Solidarity groups were formed.

Scale shift involves many of the mechanisms familiar from studies of diffusion: *emulation*, as people learn about episodes of contention elsewhere and copy or adapt them; *brokerage*, as movement missionaries or opportunistic political entrepreneurs make connections among groups that would otherwise be isolated from one another; and the *attribution of similarity* among people who did not know one another earlier or may have seen each other as strangers. An important difference between the two routes is that direct diffusion travels through existing commonalities and networks of trust, whereas mediated diffusion creates new networks and commonalities. At its most successful, upward scale shift creates new identities.

Some episodes of contention never scale upward; that is, they either fail to diffuse widely or their diffusion remains horizontal. Nondiffusion is either the result of the extreme localism or parochialism of a claim or of its demonstrated risks to claims makers. A good example of horizontal diffusion that fails to scale upward would be the "shantytowns" studied by Sarah Soule as part of the divestment movement against apartheid in the 1980s. That innovation first emerged at Columbia University in April 1985 when students blockading Hamilton Hall dragged armchairs and sofas, and eventually tarps and blankets, there from a nearby dormitory. Columbia's constructions of tarps and blankets soon spread to other campuses. At Princeton and Santa Cruz, protesters called

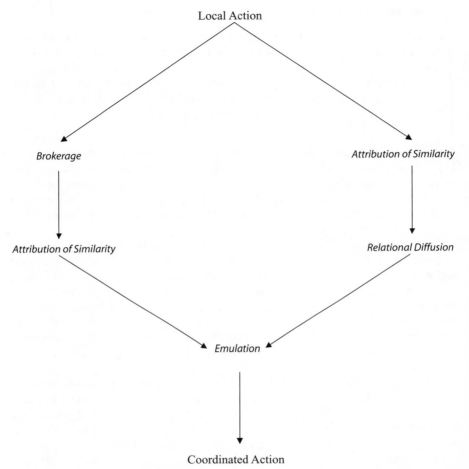

FIGURE 11.1. Scale Shift: Alternative Routes. *Source:* Tarrow and McAdam 2005: 128.

it a "camp-out"; at Harvard a "sleep-in"; whereas other students on other campuses called them "sit-outs." It was only at Cornell, in late spring, that student protesters collected scraps of wood, tar paper, and plastic to construct a shack in front of the university's administration building. That shack, as Soule reports, was the first of what later were called a shantytown, "a performance and a name that eventually spread to similar structures around the country" (Soule 1997, 1999).

Looking back, we can see that the shantytown was no more than a symbol-laden variant of the sit-in, and for that reason, it was inapplicable to other kinds of claims. Its use soon petered out as student protesters attacked other targets with other and more fitting performances. What it certainly did *not* do was to scale upward to higher levels of American politics; for that to happen, other actors would have had to employ it in public spaces less permissive than college campuses.

An innovation that *did* scale upward came during the early period of the American civil rights movement, when bus boycotts were first used by African Americans in the South. Usually dated from the Montgomery bus boycott in December 1955, the movement actually began two years later when a black minister, Theodore Jemison, organized the same kind of bus boycott in Baton Rouge, Louisiana (Tarrow and McAdam 2005: 132). But the Montgomery bus boycott, and the evocative figure of Rosa Parks who initiated it, captured the imagination of black Americans, white liberals, and especially the new television media, which diffused information about it across the country.

The spread of the movement corresponded to a classical process of relational diffusion, with an existing network of black ministers serving as the principal vehicles by which the innovation of the bus boycott spread from Baton Rouge to Montgomery and on to a host of other southern cities, but the campaign also led to the development of new church-based movement organizations throughout the South. "All over the South," writes Pat Watters, "Negroes were forming organizations in imitation of the Montgomery Improvement Association" (1971: 50). It was from this network of local organizations that the Southern Christian Leadership Conference was formed at a meeting held in Atlanta in 1957 (Clayton 1964: 12). The SCLC would remain the principal vehicle of upward scale shift throughout this period.

Many shifts in scale have the effect of institutionalizing contention as they rise into the thicket of national political institutions, with their biases and limitations. Such was the case of the nuclear freeze movement of the early 1980s. That movement began in response to the Reagan administration's plans to send medium-range nuclear missiles to Europe. It depended heavily on relational diffusion among citizens mobilized at the local level. Diffusion occurred most dramatically via the spread of local and state referenda throughout New England and elsewhere (Meyer and Kleidman 1991: 243 ff.), an innovation that would later be revived in the movement against the U.S. Patriot Act following 9/11 (Vasi and Strang 2009).

The organizers of the freeze movement were deliberately aiming at diffusion at the grassroots, avoiding the embrace of existing arms control organizations and symbolically operations far from Washington, D.C., to St. Louis (ibid.: 246). But diffusion was also mediated by existing organizations, such as the test ban and anti-ABM movements, as well as traditional pacifist and peace organizations like Physicians for Social Responsibility, and churches and religious communities. These organizations brought national constituencies and organizing experience to what had been an amateur-led grassroots movement, as David S. Meyer writes. "The nuclear disarmament, civil rights, and antiwar movements of the 1960s," he says, "had established a network of organizations from which the nuclear freeze movement would draw support and also had developed an inventory of tactics" (1990: 149–50). Inevitably, the movement moved into national politics and as it did, "the movement appeared to moderate its rhetoric and analysis" (Meyer and Kleidman 1991: 249). By 1983, it had become "a vehicle to achieve Congressional action for traditional arms control measures in the face of Reagan administration hostility (ibid.: 233).

CONCLUSIONS

The message of this chapter can be easily summarized. First, I have not argued against the tradition of research on the diffusion of contention. Research in this tradition has usefully focused on the "fact" of diffusion; it has effectively traced the pathways of diffusion across geographic and social space; and it has shown how, and under what circumstances, diffusion produces new organizations and transmits new collective action frames to broader settings. These are all important contributions to our understanding of contentious politics. In each respect, though, existing research leaves open lacunae in our understanding of the dynamics of contention. Instead, this chapter has focused on mechanisms of diffusion, on the interaction between contention and institutions, and on the frequency of diffusion between levels of the political system.

A deliberate effort to identify and trace the mechanisms of diffusion cannot fill all the lacunae in diffusion research, but it can help to produce a clearer outline of the dynamics of contention. Let us first consider the evidence for the "fact" of the near-simultaneous emergence of contention against the so-called Washington consensus on neoliberal policies in Latin America in the last decade. It is true, as Kenneth Roberts writes, that "social resistance has . . . punctured the aura of inexorability that surrounded the trends toward economic liberalization and globalization in the waning decades of the twentieth century" (Roberts 2008: 328). That social resistance was driven by powerful international forces, especially by the "policy leverage of international lenders and financial institutions, by the 'authoritative knowledge' of neoclassical economics and its transnational technocratic networks, and resurgent US hegemony in the post-Cold War era" (ibid.).

But was it driven by diffusion? A proliferation of studies on individual protest movements "can easily convey the impression that Latin America is in the midst of a generalized social backlash against market liberalism" (ibid.: 337). But the dramatic differences in the levels of social mobilization and party system institutionalization that Roberts identifies suggest rather that institutional variations and different opportunity structures are more responsible for the differences than country-to-country diffusion. Only a determined effort to trace the mechanisms by which contention arose in each country and of the similarities and differences between them can tell us whether and to what extent diffusion has been operating there.

Institutions and institutional differences frame how claims are produced and disseminated. Many students appear to see framing as a self-generating process of social construction. Although there is warrant for such a view in early accounts of framing, in Chapter 3 of this volume, Stobaugh and Snow offer a more institutionally-rooted account. It was in response to the Supreme Court's rejection of creationist thinking that the anti-evolution movement in the United States invented the idea of "intelligent design" that could be taught alongside evolution and thus challenge it. Their account demonstrates not only that time affects the framing process, but also that interaction between movements and institutions plays an important role in framing.

Stobaugh and Snow's chapter also illustrates the third argument of this chapter: that scale shift is an important part of the dynamics of contention. In the third section of this chapter, I argued that upward scale shift is an important component of diffusion and differs from horizontal diffusion because it brings new actors and new configurations of conflict into an episode of contention. Stobaugh and Snow go beyond this argument to show how downward scale shift can have similar effects. They show that after their defeat in the Supreme Court in the *Edwards* case, a second prong of the strategy of the anti-evolutionist forces in the United States was to target local and state school boards of education, "pressing them to authorize teaching creation science in the classroom and to get this perspective included alongside evolutionary theory in the textbooks that the school districts purchased."

The success of that strategy is still to be proven and in some cases, local communities have known how to defend themselves from takeovers by local anti-evolution militants. But like the shift of the nuclear freeze movement from grassroots town meetings in New England to the halls of Congress – it did bring an array of new actors and new configurations of conflict into the struggle between evolutionary and anti-evolutionary forces. It also moved the arena of conflict from the lawyerlike discussions before the United States Supreme Court to local communities in which electoral considerations and local networks could play a more important role.

These concluding comments will not end the debate about the diffusion of contentious politics, nor are they intended to do so. We have made good progress in understanding diffusion by tracing where it occurs, which geographic and social divides it crosses, and when and where it produces new movement organizations. I hope to have broadened the debate to include a more deliberate emphasis on the mechanisms of diffusion, on the role of interaction with institutions in diffusion processes, and on how the shift in the scale of contention contributes to changes in the locus of contentious interactions.

General Bibliography

Ackerman, Peter and Jack Duvall. 2000. *A Force More Powerful: A Century of Non-violent Conflict*. New York: Palgrave.

Acuff, Stewart. 2009. "Mobilizing for the Employee Free Choice Act." *The Huffington Post*. February 17 (available at www.huffingtonpost.com/stewart-acuff/mobilizing-for-the-employ-b_167153.html; accessed March 12, 2009).

Adams, Frank. 1975. *Unearthing Seeds of Fire: The Idea of Highlander*. Winston-Salem, NC: John F. Blair.

Adams, Roy. 2002. "The Wagner Act Model: A Toxic System Beyond Repair." *British Journal of Industrial Relations* 40: 114.

AFL-CIO. 2009. "What the Freedom to Join Unions Means to America's Workers and the Middle Class" (available at www.aflcio.org/joinaunion/voiceatwork/efca/whyunion.cfm; accessed June 4, 2009).

AFSCME. 2004. "Freedom of Association and Workers' Rights Violations at Resurrection Health Care: Report and Analysis under International Human Rights and Labor Rights Standards." Prepared for Worker Rights Board Hearing, Chicago, August 26, 2004.

Aksartova, Sada. 2005. "Civil Society from Abroad: U.S. Donors in the Former Soviet Union." Ph.D. dissertation, Department of Sociology, Princeton University, Princeton, NJ.

American Rights at Work. 2009. "Allies Taking Action" (available at www.americanrightsatwork.org/employee-free-choice-act/allies-taking-action/allies-taking-action-20071019-330-279.html; accessed April 30, 2009).

Andersen, Ellen Ann. 2005. *Out of the Closets and Into the Courts: Legal Opportunity Structure and Gay Rights Litigation*. Ann Arbor: University of Michigan Press.

Anderson, Benedict. 1997. *Imagined Communities*, 7th edition. London: Verso.

Andrews, Kenneth T. and Michael Biggs. 2006. "The Dynamics of Protest Diffusion: Movement Organizations, Social Networks, and News Media in the 1960 Sit-Ins." *American Sociological Review* 71: 752–777.

Appeal from the Supreme Court of Arkansas Brief for Appellee, *Epperson v. State of Arkansas*, No. 7 (filed May 11, 1968) (available on Westlaw at 1986 WL 112572).

Arsenault, Raymond. 2005. *Freedom Riders: 1961 and the Struggle for Racial Justice.* Oxford, UK: Oxford University Press.

Ash, Timothy Garton. 1983. *The Polish Solidarity.* New York: Charles Scribner's Sons.

Assayag, Jackie. 2005. "Seeds of Wrath: Agriculture, Biotechnology and Globalization," pp. 65–88 in *Globalizing India: Perspectives from Below*, edited by Jackie Assayag and Chris Fuller. London: Anthem Press.

Axelrod, Robert. 1976. *Structure of Decision.* Princeton, NJ: Princeton University Press.

Ayres, Jeffrey. 1999. "From the Streets to the Internet: The Cyber-Diffusion of Contention." *Annals of the American Academy of Political Science* 566: 132–143.

Bakhtin, Mikhail. 1981. *The Dialogic Imagination: Four Essays.* Austin: University of Texas Press.

Bambawale, O. M., A. Singh, O. P. Sharma, B. B. Bhosle, R. C. Lavekar, A. Dhandhapani, V. Kanwar, R. K. Tanwar, K. S. Rathod, N. R. Patange, and V. M. Pawar. 2004. "Performance of Bt cotton (MECH-162) under Integrated Pest Management in farmers' participatory field trial in Nanded district, Central India." *Current Science* 86: 25.

Bandy, Joe and Jackie Smith. 2005. *Coalitions Across Borders: Transnational Protest and the Neoliberal Order.* Lanham, MD: Rowman and Littlefield.

Barber, Benjamin. 1984. *Strong Democracy: Participatory Politics for a New Age.* Berkeley: University of California Press.

Barboza, David. 2003. "Development of Biotech Crops Is Booming in Asia." *New York Times* February 21: A3.

Batista, Rita, Nelson Saibo, Tiago Lourenço, and Maria Margaret Oliveira. 2008. "Microarray Analyses Reveal That Plant Mutagenesis May Induce More Transcriptomic Changes Than Transgene Insertion." *Proceedings of the National Academy of Science* 105: 3640–3645.

Beissinger, Mark. 2002. *Nationalist Mobilization and the Collapse of the Soviet State.* Cambridge, MA: Cambridge University Press.

_____. 2006. "Promoting Democracy: Is Exporting Revolution a Constructive Strategy?" *Dissent* 53: 18–24.

_____. 2007. "Structure and Example in Modular Political Phenomena: The Diffusion of Bulldozer/ Rose/ Orange/ Tulip Revolutions." *Perspectives on Politics* 5: 259–276.

Benford, Robert D. and David A. Snow. 2000. "Framing Processes and Social Movements." *Annual Review of Sociology* 26: 611–39.

Bennett, Richard M., Uma S. Kambhampati, Stephen Morse, and Yousouf Ismael. 2006. "Farm-Level Economic Performance of Genetically Modified Cotton in Maharashtra, India." *Review of Agricultural Economics* 28: 59–71.

Bennett, W. Lance. 2005. "Social Movements Beyond Borders: Understanding Two Eras of Transnational Activism," pp. 203–226 in *Transnational Protest and Global Activism*, edited by Donatella della Porta and Sidney Tarrow. Lanham, MD: Rowman and Littlefield.

Berenson, Bernard, 1952. *Rumor and Reflection.* New York: Simon and Schuster.

Bernhard, Michael H. 1993. *The Origins of Democratization in Poland: Workers, Intellectuals, and Oppositional Politics, 1976–1980.* New York: Columbia University Press.

Bernstein, Irving. 1969. *The Turbulent Years: A History of the American Worker, 1933–1941.* Boston: Houghton Mifflin.

Bieber, Florian. 2003. "The Serbian Transition and Civil Society: Roots of the Delayed Transition in Serbia." *International Journal of Politics, Culture and Society* 17: 73–90.

Biggs, Michael. 2003. "Positive Feedback in Collective Mobilization: The American Strike Wave of 1886." *Theory and Society* 32: 217–254.

———. 2005. "Strikes as Forest Fires: Chicago and Paris in the Late 19th Century." *American Journal of Sociology* 110: 1684–1714.

———. 2006. "Who Joined the Sit-ins and Why: Southern Black Students in the Early 1960s." *Mobilization* 11: 241–256.

Binder, Amy J. 2002. *Contentious Curricula: Afrocentrism and Creationism in American Public Schools*. Princeton, NJ: Princeton University Press.

Blumer, Herbert. [1939] 1972. "Collective Behavior," pp. 65–121 in *Principles of Sociology*, edited by Alfred McClung Lee. New York: Twayne.

Boal, Iain A. 2001. "Damaging Crops: Sabotage, Social Memory and the New Genetic Enclosures," pp. 146–154 in *Violent Environments*, edited by Nancy L. Peluso and Michael Watts. Ithaca, NY: Cornell University Press.

Bob, Clifford. 2005. *The Marketing of Rebellion: Insurgents, Media, and Transnational Support*. New York: Cambridge University Press.

Bockman, Johanna and Gil Eyal. 2002. "Eastern Europe as a Laboratory for Economic Knowledge: The Transnational Roots of Neoliberalism." *American Journal of Sociology* 108: 310–352.

Boehlert, Eric. 2004. "Scribes Have Kerry-Edwards 'Love Fest' Covered," July 12 (available at archive.salon.com/politics/war_room/2004/07/12/affectionate/print.html; accessed December 12, 2006).

Bohstedt, John and Dale E. Williams. 1988. "The Diffusion of Riots: The Patterns of 1766, 1795, and 1801 in Devonshire." *Journal of Interdisciplinary History* 19: 1–24.

Bondurant, Joan. 1971. *Conquest of Violence: The Gandhian Philosophy of Conflict*. Princeton, NJ: Princeton University Press.

Bonny, Sylvie. 2003. "Why Are Most Europeans Opposed to GMOs? Factors Explaining Rejection in France and Europe." *Electronic Journal of Biotechnology* 6: 50–71.

Borbieva, Noor O'Neill. 2007. "Development in the Kyrgyz Republic: Exchange, Communal Networks, and the Foreign Presence." Ph.D. dissertation, Department of Anthropology, Harvard University, Cambridge, MA.

Bordia, Prashant and Nicolas DiFonzo. 2004. "Problem Solving in Social Interactions on the Internet: Rumor as Social Cognition." *Social Psychology Quarterly* 67: 33–49.

Borger, Julian. 2000. "Workers' Rights 'Abused in US'." *The Guardian* August 30: 12.

Bownas, Richard. 2008. "Framing Farmers: The Case of GM Crops and Transnational Activist Networks in India." American Political Science Association Annual Meetings, August 29. Boston, MA.

Branch, Taylor. 1988. *Parting the Waters: America in the King Years, 1954–1963*. Gloucester, MA: Peter Smith Publisher.

Bratton, Michael, Robert Mattes, and E. Gyimah Boadi, eds. 2004. *Public Opinion, Democratization, and Market Reform*. Cambridge, UK: Cambridge University Press.

Brief for the Catholic League for Religious and Civil Rights, Amicus Curiae, in Support of Appellants, *Edwards v. Aguillard*, No. 85–1513 (filed June 19, 1986) (available on Westlaw at 1986 WL 727654).

Brief of American Civil Liberties Union and American Jewish Congress, as Amici Curiae, *Epperson v. State of Arkansas*, No. 7 (filed May 13, 1968) (available on Westlaw at 1968 WL 112573).

Brief of Amicus Curiae, American Federation of Teachers, AFL-CIO in Support of Appellees, *Edwards v. Aguillard*, No. 85-1513 (filed August 15, 1986) (available on Westlaw at 1986 WL 727655).

Brief of Amici Curiae, Biologists and Other Scientists in Support of Defendants, *Kitzmiller v. Dover Area School District*, Civil Action No. 4:04-CV-2688 (filed October 3, 2005) (available at scit.us/kitz/kitz-dibrief.pdf; accessed on October 7, 2006).

Brief of Amicus Curiae, the Discovery Institute, *Kitzmiller v. Dover Area School District*, Civil Action No. 4:04-CV-2688 (filed October 17, 2005) (available on Westlaw at 2005 WL 3136716).

Brief of the Christian Legal Society and National Association of Evangelicals as Amici Curiae Supporting Appellants, *Edwards v. Aguillard*, No. 85-1513 (filed June 19, 1986) (available on Westlaw at 1986 WL 727650).

Brinks, Daniel and Michael Coppedge. 2006. "Diffusion Is No Illusion: Neighbor Emulation in the Third Wave of Democracy." *Comparative Political Studies* 39: 463–489.

Broderick, Francis and August Meier. 1965. *Negro Protest Thought in the Twentieth Century*. Indianapolis, IN: Bobbs-Merrill.

Brody, David. 1980. *Workers in Industrial America: Essays on the Twentieth Century Struggle*. New York: Oxford University Press.

Brownmiller, Susan. 1975. *Against Our Will: Men, Women and Rape*. New York: Simon and Schuster.

Buchanan, Paul G. 1990. "'Useful Fools' as Diplomatic Tools: Organized Labor as an Instrument of US Foreign Policy in Latin America." Kellogg Institute, University of Notre Dame. Working Paper No. 136 (April 1990).

Bunce, Valerie. 1994. "Sequencing Political and Economic Reforms," pp. 46–63 in *East-Central European Economies in Transition*, edited by John Hardt and Richard Kaufman. Washington, DC: Joint Economic Committee.

———. 1999a. "The Political Economy of Postsocialism." *Slavic Review* 58: 756–793.

———. 1999b. *Subversive Institutions: The Design and the Destruction of Socialism and the State*. New York: Cambridge University Press.

———. 2003. "Rethinking Recent Democratization: Lessons from the Postcommunist Experience." *World Politics* 55: 167–192.

———. 2006. "Enabling and Enhancing Democracy: Global Patterns and Postcommunist Dynamics." Paper presented at the first meeting of the Project on Democratic Transitions, Foreign Policy Research Institute, Philadelphia.

Bunce, Valerie and Sharon Wolchik. 2006a. "Favorable Conditions and Electoral Revolutions." *Journal of Democracy* 17: 5–17.

———. 2006b. "International Diffusion and Postcommunist Electoral Revolutions." *Communist and Post-Communist Studies* 39: 283–304.

———. 2010. "Defining and Domesticating the Electoral Model: A Comparison of Slovakia and Serbia," pp. 134–154, in *Democracy and Authoritarianism in the Postcommunist World*, edited by Valerie Bunce, Michael McFaul, and Kathryn Stoner-Weiss. New York: Cambridge University Press.

———. Forthcoming. *U.S. Democracy Promotion and Electoral Change in Postcommunist Europe and Eurasia*. New York: Cambridge University Press.

Burbules, Nicholas. 1993. *Dialogue in Teaching: Theory and Practice*. New York: Teachers College Press.

Bureau of Labor Statistics. 2009, January. "Union Members in 2008." Washington, DC: U.S. Department of Labor.

Bureau of Labor Statistics. 2010, January. "Union Members in 2009." Washington, DC: U.S. Department of Labor.

Bureau of National Affairs. 2009. "Institutional Investors Urge Congress to Approve Employee Free Choice Act." *Daily Labor Report.* May 12, 2009, at A7.

Burns, Stewart. 1997. *Daybreak of Freedom: The Montgomery Bus Boycott.* Chapel Hill: University of North Carolina Press.

Bush, George. 2003. "Remarks by the President After Meeting with Members of the Congressional Conference Committee on Energy Legislation." Office of the White House Press Secretary, September 17 (available at georgewbush-whitehouse.archives .gov/news/releases/2003/09/20030917-7.html; accessed May 3, 2005).

Byrne, Jay. 2003. "The Agricultural Biotechnology Protest Industry." *Biotechnology, the Media, and Public Policy.* Washington, DC: American Enterprise Institute (available at http://www.princeton.edu/morefoodlesscarbon/reading/files/Byrne-Biotechnology-and-Public-Policy.pdf, accessed April 2, 2010).

Capital Advantage. 2008. "Bring your Advocacy Efforts into the 21st Century!" (Available at capitoladvantage.com/products/capwiz/; accessed August 13, 2008.)

Carothers, Thomas. 1999. *Aiding Democracy Abroad; The Learning Curve.* Washington, DC: Carnegie Endowment for International Peace.

———. 2004. *Critical Missions: Essays on Democracy Promotion.* Washington, DC: Carnegie Endowment for International Peace.

———.2007a. "U.S. Democracy Promotion Before and After Bush" (available at www.carnegieendowment.org/publications/index.cfm?fa=view&id=19549; accessed June 30, 2009).

———. 2007b. "The 'Sequencing' Fallacy." *Journal of Democracy* 18: 12–27.

Carragee, Kevin M. and Wim Roefs. 2004. "The Neglect of Power in Recent Framing Research." *Journal of Communication* 54: 214–233.

Carson, Clayborne. 1981. *In Struggle: SNCC and the Black Awakening of the 1960's.* Cambridge, MA: Harvard University Press.

Chabot, Sean. 2002. "Transnational Diffusion and the African-American Reinvention of the Gandhian Repertoire," pp. 97–114 in *Globalization and Resistance: Transnational Dimensions of Social Movements,* edited by Jackie Smith and Hank Johnston. Lanham, MD: Rowman and Littlefield.

———. 2003. "Crossing the Great Divide: The Gandhian Repertoire's Transnational Diffusion to the American Civil Rights Movement." Unpublished Ph.D. dissertation, University of Amsterdam.

———. 2004. "Framing, Transnational Diffusion, and African-American Intellectuals in the Land of Gandhi." *International Review of Social History* 49: 19–40.

Chabot, Sean and Jan Willem Duyvendak. 2002. "Globalization and Transnational Diffusion between Social Movements: Reconceptualizing the Dissemination of the Ghandian Repertoire and the 'Coming Out' Routine." *Theory and Society* 31: 697–740.

Chabot, Sean and Stellan Vinthagen. 2007. "Rethinking Nonviolent Action and Contentious Politics: Political Cultures of Nonviolent Opposition in the Indian Independence Movement and Brazil's Landless Workers Movement," pp. 91–121 in *Research in Social Movements, Conflicts and Change* 27, edited by Patrick G. Coy. Amsterdam: Elsevier/JAI.

Chafe, William. 1980. *Civilities and Civil Rights: Greensboro, North Carolina, and the Black Struggle for Freedom*. New York: Oxford University Press.

Chamber of Commerce. 2009. *Letter to Congress*. May 14 (available at www .chamberpost.com/2009/05/3100-companies-opposing-efca-cant-be-wrong.html; accessed May 21, 2009).

Chataway, Joanna, Joyce Tait, and David Wield. 2006. "The Governance of Agro – and Pharmaceutical Biotechnology Innovation: Public Policy and Industrial Strategy." *Technology Analysis and Strategic Management* 18: 169–185.

Chatfield, Charles. 1976. *The Americanization of Gandhi: Images of the Mahatma*. New York: Garland Press.

Choucair, Julia. 2005. "Lebanon's New Moment." *Policy Outlook*. Washington, DC: Carnegie Endowment (available at http://www.carnegieendowment.org/topic/? fa=list&type=pub&id=359&filterType=policyAndResearch&pageOn=2, accessed April 2, 2010).

Claude, Richard Pierre and Burns H. Weston, eds. 2006. *Human Rights in the World Community: Issues and Action*, 3rd edition. Philadelphia: University of Pennsylvania Press.

Clayton, Ed. 1964. *The SCLC Story*. Atlanta: The Southern Christian Leadership Conference.

Clemens, Elisabeth. 1996. "Organizational Form as Frame: Collective Identity and Political Strategy in the American Labor Movement, 1880–1920," pp. 205–226 in *Comparative Perspectives on Social Movements*, edited by Doug McAdam, John D. McCarthy, and Mayer N. Zald. New York: Cambridge University Press.

Clement, Barrie. 2006. "First Group to Stamp Out US Union Bashing." *The Independent* July 14: 54.

Cohen, Joel I. 2005. "Poor Nations Turn to Publicly Developed GM Crops." *Nature Biotechnology* 23: 27–33.

Cohen, Lizabeth. 2003. *A Consumer's Republic*. New York: Vintage.

Collected Works of Mahatma Gandhi (CWMG). 1999. CD-ROM. New Delhi: Government Publications Division.

Collins, Evelyn. 1996. "European Union Sexual Harassment Policy," pp. 23–34 in *Sexual Politics and the European Union: The Feminist New Challenge*, edited by R. Amy Elman. Providence, RI: Berghann Books.

Collins, Patricia Hill. 2000. *Black Feminist Thought: Knowledge, Consciousness, and the Politics of Empowerment*. New York: Routledge.

Compa, Lance and Jeffrey S. Vogt. 2001. "Labor Rights in the Generalized System of Preferences: A 20 Year Review." *Comparative Labor Law & Policy Journal* 22: 199–238.

Conell, Carol. 1988. "The Local Roots of Solidarity: Organization and Action in Late-Nineteenth-Century Massachusetts." *Theory and Society* 17: 365–402.

Conell, Carol and Samuel Cohn. 1995. "Learning from Other People's Actions: Environmental Variation and Diffusion in French Coal Mining Strikes, 1890–1935." *American Journal of Sociology* 101: 366–403.

Conell, Carol and Kim Voss. 1990. "Formal Organization and the Fate of Social Movements: Craft Association and Class Alliance in the Knights of Labor." *American Sociological Review* 55: 255–69.

Convention on Biological Diversity. 1992. 1760 UNTS 79; 31 ILM 818. Montreal: United Nations Environment Programme, Secretariat of the Convention on Biological Diversity (available at http://www.biodiv.org/convention/articles.asp).

Convio. 2008. "Clients" (available at www.convio.com/clients/; accessed August 13, 2008).

Cooley, Alexander. 2008. *Base Politics*. Ithaca, NY: Cornell University Press.

Corn, David. 2004. "Capital Games." *The Nation* July 30 (available at www.thenation.com/blogs/capitalgames?mm=7&yr=2004; accessed February 2, 2005).

Corner, John. 2003. "Mediated Persona and Political Culture," pp. 67–84 in *Media and the Restyling of Politics*, edited by John Corner and Dick Pels. London: Sage.

Corner, John and Dick Pels. 2003. *Media and the Restyling of Politics*. London: Sage.

Council for Biotechnology Information. 2001. "Substantial Equivalence in Food Safety Assessment." March 11 (available at www.whybiotech.com/index.asp?id=1244; accessed January 30, 2008).

Cronin, James E. 1989. "Strikes and Power in Britain, 1870–1920," pp. 79–100 in *Strikes, Wars, and Revolutions in an International Perspective: Strike Waves in the Late Nineteenth and Early Twentieth Centuries*, edited by Leopold H. Haimson and Charles Tilly. Cambridge, UK: Cambridge University Press, Editions de la Maison des Sciences de l'Homme.

Cullotta, Karen Ann. 2009. "New Owners Will Reopen Plant in Sit-In." *The New York Times* February 27: A15.

Dalton, Russell, Doh L. Shin, and Willy Jou. 2007. "Popular Conceptions of the Meaning of Democracy: Democratic Understanding in Unlikely Places." Center for the Study of Democracy, University of California at Irvine, July 3 (available at www.respositories.edlib.org/esd; accessed July 25, 2009).

Davidson, Sarah. 2008. "Forbidden Fruit: Transgenic Papaya in Thailand." *Plant Physiology* 147: 487–493.

Dawkins, Richard. 1986. *The Blind Watchmaker: Why the Evidence of Evolution Reveals a Universe without Design*. New York: W. W. Norton.

della Porta, Donatella and Sidney Tarrow. 1986. "Unwanted Children: Political Violence and the Cycle of Protest in Italy." *European Journal of Political Research* 14: 607–632.

———, eds. 2005. *Transnational Protest and Global Activism*. Lanham, MD: Rowman and Littlefield.

Delli Carpini, Michael. 2004. "Mediating Democratic Engagement: The Positive and Negative Impact of Mass Media on Citizens Engagement in Political and Civic Life," pp. 395–434 in *The Handbook of Political Communication Research*, edited by Linda Lee Kaid. Mahwah, NJ: Lawrence Erlbaum Publishers.

Demes, Pavol and Joerg Forbrig. 2007. "Civic Action and Democratic Power Shifts: On Strategies and Resources," pp. 175–190 in *Reclaiming Democracy: Civil Society and Electoral Change in Central and Eastern Europe*, edited by Joerg Forbrig and Pavol Demes. Washington, DC: German Marshall Fund.

Democracy Now. 2007. "Report: Wal-Mart Violates Worker Rights, Fosters 'Culture of Fear' to Prevent Employees from Forming Unions," *Democracy Now* radio program. May 1 (available at www.democracynow.org/2007/5/1/report_wal_mart_violates_worker_rights; accessed February 29, 2008).

Devdariani, Jaba. 2003. "The Impact of International Assistance on Georgia." *Building Democracy in Georgia* discussion paper 11. International Institute for Democracy and Electoral Assistance (available at www.idea.int/publications/georgia/upload/Book-11_scr.pdf).

Diamond, Larry. 2002. "Elections without Democracy: Thinking about Hybrid Regimes." *Journal of Democracy* 13: 21–35.

Diani, Mario. 2003. "Introduction: Social Movements, Contentious Actions and Social Networks: From 'Metaphor' to Substance?" pp. 1–20 in *Social Movements and Networks: Relational Approaches to Collective Action*, edited by Mario Diani and Doug McAdam. Oxford, UK: Oxford University Press.

DiMaggio, Paul J., Eszter Hargittai, W. Russell Neuman, and John P. Robinson. 2001. "The Social Implications of the Internet." *Annual Review of Sociology* 27: 307–336.

DiMaggio, Paul J. and Walter W. Powell. 1983. "The Iron Cage Revisited: Institutional Isomorphism and Collective Rationality in Organizational Fields." *American Sociological Review* 48: 147–160.

Djordjevic, Jasna Milsovevic. 2005. "Cinioci izborne apstenincije v Srbiji," pp. 137–156 in *Politicke stranke u Srbiji: Strukture I funksionisanje*, edited by Zorin Lutovac. Belgrade: Friedrich Ebert Stiftung/Institut drustvenih nauka.

Donohue, Thomas J. 2009. "Far from 'leveling the playing field for America's workers,' it would 'tilt the field for union organizers'." *POLITICO Debate: The Employee Free Choice Act* (available at www.politico.com/arena/archive/efca.html; accessed June 4, 2009).

Downey, Kirsten. 2009. *The Woman Behind the New Deal: The Life of Frances Perkins, FDR's Secretary of Labor and His Moral Conscience*. New York: Doubleday.

Doyle, Rodger. 2001. "U.S. Workers and the Law." *Scientific American* August 2001: 24.

Dreier, Peter and Kelly Candaele. 2008. "Why We Need EFCA." *The American Prospect* (Web edition). December 2 (available at www.prospect.org/cs/articles?article=why_we_need_efca; accessed March 4, 2009).

Dubofsky, Melvyn. 1994. *The State and Labor in Modern America*. Chapel Hill: University of North Carolina Press.

Earl, Jennifer. 2006a. "Pursuing Social Change Online: The Use of Four Protest Tactics on the Internet." *Social Science Computer Review* 24: 362–377.

———. 2006b. "Protest on the Information Highway: The Use of Four Protest Tactics Online." Paper presented at the University of Arizona, Department of Sociology's Colloquium Series, Tucson, AZ.

———. 2010. "The Dynamics of Protest-Related Diffusion on the Web." *Information, Communication and Society* 13: 209–225.

Earl, Jennifer and Katrina Kimport. 2008. "The Targets of Online Protest: State and Private Targets of Four Online Protest Tactics." *Information, Communication and Society* 11: 449–472.

———. 2009. "Movement Societies and Digital Protest: Fan Activism and Other Nonpolitical Protest Online." *Sociological Theory* 27: 220–243.

Earl, Jennifer, Katrina Kimport, Greg Prieto, Carly Rush, and Kimberly Reynoso. 2009. "Changing the World One Webpage at a Time: Conceptualizing and Explaining 'Internet Activism'." Paper presented at the 2009 Annual Meetings of the American Sociological Association, San Francisco. (Forthcoming in *Mobilization*)

Earl, Jennifer and Alan Schussman. 2003. "The New Site of Activism: On-Line Organizations, Movement Entrepreneurs, and the Changing Location of Social Movement Decision-Making." *Research in Social Movements, Conflicts and Change* 24: 155–187.

————. 2004. "Cease and Desist: Repression, Strategic Voting and the 2000 Presidential Election." *Mobilization* 9: 181–202.

————. 2007. "Contesting Cultural Control: Youth Culture and Online Petitioning," pp. 71–95 in *Digital Media and Civic Engagement*, edited by W. Lance Bennett. Cambridge, MA: MIT Press.

Edelman, Lauren B. and Mark C. Suchman. 1997. "The Legal Environments of Organizations." *Annual Review of Sociology* 23: 479–515.

Egerton, John. 1994. *Speak Now Against the Day: The Generation Before the Civil Rights Movement in the South*. Chapel Hill: North Carolina Press.

Elkins, Zachary and Beth Simmons. 2005. "On Waves, Clusters, and Diffusion: A Conceptual Framework." *The Annals of the American Academy of Political and Social Sciences* 598: 33–51.

Ellingson, Stephen. 1995. "Understanding the Dialect of Discourse and Collective Action: Public Debate and Rioting in Antebellum Cincinnati." *American Journal of Sociology* 101: 100–144.

Entman, Robert. 1993. "Framing: Towards Clarification of a Fractured Paradigm." *Journal of Communication* 43: 51–58.

Esser, Frank and Barbara Pfetsch. 2004. *Comparing Political Communication*. Cambridge, UK: Cambridge University Press.

ETC. 2007. ETC Group Communiqué #95, May/June 2007, Issue # 95, Terminator: The Sequel (available at www.etcgroup.org/en/about/).

The European Parliament and The Council. 2001. *Official Journal of the European Community* L106;1–38.

Ewen, Stuart. 1998. *PR: A Social History of Spin*. New York: Basic Books.

Falkner, Robert. 2000. "Regulating Biotech Trade: The Cartagena Protocol on Biosafety." *International Affairs* 76: 299–313.

Farley, Lin. 1978. *Sexual Shakedown. The Sexual Harassment of Women on the Job*. New York: McGraw-Hill.

Farmer, James. 1985. *Lay Bare the Heart: An Autobiography of the Civil Rights Movement*. Fort Worth: Texas Christian University Press.

Ferguson. John-Paul and Thomas A. Kochan. 2008. "Sequential Failures in Workers' Right to Organize." MIT Sloan School of Management. Institute for Work and Employment Research (March) (available at www.americanrightsatwork.org/dmdocuments/sequential_failures_in_workers_right_to_organize_3_25_2008.pdf; accessed May 24, 2009).

Ferree, Myra M., William A. Gamson, Jürgen Gerhards, and Dieter Rucht. 2002. *Shaping Abortion Discourse: Democracy and the Public Sphere in Germany and the United States*. Cambridge, UK and New York: Cambridge University Press.

Fine, Sidney. 1969. *Sit-Down: The General Motors Strike of 1936–1937*. Ann Arbor: University of Michigan Press.

Fink, Leon. 1983. *Workingmen's Democracy: The Knights of Labor and American Politics*. Chicago: University of Illinois Press.

Finkel, Steven F., Aníbal Pérez-Liñan, Mitchell A. Seligson, and Dinorah Azpuru. 2006. "Effects of US Foreign Assistance on Democracy Building: Results of a Cross-National Quantitative Study." Final Report, USAID, version #34.

Fischer, Louis. 1962. *The Essential Gandhi: An Anthology*. New York: Vintage.

Fischer, Sabine. 2005. "The EU's Strategy of 'New Neighborhood' and its Impact on International Relations of the Former Soviet Union." Paper presented at the annual meeting of the International Studies Association, Honolulu, HI, March 1–5.

Fish, M. Steven. 1998. "Democratization's Prerequisites." *Post-Soviet Affairs* 14: 212–247.

_____. 2005. *Democracy Derailed in Russia: The Failure of Open Politics*. Cambridge, UK: Cambridge University Press.

Foot, Kirsten A. and Steven M. Schneider. 2002. "Online Action in Campaign 2000: An Exploratory Analysis of the U.S. Political Web Sphere." *Journal of Broadcasting and Electronic Media* 46: 222–244.

Foran, John. 2005. *Taking Power: On the Origins of Third World Revolutions*. New York: Cambridge University Press.

Forrest, Barbara and Paul R. Gross. 2003. *Creationism's Trojan Horse: The Wedge of Intelligent Design*. New York: Oxford University Press.

"Fox Posts Reporter's Kerry Spoof on Website." 2004. *Los Angeles Times*, October 02 (http://articles.latimes.com/2004/oct/02/nation/na-fox2).

Fox, Richard. 1997. "Passage from India," pp. 65–82 in *Between Resistance and Revolution: Cultural Politics and Social Protest*, edited by Richard Fox and Orin Starn. New Brunswick, NJ: Rutgers University Press.

Franzosi, Roberto. 1995. *The Puzzle of Strikes: Class and State Strategies in Postwar Italy*. Cambridge, UK: Cambridge University Press.

Freeman, Richard and Joel Rogers. 1999. *What Workers Want*. Ithaca, NY: Cornell ILR Press.

Freire, Paulo. 2000. *Pedagogy of the Oppressed: 30th Anniversary Edition*. New York: Continuum.

Friedman, Gabrielle S. and James Q. Whitman. 2003. "The European Transformation of Harassment Law: Discrimination versus Dignity." *Columbia Journal of European Law* 9: 241–74.

Friedman, Gerald. 1998. *State-Making and Labor Movements: France and the United States, 1876–1914*. Ithaca, NY: Cornell University Press.

Friedman, Sheldon and Stephen Wood. 2001. "Employers' Unfair Advantage in the United States of America: Symposium on the Human Rights Watch Report on the State of Workers' Freedom of Association in the United States." *British Journal of Industrial Relations* 39: 585.

Friends of the Earth International. 2006. *Who Benefits from GM Crops? Monsanto and the Corporate-Driven Genetically Modified Crop Revolution*. Amsterdam: Friends of the Earth International.

Fuhrmann, Matthew. 2006. "A Tale of Two Social Capitals: Revolutionary Collective Action in Kyrgyzstan." *Problems of Postcommunism* 53: 16–29.

Fukic, Marko and Zeljko Capin. 1999. "Vladimir Meciar, bivsi premijer Republike Slovacke: Hrvatski prijatelji voci izbora mogu uciti na nasim pogreskama." *Vecernji list*.

Fukuda-Parr, Sakiko, ed. 2007. *The Gene Revolution: GM Crops and Unequal Development*. London: Earthscan.

Furchtgott-Roth, Diana. 2009. "After Card Check, Don't Forget Binding Arbitration." Hudson Institute. RealClearMarkets.com. May 7 (available at www.hudson.org/index.cfm?fuseaction=publication_details&id=6227; accessed May 24, 2009).

Gamson, William A. 1992. "The Social Psychology of Collective Action," pp. 53–76 in *Frontiers in Social Movement Theory*, edited by Aldon Morris and Carol McClurg Mueller. New Haven, CT: Yale University Press.

Ganev, Venelin I. 2007. *Preying on the State: The Transformation of Bulgaria after 1989*. Ithaca, NY: Cornell University Press.

Gans, Herbert J. 2003. *Democracy and the News*. New York: Oxford University Press.

Gaonkar, Dilip Parameshwar and Elizabeth A. Povinelli. 2003. "Technologies of Public Forms: Circulation, Transfiguration, Recognition." *Public Culture* 15: 385–397.

Garber, Larry and Glenn Cowan. 1993. "The Virtues of Parallel Vote Tabulations." *Journal of Democracy* 4: 95–107.

Garrido, Maria and Alexander Halavais. 2003. "Mapping Networks of Support for the Zapatista Movement: Applying Social-Networks Analysis to Study Contemporary Social Movements," pp. 165–184 in *Cyberactivism: Online Activism in Theory and Practice*, edited by Martha McCaughey and Michael D. Ayers. New York: Routledge.

Garrow, David. 1986. *Bearing the Cross: Martin Luther King, Jr. and the Southern Christian Leadership Conference*. New York: Harper.

Gaskell, George, Agnes Allansdottir, Nick Allum, Cristina Corchero, Claude Fischler, Jürgen Hampel, Jonathan Jackson, Nicole Kronberger, Niels Mejlgaard, Gemma Revuelta, Camilla Schreiner, Sally Stares, Helge Torgersen, and Wolfgang Wagner 2006. *Europeans and Biotechnology in 2005: Patterns and Trends*. A Report to the European Commission's Directorate-General for Research. Final report on Eurobarometer 64.3. Brussels: EU Commission (available at www.goldenrice.org/PDFs/Eurobarometer_2005.pdf).

Geisler, Norman. 1982. *The Creator in the Courtroom: Scopes II*. Grand Rapids, MI: Baker Books.

Gel'man, Vladimir. 2005. "Political Opposition in Russia: A Dying Species?" *Post-Soviet Affairs* 3: 226–246.

Getman, Julius. 2001. "A Useful Step." *British Journal of Industrial Relations* 39: 591.

———. 2003. "The National Labor Relations Act: What Went Wrong; Can We Fix It?" *Boston College Law Review* December 45: 125.

Gibson, John. 2004. "The Big Story with John Gibson." (FOX News television broadcast) October 15.

Gitlin, Todd. 1980. *The Whole World Is Watching: Mass Media in the Making and the Unmaking of the New Left*. Berkeley: University of California Press.

Glascock, Ned. 2000. "Rights Group Targets Firms." *Raleigh News & Observer*. August 31: A3.

Gleditsch, Kristian Skrede and Michael D. Ward. 2006. "Diffusion and the International Context of Democratization." *International Organization* 60: 911–933.

Glenn, John, III. 2000. *Framing Democracy: Civil Society and Civic Movements in Eastern Europe*. Stanford, CA: Stanford University Press.

GM Watch. 2006. "Mortality in Sheep Flocks after grazing on Bt Cotton fields – Warangal District, Andhra Pradesh." *GM Watch* (available at www.gmwatch.org/index. php?option=com_content&view=article&id=6416).

Goati, V. 2000. "The Nature of the Order and the October Overthrow in Serbia," pp. 45–58 in *Revolution and Order: Serbia After October 2000*, edited by Ivana Spasic and Milan Subotic. Belgrade: Belgrade Institute for Philosophy and Sociology.

Gold, Ann Grodzins. 2003. "Vanishing: Seeds' Cyclicality." *Journal of Material Culture* 8: 255–272.

Gonsalves, Carol, David R. Lee, and Dennis Gonsalves. 2007. "The Adoption of Genetically Modified Papaya in Hawaii and Its Implications for Developing Countries." *Journal of Development Studies* 43: 177–191.

Gonyea, Don. 2008. "Ex-Press Aide McClellan Blasts Bush on Iraq." *NPR* May 28 (available at www.npr.org/templates/story/story.php?storyId=90907249; accessed August 2, 2008).

Gould, Roger. 1991. "Multiple Networks and Mobilization in the Paris Commune, 1871." *American Sociological Review* 56: 716–729.

Graaf, Henk van de and Rob Hoppe. 1992. *Beleid en politiek*. Muiderberg, Netherlands: Coutinho.

Graff, G. D., G. Hochman, and D. Zilberman. 2009. "The Political Economy of Agricultural Biotechnology Policies." *AgBioForum* 1: 34–46.

Greenhouse, Steven. 2000. "Report Faults Laws for Slowing Growth of Unions." *The New York Times* October 24: A20.

———. 2005. "Labor to Press for Workers' Right to Join Unions." *The New York Times* December 9: A18.

———. 2008a. "After Push for Obama, Unions Seek New Rules." *The New York Times* November 8: A33.

———. 2008b. "Workers at Pork Plant in North Carolina Vote to Unionize After a 15-Year Fight." *The New York Times* December 13: A10.

Greenpeace International. 2007. *Genetically Engineered Maize: The Reality Behind the Myths*. Amsterdam: Greenpeace International.

Gregg, Richard. 1959. *The Power of Nonviolence*. Philadelphia: J. B. Lippincott.

Gross, James A. 2002. "Book Review: Unfair Advantage: Workers' Freedom of Association in the United States under International Human Rights Standards." *University of Pennsylvania Journal of Labor and Employment Law* 4 (Spring): 699.

Gruère, Guillaume P., Purvi Mehta-Bhatt, and Debdatta Sengupta. 2008. "Bt Cotton and Farmer Suicides in India. Reviewing the Evidence." International Food Policy Research Institute Discussion Paper No. 808. October. Washington, DC: IFPRI.

Gupta, Anil K. and Vikas Chandak. 2005. "Agricultural Biotechnology in India: Ethics, Business and Politics." *International Journal of Biotechnology* 7 (1–3): 212–227.

Hagopian, Frances and Scott P. Mainwaring. 2005. *The Third Wave of Democratization in Latin America: Advances and Setbacks*. Cambridge, UK: Cambridge University Press.

Halberstam, David. 1998. *The Children*. New York: Random House.

Hamburger, Tom. 2009. "Unions See Key Bill Slip Away; Business Interests Outmaneuver Labor to Erode Senate Support for 'Card Check.'" *The Los Angeles Times* May 9: A1.

Harsin, Jayson. 2006. "The Rumor Bomb: A Convergence Theory of American Mediated Politics." *Southern Review: Communication, Politics & Culture*: 39: 84–110.

———. 2008. "The Rumor Bomb: On Convergence Culture and Politics." *Flow TV* 9.04 (available at http://flowtv.org/?p=2259; accessed June 1, 2009).

Healy, Patrick. 2004. "Kerry Looks to Clarify Stance, Views on Iraq." *Boston Globe* September 22 (available at www.boston.com/news/nation/articles/2004/09/22/kerry_looks_to_clarify_stance_views_on_iraq?pg=full; accessed January 14, 2005).

Heath, Chip and Dan Heath. 2007. *Made to Stick: Why Some Ideas Survive and Others Die*. New York: Random House.

Hedström, Peter. 1994. "Contagious Collectivities: On the Spatial Diffusion of Swedish Trade Unions, 1890–1949." *American Journal of Sociology* 99: 1157–1179.

Hedström, Peter, Rickard Sandell, and Carlotta Stern. 2000. "Mesolevel Networks and the Diffusion of Social Movements." *American Journal of Sociology* 106: 145–172.

Heins, Volker. 2008. *Nongovernmental Organizations in International Society: Struggles over Recognition*. New York: Palgrave Macmillan.

Herd, Graeme. 2005. "Colorful Revolutions and the CIS." *Problems of Postcommunism* 52: 3–18.

Herring, Ronald J. 2005. "Miracle Seeds, Suicide Seeds and the Poor: GMOs, NGOs, Farmers and the State," pp. 203–232 in *Social Movements in India: Poverty, Power, and Politics*, edited by Raka Ray and Mary Fainsod Katzenstein. Lanham, MD: Rowman and Littlefield.

———. 2006. "Why Did 'Operation Cremate Monsanto' Fail? Science and Class in India's Great Terminator Technology Hoax." *Critical Asian Studies* 38: 467–493.

———. 2007a. "The Genomics Revolution and Development Studies: Science, Politics and Poverty." *Journal of Development Studies* 43: 1–30.

———. 2007b. "Stealth Seeds: Biosafety, Bioproperty, Biopolitics." *Journal of Development Studies* 43: 130–157.

———. 2007c. *Transgenics and the Poor: Biotechnology in Development Studies.* Oxon/London: Routledge.

———. 2008a. "Opposition to Transgenic Technologies: Ideology, Interests, and Collective Action Frames." *Nature Reviews Genetics* 9: 458–463.

———. 2008b. "Whose Numbers Count? Probing Discrepant Evidence on Transgenic Cotton in the Warangal District of India." *International Journal of Multiple Research Approaches* 2: 145–159.

———. 2009a. "China, Rice, and GMOs: Navigating the Global Rift on Genetic Engineering." *The Asia-Pacific Journal: Japan Focus* January 15 (available at japanfocus.org/_Ron_Herring-China_Rice_and_GMOs_Navigating_the_Global_Rift_on_Genetic_Engineering; accessed May 2, 2009).

———. 2009b. "Persistent Narratives: Why Is the 'Failure of Bt Cotton in India' Story Still With Us?" *AbBioForum [The Journal of Agrobiotechnology Economics and Management]* 12: 14–22.

Herring, Ronald and Millind Kandlikar. 2009. "Illicit Seeds: Intellectual Property and the Underground Proliferation of Agricultural Biotechnologies," pp. 56–79 in *The Politics of Intellectual Property: Contestation over the Ownership, Use, and Control of Knowledge and Information*, edited by Sebastian Haunss and Kenneth C. Shadlen. Cheltenham, UK: Edward Elgar.

Ho, Mae-Wan. 2000. *Genetic Engineering.* New York: Continuum.

Hopgood, Stephen. 2006. *Keepers of the Flame: Understanding Amnesty International.* Ithaca, NY: Cornell University Press.

Hospital Business Week. 2007. "International Watchdog Group Singles Out Resurrection for Anti-Union Violations." PR Newswire, September 19: 130.

Howard, Marc Morjé and Philip B. Roessler. 2006. "Liberalizing Electoral Outcomes in Competitive Authoritarian Regimes." *American Journal of Political Science* 50: 443–455.

Human Rights Watch. 2000. *Unfair Advantage: Workers' Freedom of Association in the United States under International Human Rights Standards*, revised edition (2004). Ithaca, NY: Cornell University Press.

———. 2001a. *Fingers to the Bone: United States Failure to Protect Child Farmworkers.* New York: Human Rights Watch.

———. 2001b. *Hidden in the Home: Abuse of Domestic Workers with Special Visas in the United States.* New York: Human Rights Watch.

———. 2005. *Blood, Sweat, and Fear: Workers' Rights in the U.S. Meat and Poultry Industry.* New York: Human Rights Watch.

——— 2007. *Discounting Rights: Wal-Mart's Violations of US Workers' Right to Freedom of Association*. New York: Human Rights Watch.

———. 2009a. *The Employee Free Choice Act: A Human Rights Imperative*. Briefing Paper. January 2009.

———. 2009b. *A Strange Case:* European Companies in the United States and International Standards on Workers' Freedom of Association* [*the title is borrowed from Robert Louis Stevenson's *The Strange Case of Dr. Jekyll and Mr. Hyde*]. New York: Human Rights Watch.

ILO Committee on Freedom of Association. 2003. Complaint against the United States. Case No. 2227, Report No. 332.

———. 2006. Complaint against the United States, Case No. 2292, Report No. 343.

———. 2007. Complaint against the United States, Case No. 2460, Report No. 344.

———. 2008. Complaint against the United States, Case No. 2524, Report No. 349.

Ingersoll, Thomas N. 1999. "'Riches and Honour Were Rejected by Them as Loathsome Vomit': The Fear of Leveling in New England," pp. 46–66 in *Inequality in Early America*, edited by Gardina Pestana and Sharon V. Salinger. Hanover, NH: University Press of New England.

Initiated Act No. 1, Ark. Acts 1929; *Ark. Stat. Ann.* 80–1627, 80–1628.

Isaac, Larry, Steve McDonald, and Greg Lukasik. 2006. "Takin' It from the Streets: How the Sixties Mass Movement Revitalized Unionization." *American Journal of Sociology* 112: 46–96.

Israel, Milton. 1994. *Communications and Power: Propaganda and the Press in the Indian National Struggle, 1920–1947*. Cambridge: Cambridge University Press.

Jackson, Maurice, Eleanora Petersen, James Bull, Sverre Monsen, and Patricia Richmond. 1960. "The Failure of an Incipient Social Movement." *Pacific Sociological Review* 3: 35–40.

Jacoby, Wade. 2004. *The Enlargement of the European Union and NATO: Ordering from the Menu in Central Europe*. Cambridge, UK: Cambridge University Press.

———. 2006. "Inspiration, Coalition and Substitution." *World Politics* 58: 623–651.

James, Clive. 2008. *Global Status of Commercialized Biotech/GM Crops: 2008*. ISAAA Brief No. 39. Ithaca, NY: International Service for the Acquisition of Agri-Biotech Applications.

Jamieson, Kathleen Hall. 1988. *Eloquence in the Electronic Age*. New York: Oxford University Press.

Jasanoff, Shiela. 2005. *Designs on Nature*. Princeton, NJ: Princeton University Press.

Jasinski, James. 2001. *A Sourcebook on Rhetoric: Key Concepts in Contemporary Rhetorical Studies*. Thousand Oaks, CA: Sage Publications.

Jayaraman, K. S. 2001. "Illegal Bt Cotton in India Haunts Regulators." *Nature Biotechnology* 19: 1090.

———. 2004. "India Produces Homegrown GM Cotton." *Nature Biotechnology* 22: 255–256.

Jenkins, Henry. 2006. *Convergence Culture: Where Old and New Media Collide*. New York: NYU Press.

Jenkins, J. Craig and Craig M. Eckert. 1986. "Channeling Black Insurgency: Elite Patronage and Professional Social Movement Organizations in the Development of the Black Movement." *American Sociological Review* 51: 812–829.

Jennings, Ray. 2009. "Serbia's Bulldozer Revolution: Evaluating Internal and External Factors in the Successful Democratic Breakthrough in Serbia." Center for Democracy, Development and the Rule of Law (CDDRL), Working Paper, Freeman Spogli Institute for International Studies, Stanford University.

Jeyaratnam, J. 1990. "Acute Pesticide Poisoning: A Major Global Health Problem." *World Health Statistics Quarterly* 43: 139–144.

Jha, Manoranjan. 1973. *Civil Disobedience and After.* Delhi: Meenakshi Prakasham.

Joshi, Rajesh and Andrew Draper. 2004. "Maersk Target of Protest by Thousands of Truckers: Company Accused of 'Threatening, Intimidating and Terminating Drivers.'" *Lloyd's List* September 6: 3.

Joshi, Sharad. 2003. "Biotechnologists Too Are Bound by Scientific Methods." *Economic and Political Weekly* September 6: 3851–3854.

Jurisdictional Statement of Appellants, *Epperson v. State of Arkansas*, No. 7 (filed on October 20, 1967) (available on Westlaw at 1967 WL 129525).

Kandelaki, Giorgi. 2005. "Rose Revolution: A Participant's Story." USIP.

Kapur, Sudarshan. 1992. *Raising Up a Prophet: The African-American Encounter with Gandhi.* Boston: Beacon Press.

Kapuscinski, Ryszard. 2006. *The Emperor.* Raleigh, NC: Pentland Press.

Katz, Michael B. 1986. *In the Shadow of the Poorhouse: A Social History of Welfare in America.* New York: Basic Books.

Kaush, Kristina and Richard Youngs. 2009. "Algeria: Democratic Transition Case Study." CDDRL Working Paper, Freeman Spogli Institute for International Studies, Stanford University.

Keck, Margaret and Kathryn Sikkink. 1998. *Activists Beyond Borders: Advocacy Networks in International Politics.* Ithaca, NY: Cornell University Press.

Kenney, Padraic. 2002. *Carnival of Revolution: Central Europe, 1989.* Princeton, NJ: Princeton University Press.

Kerry, John. "2004 Democratic National Convention Acceptance Address" (available at www.americanrhetoric.com/speeches/convention2004/johnkerry2004dnc.htm; accessed September 20, 2005).

Killian, Lewis. 1984. "Organization, Rationality and Spontaneity in the Civil Rights Movement." *American Sociological Review* 49: 770–783.

King, Martin Luther, Jr. 1958. *Stride toward Freedom: The Montgomery Story.* New York: Harper.

———. 1963. *Why We Can't Wait.* New York: Harper and Row.

Kling, J. 2009. "First US Approval for a Transgenic Animal Drug." *Nature Biotechnology* 27: 302–304.

Kniazev, Aleksandr. 2005. *Gossudarstvennyi perevorot. 24 Marta 2005g v Kirgizii.* Moscow: Europa.

Kropowski, Jean. 2004. "The Web: E-mail's Last-Minute Vote-Getting." United Press International. November 2 (available at www.lexisnexis.com; accessed September 15, 2005).

Kornhauser, William. 1959. *The Politics of Mass Society.* Glencoe, IL: Free Press.

Kraus, Henry. 1947. *The Many and the Few.* Urbana and Chicago: University of Illinois Press.

Kubicek, Paul. 2005. "The European Union and Democratization in Ukraine." *Communist and Post-Communist Studies* 38: 269–292.

Kubik, Jan. 1994. *The Power of Symbols Against the Symbols of Power: The Rise of Solidarity and the Fall of State Socialism in Poland*. University Park: Pennsylvania State University Press.

_____. 2009 "Solidarity," pp. 3072–3080 in *International Encyclopedia of Revolution and Protest 1500-Present*, edited by Immanuel Ness. Oxford, UK: Blackwell Publishing.

Kurtz, Howard. 2004. "Campaign '04, bar trivia '05." *Washington Post*. November 1 (available at www.washingtonpost.com/ac2/wp-dyn/A14460-2004Oct31?language=printer; accessed September 15, 2005).

Kuzio, Taras. 2005. "From Kuchma to Yushchenko: Orange Revolution in Ukraine." *Problems of Postcommunism* 52: 29–44.

Laba, Roman. 1991. *The Roots of Solidarity: A Political Sociology of Poland's Working Class Democratization*. Princeton, NJ: Princeton University Press.

Lakoff, George. 2004. *Don't Think of an Elephant: Know Your Values and Frame the Debate*. New York: Chelsea Green Publishing.

Lakoff, George and Mark Johnson. 1980. *Metaphors We Live By*. Chicago: University of Chicago Press.

Landler, Mark. 2007. "Norway Backs Its Ethics With Its Cash." *The New York Times* May 4: C1.

Latour, Bruno. 2004. "Scientific Objects and Legal Objectivity" (available at www.ensmp.fr/~latour/articles/article/088.html; accessed May 2, 2009).

Layne-Farrar, Anne. 2009. "An Empirical Assessment of the Employee Free Choice Act: The Economic Implications." LECG Consulting (March 3, 2009).

Lazic, Mladen. 1999. *Protest in Belgrade*. Budapest: Central European University Press.

Leader, Sheldon. 2002. "Choosing an Interpretation of the Right to Freedom of Association." *British Journal of Industrial Relations* 40: 114.

Leary, Virginia A. 2003. "The Paradox of Workers' Rights as Human Rights," pp. 22–47 in *Human Rights, Labor Rights, and International Trade*, edited by Lance A. Compa and Stephen F. Diamond. Philadelphia: University of Pennsylvania Press.

LeBon, Gustave. [1897] 1960. *The Crowd: A Study of the Popular Mind*. New York: Viking Press.

Lee, Chang Kil and David Strang. 2006. "The International Diffusion of Public Sector Downsizing." *International Organization* 60: 883–909.

Leopold, Les. 2007. *The Man Who Hated Work and Loved Labor: The Life and Times of Tony Mazzocchi*. White River Junction, VT: Chelsea Green.

Levitsky, Steven and Lucan A. Way. 2002. "The Rise of Competitive Authoritarianism." *Journal of Democracy* 13: 51–65.

_____. 2005. "International Linkage and Democratization." *Journal of Democracy* 16: 20–34.

_____. forthcoming. *Competitive Authoritarianism: Hybrid Regimes after the Cold War*. Cambridge, UK: Cambridge University Press.

Lewis, John. 1998. *Walking with the Wind: A Memoir of the Movement*. New York: Harcourt Brace.

Lezaun, J. 2004. "Genetically Modified Foods and Consumer Mobilization in the UK." *TECHNIKFOLGENABSCHÄTZUNG Theorie und Praxis* Nr. 3, 13. Jahrgang – Dezember 2004, S. 49–56

Lichbach, Mark I. 1998. *The Rebel's Dilemma: Economics, Cognition, and Society*. Ann Arbor, MI: University of Michigan Press.

Lichtenstein, Nelson. 2002. *State of the Union: A Century of American Labor.* Princeton, NJ: Princeton University Press.

―――. 2003. "The Rights Revolution." *New Labor Forum* 12 (1): 60–73.

Lindberg, Staffan. 2006. *Democracy and Elections in Africa.* Baltimore: Johns Hopkins University Press.

―――. 2009. *Democratization by Election: A New Mode of Transition?* Baltimore: Johns Hopkins University Press.

Linder, Douglas O. 2005. "Tennessee vs. John Scopes." *Famous Trials in American History* April 25 (available at http://www.law.umkc.edu/faculty/projects/ftrials/scopes/scopes.htm; accessed October 1, 2006).

Logan, John. 2006. "The Union Avoidance Industry in the United States." *British Journal of Industrial Relations* 44: 651.

Lomax, Louis E. 1960. "The Negro Revolt Against 'The Negro Leaders.'" *Harper's Magazine* June 220: 41–48.

Lust-Okar, Ellen. 2004. "Divided They Rule: The Management and Manipulation of Political Opposition." *Comparative Politics* 1: 159–179.

―――. 2005. "Elections Under Authoritarianism: Preliminary Lessons from Jordan." Unpublished paper, Department of Political Science, Yale University, New Haven, CT.

Lybbert, Travis J. 2003. "Humanitarian Use Technology Transfer: Issues and Approaches." *International Journal of Food, Agriculture & Environment* 1 (3–4): 95–99.

MacFarquhar, Neil. 2005. "Big Beirut Rally Wants Syria Out." *The New York Times* March 15: A5, p.1.

Madsen, S. T. 2001. "The View from Vevey." *Economic and Political Weekly.* September 29: 3733–3742.

Markoff, John. 1996. *Waves of Democracy: Social Movements and Political Change.* Thousand Oaks, CA: Pine Forge Press.

Marks, Gary and Doug McAdam. 1996. "Social Movements and the Changing Structure of Political Opportunity in the European Union," pp. 95–112 in *Governance in the Euro-Polity*, edited by George Marks, Fritz Scharpf, Philippe Schmitter, and Wolfgang Streek. London: Sage Publications.

McAdam, Doug. 1982. *Political Process and the Development of Black Insurgency, 1930–1970.* Chicago: University of Chicago Press.

―――. 1983. "Tactical Innovation and the Pace of Insurgency." *American Sociological Review* 48: 735–754.

―――. 1988. *Freedom Summer.* New York: Oxford University Press.

―――. 1996. "The Framing Function of Movement Tactics: Strategic Dramaturgy in the American Civil Rights Movement," pp. 338–355 in *Comparative Perspectives on Social Movements*, edited by Doug McAdam, John McCarthy, and Mayer Zald. New York: Cambridge University Press.

―――. 1999. *Political Process and the Development of Black Insurgency*, 2nd edition. Chicago: University of Chicago Press.

McAdam, Doug and Dieter Rucht. 1993. "The Cross-National Diffusion of Movement Ideas." *Annals of the American Academy of Political and Social Science* 528: 56–74.

McAdam, Doug and William H. Sewell, Jr. 2001. "It's About Time: Temporality in the Study of Social Movements and Revolutions," pp. 89–125 in *Silence and Voice in the Study of Contentious Politics*, edited by Ronald R. Aminzade, Jack A. Goldstone,

Doug McAdam, Elizabeth J. Perry, William H. Sewell, Jr., Sidney Tarrow, and Charles Tilly. Cambridge, UK: Cambridge University Press.

McAdam, Doug and Sidney Tarrow. 2009. "On the Reciprocal Relationship between Elections and Social Movements." Paper Presented at the Conference to Honor Hanspeter Kriesi, June 2009. Zurich, Switzerland.

McAdam, Doug, Sidney Tarrow, and Charles Tilly. 2001. *Dynamics of Contention*. Cambridge, UK: Cambridge University Press.

_____. 2009. "Comparative Perspectives on Contentious Politics," pp. 260–290 in *Comparative Perspectives: Rationality, Culture, and Structure*, edited by Mark Irving Lichbach and Alan S. Zuckerman. Cambridge, UK: Cambridge University Press.

McCarthy, John D. and Clark McPhail. 1998. "The Institutionalization of Protest in the United States," pp. 83–110 in *The Social Movement Society: Contentious Politics for a New Century*, edited by David S. Meyer and Sidney Tarrow. Lanham, MD: Rowman and Littlefield.

McCarthy, John D. and Mayer N. Zald. 1977. "Resource Mobilization and Social Movements: A Partial Theory." *American Journal of Sociology* 82: 1212–1241.

McCartin, Joseph A. 1997. *Labor's Great War: The Struggle for Industrial Democracy and the Origins of Modern American Labor Relations 1912–1921*. Chapel Hill: University of North Carolina Press.

_____. 2005. "Democratizing the Demand for Workers' Rights: Toward a Re-framing of Labor's Argument." *Dissent* Winter: 61–66.

McChesney, Robert and Dan Schiller. 2002. "The Political Economy of International Communications: Foundations for the Emerging Global Debate over Media Ownership and Regulation." Paper prepared for the UNRISD Programme on Information Technologies and Social Development as part of UNRISD background work for the World Summit on the Information Society, June (available at www.unrisd.org/80256B3C005BCCF9/(httpAuxPages)/C9DCBA6C7DB78C2AC1256BDF0049A774/$file/mcchesne.pdf; accessed May 15, 2008).

McFaul, Michael. 2005. "Transitions from Postcommunism." *Journal of Democracy* 16 (3): 5–19.

_____. 2007. "Ukraine Imports Democracy: External Influences on the Orange Revolution." *International Security* 32 (2): 45–83.

McGovern, George. 2008. "My Party Should Respect Secret Union Ballots." *The Wall Street Journal*. August 8: A13.

McHughen, A. 2000. *Pandora's Picnic Basket: The Potential and Hazards of Genetically Modified Foods*. Oxford, UK: Oxford University Press.

McKinley, James C., Jr. 2006. "In a Presidential Tone, Calderon Rejects Recount." *The New York Times* July 13: Section A5: 8.

McNair, Brian. 2006. *Cultural Chaos: Journalism, News and Power in a Globalised World*. London: Routledge.

_____. 2007. *An Introduction to Political Communication*. London: Routledge.

McNatt, Robert. 2000. "The List: Union Busters." *Business Week* September 11: 14.

McPhail, Clark. 1991. *The Myth of the Maddening Crowd*. New York: Aldine De Gruyter.

Media Matters for America. 2004. "As evidence mounts of GOP connection to anti-Kerry Swift Boat Vets, Hume and Dole deny the obvious," August 26 (available from http://mediamatters.org/research/200408260008).

Meier, August and Elliott Rudwick. 1973. *CORE: A Study in the Civil Rights Movement, 1942–1968*. New York: Oxford University Press.

Meladze, Giorgi. 2005. "Civil Society: A Second Chance for Post-Soviet Democracy: A Eurasianet Commentary." (available at /www.eurasianet.org/departments/civilsociety/articles/eavo90605.shtml; accessed May 3, 2009)

Mencher, Melvin. 2000. *News Reporting and Writing, 8th edition.* Boston: McGraw-Hill.

Mendelson, Sarah and Theodore Gerber. 2005. "Local Activist Culture and Transnational Diffusion: An Experiment in Social Marketing among Human Rights Groups in Russia." Unpublished paper.

Merry, Sally Engle. 2003. "Constructing a Global Law – Violence Against Women and the Global Human Rights System." *Law and Social Inquiry* 28: 941–979.

Meyer, David S. 1990. *A Winter of Discontent: The Nuclear Freeze and American Politics.* New York: Praeger.

Meyer, David S. and Rob Kleidman. 1991. "The Nuclear Freeze Movement in the United States," pp. 231–262 in *Peace Movements in Western Europe and the United States. International Social Movement Research 3*, edited by Bert Klandermans. Greenwich, CT: JAI Press.

Meyer, David S. and Debra C. Minkoff. 2004. "Conceptualizing Political Opportunity." *Social Forces* 82: 1457–1492.

Miller, Henry I. 1999. "Substantial Equivalence." *Nature.* November 11 (17): 1042–1043.

Miller, Henry I. and Gregory Conko. 2000. "The Science of Biotechnology Meets the Politics of Global Regulation." *Issues in Science and Technology* 1: 47–54.

Milligan, Susan. 2004. "Kerry Criticized for French Connection." *Boston Globe* April 12 (available at www.boston.com/news/globe/living/articles/2004/04/12/kerry_criticized_for_french_connection/; accessed September 21, 2005).

Minkoff, Debra C. 1995. "Interorganizational Influences on the Founding of African American Organizations, 1955–1985." *Sociological Forum* 10: 51–79.

———. 1997. "The Sequencing of Social Movements." *American Sociological Review* 62: 779–799.

Mitchell, Lincoln Abraham. 2009. *Uncertain Democracy: U.S. Foreign Policy and Georgia's Rose Revolution.* Philadelphia: University of Pennsylvania Press.

Mongelluzzo, Bill. 2005. "Teamsters Pushes Maersk Driver Protest; Union Hits Carrier's Shareholders Meeting." *Journal of Commerce Online* April 19, 2005.

———. 2006. "Teamsters Want Maersk to Abide by UN Workers Rules." *Journal of Commerce Online* April 11, 2006.

Morin, Richard and Dana Milbank. 2004. "Most Think Truth Was Stretched to Justify War in Iraq." *Washington Post* February 13 (available at http://www.washingtonpost.com/ac2/wp-dyn/A37340–2004Feb12?language=printer; accessed September 20, 2005).

Morris, Aldon. 1981. "Black Southern Student Sit-In Movement: An Analysis of Internal Organization." *American Sociological Review* 46: 744–767.

———. 1984. *The Origins of the Civil Rights Movement: Black Communities Organizing for Change.* New York: Free Press.

Muggeridge, Malcolm. 2008. "Organized Labor's International Law Project? Transforming Workplace Rights into Human Rights." National Right-To-Work Committee. *Engage* February (9) 1: 98.

Muiznieks, Nils R. 1995. "The Influence of the Baltic Popular Movements on the Process of Soviet Disintegration." *Europe-Asia Studies* 47 (1): 3–25.

Murray, Pauli. 1987. *Song in a Weary Throat: An American Pilgrimage*. New York: Harper and Row.

Myers, Daniel J. 1994. "Communication Technology and Social Movements: Contributions of Computer Networks to Activism." *Social Science Computer Review* 12: 251–260.

_____. 1997. "Racial Rioting in the 1960s: An Event History Analysis of Local Conditions." *American Sociological Review* 62: 94–112.

_____. 2000. "The Diffusion of Collective Violence: Infectiousness, Susceptibility, and Mass Media Networks." *American Journal of Sociology* 106: 173–208.

Naik, Gopal, Matin Qaim, Arjunan Subramanian, and David Zilberman. 2005. "Bt Cotton Controversy: Some Paradoxes Explained." *Economic and Political Weekly* April 9: 1514–1517.

Naim, Moises. 2005. *Illicit: How Smugglers, Traffickers and Copycats Are Hijacking the Global Economy*. New York: Doubleday.

Nanda, Meera. 2003. *Prophets Facing Backwards: Postmodern Critiques of Science and Hindu Nationalism in India*. New Brunswick, NJ: Rutgers University Press.

Narayanamoorthy, A. and S. S. Kalamkar. 2006. "Is Bt Cotton Cultivation Economically Viable for Indian Farmers? An Empirical Analysis." *Economic and Political Weekly* 41 (26): 2716–2724.

Neier, Aryeh. 2002. *Taking Liberties: Four Decades in the Struggle for Rights*. New York: Public Affairs Press.

Noddings, Nel. 1991. *Caring: A Feminist Approach to Ethics and Moral Education*. Berkeley: University of California Press.

Noonan, Rita K. 1995. "Women against the State: Political Opportunities and Collective Action Frames in Chile's Transition to Democracy." *Sociological Forum* 19: 81–111.

Nygren, Bertil. 2005. "The Beauty and the Beast: When Electoral Democracy Hit Eurasia." Unpublished paper.

Oberschall, Anthony. 1989. "The 1960 Sit-Ins: Protest Diffusion and Movement Take-Off." *Research in Social Movements, Conflict, and Change* 11: 31–53.

Olesen, Thomas. 2005. *International Zapatismo: The Construction of Solidarity in the Age of Globalization*. London: ZED Books.

Olson, Mancur. 1965. *The Logic of Collective Action: Public Goods and the Theory of Groups*. Cambridge, MA: Harvard University Press.

Olzak, Susan and Emily Ryo. 2007. "Organizational Diversity, Vitality and Outcomes in the Civil Rights Movement." *Social Forces* 85: 1561–1591.

Oppenheimer, Martin. 1989. *The Sit-In Movement of 1960*. Brooklyn, NY: Carlson.

Osa, Maryjane. 2001. "Mobilization Structures and Cycles of Protest: Post-Stalinist Contention in Poland, 1954–9." *Mobilization* 6: 211–31.

Oxfam America. 2004. *Like Machines in the Fields: Workers Without Rights in American Agriculture*. Boston: Oxfam America.

Paarlberg, Robert L. 2001. *The Politics of Precaution: Genetically Modified Crops in Developing Countries*. Baltimore: Johns Hopkins University Press.

_____. 2008. *Starved for Science: How Biotechnology Is Being Kept Out of Africa*. Cambridge, MA: Harvard University Press.

Panagariya, Arvind. 2000. "Shoes on the Other Foot: Stunning Indictment of Laws Governing Workers' Rights in the United States." *The Economic Times* (India) December 20: 1.

Papava, Vladimer. 2005. *Necroeconomics: The Political Economy of Post-Communist Capitalism.* New York: Universe.

Park, Robert E. and E. W. Burges. 1921. *Introduction to the Science of Sociology.* Chicago: University of Chicago Press.

Pavlovic, Dusan. 2005. *Akteri I modeli: ogledi o politici u Srbiji pod Milosevic.* Belgrade: B92.

Pedriana, Nicholas. 2006. "From Protective to Equal Treatment: Legal Framing Process and Transformation of the Women's Movement in the 1960s." *American Journal of Sociology* 111: 1718–1761.

Pendleton, S. C. 1998. "Rumor Research Revisited and Expanded." *Language & Communication* 1: 69–86.

Pesticide Action Network International. 2007. *Genetic Engineering and Pesticides. A PAN International Position Paper* (available at www.pan-international.org/panint/files/WG2%20Genetic%20Engineering%20and%20Pesticides.pdf; accessed June 11, 2009).

Petras, James and Maurice Zeitlin. 1967. "Miners and Agrarian Radicalism." *American Sociological Review* 32: 578–586.

Petrova, Tsvetlana. 2010. "A Postcommunist Transition in Two Acts: The 1996–1997 Anti-Government Struggle in Bulgaria as a Bridge between the First and Second Waves of Transition in Eastern Europe," pp. 107–133 in *Democracy and Authoritarianism in the Postcommunist World*, edited by Valerie Bunce, Michael McFaul, and Kathryn Stoner-Weiss. Cambridge, UK: Cambridge University Press.

Pew Center for People and the Press. 2008. "The Internet's Broader Role in 2008." January 11 (available at pewresearch.org/pubs/689/the-internets-broader-role-in-campaign-2008; accessed December 2, 2008).

Pfeffer, Paula. 1990. *A. Philip Randolph, Pioneer of the Civil Rights Movement.* Baton Rouge: Louisiana State University Press.

Pimbert, Michel P. and Tom Wakeford. 2002. "Prajateerpu: A Citizens Jury/Scenario Workshop on Food and Farming Futures for Andhra Pradesh." *Economic and Political Weekly* July 6: 2778–2788.

Pinard, Maurice. 1971. *The Rise of a Third Party: A Study in Crisis Politics.* Montreal: McGill Queen's University Press.

Pinstrup-Andersen, Per and Ebbe Schiøler. 2000. *Seeds of Contention: World Hunger and the Global Controversy over GM Crops.* Baltimore: Johns Hopkins University Press.

Piven, Frances Fox and Richard Cloward. 1977. *Poor People's Movements.* New York: Pantheon Books.

Polletta, Francesca. 1998. "'It Was Like a Fever...' Narrative and Identity in Social Protest." *Social Problems* 45: 137–159.

———. 2002. *Freedom Is an Endless Meeting: Democracy in American Social Movements.* Chicago: University of Chicago Press.

Pope, James Gray. 2002. "The Thirteenth Amendment Versus the Commerce Clause: Labor and the Shaping of American Constitutional Law, 1921–1957." *Columbia Law Review* 102: 1.

Powledge, Fred. 1991. *Free at Last? The Civil Rights Movement and the People Who Made It.* Boston: Little, Brown and Company.

Pray, Carl E., Jikun Huang, Ruifa Hu, and Scott Rozelle. 2002. "Five Years of Bt Cotton in China – the Benefits Continue." *The Plant Journal* 31 (4): 423–430.

Pray, Carl E. and Anwar Naseem. 2007. "Supplying Crop Biotechnology to the Poor: Opportunities and Constraints." *Journal of Development Studies* 43 (1): 192–217.

Pribicevic, Ognjen. 2004. "Serbia After Milosevic." *Southeast Europe and Black Sea Studies* 4 (1): 107–118.

Radnitz, Scott. 2006. "What Really Happened in Kyrgyzstan?" *Journal of Democracy* 17 (2): 132–146.

———. 2010. "A Horse of a Different Color: Revolution and Regression in Kyrgyzstan," in *Democracy and Authoritarianism in the Post Communist World*, edited by Valerie Bunce, Michael McFaul, and Kathryn Stoner-Weiss. Cambridge, UK: Cambridge University Press.

Raines, Howell. 1977. *My Soul Is Rested*. New York: Penguin.

Ransby, Barbara. 2003. *Ella Baker and the Black Freedom Movement: A Radical Democratic Vision*. Chapel Hill: University of North Carolina Press.

Rao, C. Kameswara. 2007a. "Causes of Death of Cattle and Sheep in the Telengana Region of Andhra Pradesh in India" (available at www.plantbiotechnology.org.in/issues.html; accessed May 30, 2009).

———. 2007b. "Why Do Cattle Die Eating Bt Cotton Plants Only in the Telengana Region of Andhra Pradesh in India?" Foundation for Biotechnology Awareness and Education (available at www.plantbiotechnology.org.in/issues.html; accessed May 25, 2009).

Raudabaugh, John N. 2008. "Statement before the Senate Republican Conference." July 21, 2008 (available at www.hrpolicy.org/downloads/2008/SFX7C77.pdf; accessed June 2, 2009).

Reddy, A. Vinayak and G. Bhaskar, eds. 2005. *Rural Transformation in India: The Impact of Globalisation*. New Delhi: New Century Publications.

Reid, Andy. 2003. "Package of Bones Arrives at Brown-Waite's Office." *Tampa Tribune* April 1 (available at www.lexisnexis.com; accessed September 15, 2005).

Rich, Frank. 2004. "How Kerry Became a Girlie Man." *The New York Times* September 5 (available at lexisnexis.com; accessed September 21, 2005).

Roberts, Kenneth M. 2008. "The Mobilization of Opposition to Economic Liberalization," pp. 327–349 in *Annual Review of Political Science*, vol. 11, edited by Margaret Levi, Simon Jackman, and Nancy Rosenblum. Palo Alto, CA: Annual Reviews.

Robinson, Jo Ann. 1987. *The Montgomery Bus Boycott and the Women Who Started It: The Memoir of Jo Ann Gibson Robinson*. Knoxville: University of Tennessee Press.

Rodenbeck, Max. 2005. "A New Lebanon?" *New York Review of Books* 52 (7) (available at www.nybooks.com/articles/17952; accessed August 9, 2009).

Rogers, Everett. 1983. *Diffusion of Innovations*, 3rd edition. New York: Free Press.

———. 1995. *Diffusion of Innovations*, 4th edition. New York: Free Press.

Roggeband, Conny. 2002. *Over de grenzen van de politiek. Een vergelijkende studie naar de opkomst en ontwikkeling van de vrouwenbeweging tegen seksueel geweld in Nederland en Spanje*. Assen, Netherlands: van Gorcum.

———. 2004. "'Immediately I Thought We Should Do the Same Thing': International Inspiration and Exchange in Feminist Action against Sexual Violence." *European Journal of Women's Studies* 11 (2): 159–175.

———. 2007. "Translators and Transformers. International Inspiration and Exchange in Social Movements." *Social Movement Studies* 6 (3): 247–261.

Roggeband, Conny and Mieke Verloo. 1999. "Global Sisterhood and Political Change. The Unhappy 'Marriage' of Women's Movements and Nation States," pp. 177–194 in *Expansion and Fragmentation: Internationalization, Political Change and the*

Transformation of the Nation State, edited by Kees Kersbergen et al. Amsterdam: Amsterdam University Press.

Romero, Simon. 2007. "Students Emerge as a Leading Force Against Chávez." *New York Times* November 10: Section A3:3.

Rosenkrantz, Holly. 2009. "Social Investment Funds Back Labor Union Organizing Measure." *Bloomberg News* May 11 (available at /www.bloomberg.com/apps/news?pid=20601110&sid=aITL6dFsvEMM; accessed June 3, 2009).

Roth, Silke. 2003. *Building Movement Bridges: The Coalition of Labor Union Women.* Westport, CT: Praeger.

Rothchild, Eric. 2005. "Transcript of Opening Statement by Plaintiff." *Dover Trial Transcripts* September 26, 2005 (available at www.aclupa.org/downloads/Day1AMSession.pdf; accessed October 7, 2006).

Rothman, Franklin Daniel and Pamela E. Oliver. 1999. "From Local to Global: The Anti-Dam Movement in Southern Brazil, 1979–1992." *Mobilization* 4: 41–57.

Rubenstein, Michael. 1987. *The Dignity of Women at Work: A Report on the Problem of Sexual Harassment in the Member States of the European Communities.* Luxembourg: Office for Official Publications of the European Communities.

Rude, George. 1964. *The Crowd in History, 1730–1848.* New York: John Wiley and Sons.

Sageman, Mark. 2004. *Understanding Terror Networks.* Philadelphia: University of Pennsylvania Press.

Saguy, Abigail C. 2002. "International Crossways: Traffic in Sexual Harassment Policy." *European Journal of Women's Studies* 9 (3): 249–262.

Sato, Kyoko. 2007. "Meanings of Genetically Modified Food and Policy Change and Persistence: The Cases of France, Japan and the United States." PhD dissertation, Department of Sociology, Princeton University, Princeton, NJ.

Schedler, Andreas. 2006. *Electoral Authoritarianism: The Dynamics of Unfree Competition.* Boulder, CO: Lynne Rienner.

Schneiberg, Marc and Sarah A. Soule. 2004. "Institutionalization as a Contested, Multi-Level Process: Rate Regulation in American Fire Insurance," pp. 122–160 in *Social Movements and Organizational Theory*, edited by Jerry Davis, Doug McAdam, Dick Scott, and Mayer Zald. New York: Cambridge University Press.

Schurman, Rachel. 2004. "Fighting 'Frankenfoods': Industry Opportunity Structures and the Efficacy of the Anti-Biotech Movement in Western Europe." *Social Problems* 51 (2): 243–268.

Schurman, Rachel and William Munro. 2006. "Ideas, Thinkers and Social Networks: The Process of Grievance Construction in the Anti-Genetic Engineering Movement." *Theory and Society* 35: 1–38.

Scoones, Ian. 2008. "Mobilizing Against GM Crops in India, South Africa and Brazil." *Journal of Agrarian Change* 8 (2): 315–344.

Searles, Ruth and J. Allen Williams, Jr. 1962. "Negro College Students' Participation in Sit-Ins." *Social Forces* 40: 215–220.

Seshachari, Candadai. 1969. *Gandhi and the American Scene: An Intellectual History and Inquiry.* Bombay: Nachiketa.

Shaw, Randy. 2008. *Beyond the Fields: César Chávez, the UFW, and Struggle for Justice in the 21st Century.* Berkeley, CA: University of California Press.

Shelton, Anthony M. 2007. "Considerations on the Use of Transgenic Crops for Insect Control." *Journal of Development Studies* 43 (5): 890–900.

Shiva, Vandana. 1997. *Biopiracy: The Plunder of Nature and Knowledge.* Boston: South End Press.

———. 2006a. "Resources, Rights and Regulatory Reform." *Context* 3 (Spring/ Summer) 1: 85–91.

———. 2006b. "The Pseudo-Science of Biotech Lobbyists." Irish Seed Saver Association. February 27 (available at http://mra.e-contentmanagement.com/archives/ vol/2/issue/2/article/2364/whose-numbers-count).

Shiva, Vandana, Ashok Emani, and Asfar H. Jafri. 1999. "Globalization and Threat to Seed Security: Case of Transgenic Cotton Trials in India." *Economic and Political Weekly* March 6–12: 601–613.

Shiva, Vandana, Afsar H. Jafri, Ashok Emani, and Manish Pande. 2000. *Seeds of Suicide: The Ecological and Human Costs of Globalization of Agriculture.* Delhi: Research Foundation for Science, Technology and Ecology.

Shorter, Edward and Charles Tilly. 1974. *Strikes in France 1830–1968.* Cambridge, UK: Cambridge University Press.

Shridharani, Krishnalal. 1939. *War without Violence.* New York: Harcourt Brace.

Silitski, Vitali. 2005a. "Is the Age of Post-Soviet Electoral Revolutions Over?" *Democracy at Large* 1: 8–10.

———. 2005b. *The Long Road from Tyranny: Post-Communist Authoritarianism and Struggle for Democracy in Serbia and Belarus.* Unpublished book manuscript.

———. 2010. "Contagion Deterred: Preemptive Authoritarianism in the Former Soviet Union (the Case of Belarus)," pp. 274–299 in *Democracy and Authoritarianism in the Postcommunist World*, edited by Valerie Bunce, Michael McFaul, and Kathryn Stoner-Weiss. New York: Cambridge University Press.

Silver, Nate. 2009. "EFCA's backers still have work to do." *FiveThirtyEight: Politics Done Right.* March 17 (available at www.fivethirtyeight.com/2009/03/ efcas-backers-still-have-work-to-do.html; accessed June 2, 2009).

Simmons, Beth A., Frank Dobbin, and Geoffrey Garrett. 2006. "Introduction: The International Diffusion of Liberalism." *International Organization* 60: 781–810.

Simmons, Beth and Zachary Elkins. 2004. "The Globalization of Liberalization Policy: Diffusion in the International Political Economy." *The American Political Science Review* 98: 171–189.

Singer, Benjamin D. 1970. "Mass Media and Communication Processes in the Detroit Riot of 1967." *Public Opinion Quarterly* 34: 236–245.

Singh, Harnam. 1962. *The Indian National Movement and American Opinion.* New Delhi: Rama Krishna.

Skocpol, Theda. 2004. *Diminished Democracy: From Membership to Management in American Civic Life.* Norman: University of Oklahoma Press.

Skocpol, Theda, Marshall Ganz, and Ziad Munson. 2000. "A Nation of Organizers: The Institutional Origins of Civic Voluntarism in the United States." *American Political Science Review* 94: 527–546.

Snow, David A. 2004. "Framing Processes, Ideology, and Discursive Fields," pp. 380–412 in *The Blackwell Companion to Social Movements*, edited by David A. Snow, Sarah Soule, and Hanspeter Kriesi. Oxford, UK: Blackwell Publishing.

Snow, David A. and Robert D. Benford. 1988. "Ideology, Frame Resonance, and Participant Mobilization." *International Social Movement Research* 1: 197–217.

———. 1992. "Master Frames and Cycles of Protest," pp. 133–155 in *Frontiers in Social Movement Theory*, edited by Aldon D. Morris and Carol McClurg Mueller. New Haven, CT: Yale University Press.

————. 1999. "Alternative Types of Cross-national Diffusion in the Social Movement Arena," pp. 23–39 in *Social Movements in a Globalizing World*, edited by Donatella della Porta, Hanspeter Kriesi, and Dieter Rucht. New York: St. Martin's Press.

Snow, David A. and Jason D. Clark-Miller. 2005. "Frame Articulation and Elaboration in a Right Wing Group: An Empirical Examination of Framing Processes." Unpublished paper.

Soule, Sarah A. 1997. "The Student Divestment Movement in the United States and Tactical Diffusion." *Social Forces* 75: 855–83.

————. 1999. "The Diffusion of an Unsuccessful Innovation." *Annals of the American Academy of Political and Social Science* 566: 120–131.

————. 2004. "Diffusion Processes within and Across Movements," pp. 294–310 in *The Blackwell Companion to Social Movements*, edited by David A. Snow, Sarah A. Soule, and Hanspeter Kreisi. Malden, MA: Blackwell Publishing.

Soule, Sarah A. and Yvonne Zylan. 1997. "Runaway Train? The Diffusion of State Level Reform in ADC/AFDC Eligibility Requirements, 1950–1967." *American Journal of Sociology* 103: 733–762.

Spasic, Ivana and Milan Subotic. 2000. *Revolution and Order: Serbia After October 2000*. Belgrade: Belgrade Institute for Philosophy and Sociology.

Spilerman, Seymour. 1976. "Structural Characteristics of Cities and the Severity of Racial Disorders." *American Sociological Review* 41: 771–93.

St. Protich, Milan. 2005. *Izneverena revolutiutsija*. Belgrade: Chigoya.

Staniszkis, Jadwiga. 1984. *Poland's Self-Limiting Revolution*. Princeton, NJ: Princeton University Press.

Starr, Harvey and Christina Lundborg. 2003. "Democratic Dominoes Revisited." *Journal of Conflict Resolution* 47 (4): 490–519.

States News Service. 2009. "Business Leaders from 12 States Blitz Capitol Hill to Oppose Card Check Bill 'Compromise'." US Chamber of Commerce, June 3 (available at www.uschamber.com/press/releases/2009/june/090603_states.htm).

Steinberg, Marc. 1999. "The Talk and Back Talk of Collective Action: A Dialogic Analysis of Repertoires of Discourse among Nineteenth-Century English Cotton Spinners." *American Journal of Sociology* 105: 736–780.

Stokes, Susan C. 1995. *Cultures in Conflict: Social Movements and the State in Peru*. Berkeley: University of California Press.

Stone, Deborah A. 1989. "Causal Stories and the Formation of Policy Agendas." *Political Science Quarterly* 104: 281–300.

Stone, Glenn Davis. 2002. "Biotechnology and Suicide in India." *Anthropology News* 43 (5): 5.

————. 2007. "Agricultural Deskilling and the Spread of Genetically Modified Cotton." *Current Anthropology* 48: 67–103.

Strang, David and John W. Meyer. 1993. "Institutional Conditions for Diffusion." *Theory and Society* 22: 487–511.

Strang, David and Sarah A. Soule. 1998. "Diffusion in Organizations and Social Movements: From Hybrid Corn to Poison Pills." *Annual Review of Sociology* 24: 265–290.

Swanson, David. 2004. "Transnational Trends in Political Communication: Conventional Views and New Realities," pp. 45–63 in *Comparing Political Communication*, edited by Frank Esser and Barbara Pfetsch. Cambridge, UK: Cambridge University Press.

Swidorski, Carl. 2003. "From the Wagner Act to the Human Rights Watch Report: Labor and Freedom of Expression and Association, 1935–2000." *New Political Science* 25 (March 2003): 55.

Szymanski, Ann-Marie E. 2003. *Pathways to Prohibition: Radicals, Moderates, and Social Movement Outcomes*. Durham, NC: Duke University Press.

Tait, Joyce. 2001. "More Faust Than Frankenstein." *Journal of Risk Research* 4 (2): 175–189.

Tarde, Gabriel. 1903. *The Laws of Imitation*. New York: Henry Holt.

Tarrow, Sidney. 1998a. *Dynamics of Contention*. Cambridge, UK: Cambridge University Press.

_____. 1998b. "Fishnets, Internets, and Catnets: Globalization and Transnational Collective Action," pp. 228–244 in *Challenging Authority: The Historical Study of Contentious Politics*, edited by Michael P. Hanagan, Leslie P. Moch, and Wayne Te Brake. Minneapolis: University of Minnesota Press.

_____. 1998c. *Power in Movement: Social Movements and Contentious Politics*. New York and Cambridge: Cambridge University Press.

_____. 2005. *The New Transnational Activism*. Cambridge, UK: Cambridge University Press.

Tarrow, Sidney and Donatella della Porta. 2005. "Globalization, Complex Internationalism and Transnational Contention," pp. 227–246 in *Transnational Protest and Global Activism*, edited by Donatella della Porta and Sidney Tarrow. Lanham, MD: Rowman and Littlefield.

Tarrow, Sidney and Doug McAdam. 2005. "Scale Shift in Transnational Contention," pp. 121–147 in *Transnational Protest and Global Activism*, edited by Donatella della Porta and Sidney Tarrow. Lanham, MD: Rowman and Littlefield Publishers.

Teamsters, International Brotherhood of. 2004. "Workers' Rights Violations at Maersk: Report and Analysis; Actions by U.S. Divisions of Maersk Corporation in Light of International Human Rights and Labor Rights Standards." June 1: 19.

_____. 2009. "Alaska First Student Workers Choose Teamsters Union" (available at www.teamster.org/content/alaska-first-student-workers-choose-teamsters-union, accessed April 27, 2009).

Teeth Maestro. 2008. "Monsanto – genetically modified BT Cotton 'terminator' seeds being introduced in Pakistan." Teeth Maestro blog (available at teeth.com.pk/blog/2008/05/18/monsanto-gm-terminator-seeds).

Tendulkar, D.G. 1960. *Mahatma*, 8 vols. Delhi: Government Publications Division.

Teorell, Jan and Axel Hadenius. 2009. "Election as Levers of Democracy: A Global Inquiry," pp. 77–100 in *Democratization by Elections: A New Mode of Transition?* edited by Staffan Lindberg. Baltimore, MD: Johns Hopkins University Press.

Terchek, Ronald. 1998. *Gandhi: Struggling for Autonomy*. Lanham, MD: Rowman and Littlefield.

Thies, Janice E. and Medha H. Devare. 2007. "An Ecological Assessment of Transgenic Crops." *Journal of Development Studies* 43 (1): 97–129.

Thurman, Howard. 1979. *With Head and Heart: The Autobiography of Howard Thurman*. San Diego, CA: Harcourt Brace.

Thussu, D. K. 1998. *Electronic Empires*. London: Arnold Publishers.

Tiberghien, Yves. 2007. "Europe: Turning Against Agricultural Biotechnology in the Late 1990s," pp. 51–68 in *The Gene Revolution: GM Crops and Unequal Development*, edited by Sakiko Fukuda-Parr. London: Earthscan.

Tilly, Charles. 1986. *The Contentious French*. Cambridge, MA: Harvard University Press.

———. 1995a. *Popular Contention in Great Britain, 1754–1834*. Cambridge, MA: Harvard University Press.

——— 1995b. "Contentious Repertoires in Great Britain, 1758–1834," pp. 15–42 in *Repertoires and Cycles of Collective Action*, edited by Mark Traugott. Durham, NC: Duke University Press.

———. 2004. *Social Movements*. Boulder, CO: Paradigm Press.

———. 2008. *Contentious Performances*. New York: Cambridge University Press.

Tilly, Charles and Sidney Tarrow. 2006. *Contentious Politics*. Boulder, CO: Paradigm Publishers.

Toumey, Christopher P. 1994. *God's Own Scientists: Creationists in a Secular World*. New Brunswick, NJ: Rutgers University Press.

Traugott, Mark. 1995. *Repertoires and Cycles of Collective Action*. Durham, NC: Duke University Press.

Trejo, Guillermo, 2004. "The Political Foundations of Ethnic Mobilization and Territorial Conflict in Mexico, 1975–2000," pp. 355–386 in *Federalism and Territorial Cleavages*, edited by Ugo Amoretti and Nancy Bermeo. Baltimore: Johns Hopkins University Press.

Tucker, Joshua A. 2007. "Enough! Electoral Fraud, Collective Action Problems, and the Second Wave of Post-Communist Democratic Revolutions." *Perspectives on Politics* 5 (3): 535–551.

Turner, Ralph H. and Lewis M. Killian. 1987. *Collective Behavior*. Englewood Cliffs, NJ: Prentice Hall.

Vaissy, Justin. 2003. "American Francophobia Takes a New Turn." *French Politics, Culture and Society* 21 (2): 33–51.

Valiente, Celia. 1998. "Sexual Harassment in the Workplace: Equality Policies in Post-authoritarian Spain," pp. 169–179 in *Politics of Sexuality: Identity, Gender and Citizenship*, edited by Terrell Carver and Veronique Mottier. London: Routledge.

Van Cott, Donna Lee. 2005. *From Movements to Parties in Latin America: The Evolution of Ethnic Politics*. Cambridge, UK: Cambridge University Press.

Van de Walle, Nicolas, 2005. "Why Do Oppositions Coalesce in Electoral Autocracies?" *Einaudi Center for International Studies Working Paper Series* 1–5, Cornell University.

———. 2006. "Tipping Games: When Do Opposition Parties Coalesce?," pp. 77–94 in *Electoral Authoritarianism: The Dynamics of Unfree Competition*, edited by Andreas Schedler. Boulder, CO: Lynne Rienner.

Vasi, Ion Bogdan and David Strang. 2009. "Civil Liberty in America: The Diffusion of Municipal Bill of Rights Resolutions after the Passage of the USA PATRIOT Act." *American Journal of Sociology* 114 (6): 1716–1764.

Venkateshwarlu, K. 2007. "Fatal Feed." *Frontline* 24 (8): 48–50.

Verloo, Mieke. 2005. "Mainstreaming Gender Inequality: A Critical Frame Analysis Approach." *The Greek Review of Social Research* 117: 11–34.

Vidal, John. 2006. "Outcrop of Deaths." *Guardian*. (available at http://www.guardian.co.uk/society/2006/may/10/environment)

Voss, Kim. 1988. "Labor Organization and Class Alliance: Industries, Communities, and the Knights of Labor." *Theory and Society* 17: 329–64.

———. 1993. *The Making of American Exceptionalism: The Knights of Labor and Class Formation in the Nineteenth Century*. Ithaca, NY: Cornell University Press.

Wallsten, Peter and Mark Z. Barabak. 2004. "Bush campaign steps up attacks." *Los Angeles Times* August 13. (available at http://articles.latimes.com/2004/aug/13/nation/na-campaign13; accessed June 1, 2009)

Walsh-Russo, C. 2004. "Diffusion and Social Movements: A Review of the Literature." Unpublished Paper, Department of Sociology, Columbia University.

Walton, John and David Seddon. 1994. *Free Markets and Food Riots: The Politics of Economic Adjustment*. Oxford, UK: Blackwell Publishing.

Watters, Pat. 1971. *Down to Now: Reflections on the Southern Civil Rights Movement*. New York: Pantheon.

Way, Lucan. 2005a. "Authoritarian State-Building and the Sources of Regime Competitiveness in the Fourth Wave: The Cases of Belarus, Moldova, Russia and Ukraine." *World Politics* 57: 231–261.

_____. 2005b. "Ukraine's Orange Revolution: Kuchma's Failed Authoritarianism." *Journal of Democracy* 16 (2): 131–145.

Wehr, Paul. 1960. "The Sit-Down Protests: A Study of a Passive Resistance Movement in North Carolina." Master's thesis, Department of Sociology and Anthropology, University of North Carolina at Chapel Hill.

Weighardt, Florian. 2006. "European GMO Labeling Thresholds Impractical and Unscientific." *Nature Biotechnology* 24: 23–25.

Weiss, Marley S. 2003. "Two Steps Forward, One Step Back – Or Vice Versa: Labor Rights Under Free Trade Agreements from NAFTA, Through Jordan, via Chile, to Latin America, and Beyond." *University of San Francisco Law Review* 37 (Spring 2003): 689.

Wejnert, Barbara. 2002. "Integrating Models of Diffusion of Innovations: A Conceptual Framework." *Annual Review of Sociology* 28: 297–326.

_____. 2005. "Diffusion, Development, and Democracy, 1800–1999." *American Sociological Review* 70 (1): 53–81.

Weyerman, Reto. 2005. "A Silk Road to Democracy? FAST Country Risk Profile: Kyrgyzstan." Working paper, Swiss Peace Foundation.

Weyland, Kurt. 2005. "Theories of Policy Diffusion: Lessons from Latin American Pension Reform." *World Politics* 57: 262–295.

_____. 2006. *Bounded Rationality and Policy Diffusion: Social Sector Reform in Latin America*. Princeton, NJ: Princeton University Press.

Wheatley, Jonathan. 2005. *Georgia from National Awakening to Rose Revolution: Delayed Transition in the Former Soviet Union*. Oxford, UK: Oxford University Press.

Wheeler, Hoyt N. 2001. "The Human Rights Watch Report from a Human Rights Perspective." *British Journal of Industrial Relations* 39: 591.

Wikipedia. 2006. "Kitzmiller v. Dover Area District." *Wikipedia* (available at en.wikipedia.org/wiki/Kitzmiller_v._Dover_Area_School_District_trial documents; accessed October 7, 2006).

Winston, M. 2002. *Travels in Genetically Modified Zone*. Cambridge, MA: Harvard University Press.

Witt, Matt and Rand Wilson. 1999. "The Teamsters' UPS Strike of 1997: Building a New Labor Movement." *Labor Studies Journal* 24 (1): 58–73.

Witte, James C. 2008. "The Changing Face of Yahoo: From Portal, to Search to Collective Intelligence." Paper presented at the Annual Meetings of the American Sociological Association. Boston, MA.

Wittner, Lawrence. 1969. *Rebels against War: The American Peace Movement, 1941–1960.* New York: Columbia University Press.

Wolff, Miles. 1970. *Lunch at the Five and Ten: The Greensboro Sit-Ins: A Contemporary History.* New York: Stein and Day.

Wood, Elisabeth Jean. 2003. *Insurgent Collective Action and Civil War in El Salvador.* Cambridge, UK: Cambridge University Press.

Youngdahl, Jay. 2009. "Solidarity First: Labor Rights Are Not the Same as Human Rights." *New Labor Forum* 18: 31–37.

Zippel, Kathrine. 2006. *The Politics of Sexual Harassment: A Comparative Study of the United States, the European Union, and Germany.* Cambridge, UK: Cambridge University Press.

Index